Absolute Beginner's Guide
to Programming

Absolute Beginner's Guide to Programming

Greg Perry

A Division of Prentice Hall Computer Publishing
11711 North College, Carmel, Indiana 46032 USA

One man's humor and wisdom keeps me going through some tiring hours of writing. Thanks Rush, for your excellence in broadcasting.

Trademarks

Publisher
Richard K. Swadley

Acquisitions Manager
Jordan Gold

Acquisitions Editor
Stacy Hiquet

Development Editor
Rosemarie Graham

Production Editor
Tad Ringo

Copy Editor
Greg Horman

Editorial Coordinators
Rebecca S. Freeman
Bill Whitmer

Editorial Assistant
Sharon Cox

Technical Editor
Brad Hiquet

Cover Designer
Dan Armstrong

Inside Illustrator
Chris Rozzi

**Director of Production
and Manufacturing**
Jeff Valler

Production Manager
Corinne Walls

Imprint Manager
Matthew Morrill

Book Designer
Michele Laseau

Production Analyst
Mary Beth Wakefield

Proofreading/Indexing Coordinator
Joelynn Gifford

Graphics Image Specialists
Dennis Sheehan
Sue VandeWalle
Roger Morgan

Production
Katy Bodenmiller, Christine Cook,
Lisa Daugherty, Brook Farling,
Dennis Clay Hager, Howard Jones,
John Kane, Sean Medlock,
Juli Pavey, Angela Pozdol,
Linda Quigley, Michelle Self,
Susan Shepard, Greg Simsic,
Angie Trzepacz

Indexer
Loren Christopher Malloy

Overview

Introduction xxi

1   Your Computer Is a Tool 3

2   The Computer's Background 29

3   What Is a Program? 55

4   Designing the Program 81

5   The Programming Process..111

6   Programming Languages: The Early Years 135

7   Programming Languages: Modern Day 165

8   Your First Language: QBasic 197

9   Data Processing with QBasic...221

10 Managing Data and Disk Files 253

11 Having Fun with QBasic 279

12 Program Algorithms 305

13 How Companies Program 339

14 The Future of Programming 369

A   Where Do You Go from Here? 389

B   ASCII Table..407

Glossary 417

Index 431

Contents

Introduction xxi

1   Your Computer Is a Tool 3
What a Computer Does 4
Common Misconceptions 6
    Myth 1: "Only Math Experts Can Program Computers" 8
    Myth 2: "Computers Make Mistakes" 8
    Myth 3: "Computers Are Difficult to Use" 9
Computers Benefit Many 11
    Computers in the Home 11
    Computers in Business 14
Computers in the Job Market 16
People and Computers 18
It Takes More Than a Computer 19
    The Hardware 19
    The Software 22
    The People 23
    The Data 23
    The Procedures 24
    Spread the Word 25
Chapter Highlights 25

2   The Computer's Background 29
A Quick Overview 30
    The First Generation 30
    The Second Generation 32
    The Third Generation 33
The True Beginnings 34
Today's Computers 38
The Types of Computers 39
    Supercomputers 40
    Mainframes 41

ix

Minicomputers 42
Microcomputers 43
The Computer's Hardware 44
    The System Unit 45
    Disks 47
    The Keyboard 48
    The Monitor 49
    The Printer 49
The Operating System 49
Chapter Highlights 51

3 What Is a Program? 55
The Need for Programs 56
Programs, Programs, Everywhere 59
Programs As Directions 59
    Programs Are Saved Instructions 62
    Art or Science? 65
    Speak the Language 67
The Language Translator 71
    Interpreters 71
    Compilers 73
Accuracy Is Everything 74
Chapter Highlights 77

4 Designing the Program 81
The Need for Design 82
Program Design 83
    Step 1: Define the Output 85
    Step 2: Develop the Logic 94
    Step 3: Write the Program 107
Chapter Highlights 108

5 The Programming Process 111
The Editor 112
    Line Editors 113
    Full-Screen Editor 116
Structured Programming 121
    Sequence 126
    Decision (Selection) 127
    Looping (Repetition and Iteration) 128

Testing the Program 130
The Program Language 131
Chapter Highlights 132

6 Programming Languages: The Early Years 135
Storage of Programs and Data 136
Binary Arithmetic 139
The First Programs 144
Enter the Keyboard 145
Getting Closer to English 149
  The FORTRAN Language 149
  The Business of COBOL 152
Other Languages Through the Years 156
Chapter Highlights 161

7 Programming Languages: Modern Day 165
Structured Programming with Pascal 166
C 169
  The Success of C 170
The C Language 172
  C++: A Better C 176
The BASICs 178
  Graphical Programming with Visual Basic 184
  Visual Basic for DOS 190
Which Language Is Best? 190
Chapter Highlights 193

8 Your First Language: QBasic 197
Getting Started 198
Delving into QBasic 202
Storing Data 204
Assigning Values 206
Looking at Values 208
  Using the Semicolon 210
  Printing with Commas 211
Printing on the Printer 213
Clearing the Screen 214
Math with QBasic 214
Chapter Highlights 218

9   Data Processing with QBasic **221**
Getting Keyboard Data with *INPUT* 222
Inputting Strings and Multiple Variables 225
Combining *PRINT* and *INPUT* 226
Comparing Data with *IF* 232
The Relational Test Options 234
The *SELECT CASE* Statement 236
Looping Statements 237
The *FOR-NEXT* Loop 238
The *DO-WHILE* Loop 246
The *DO-UNTIL* Loop 247
Chapter Highlights 249

10   Managing Data and Disk Files **253**
Introduction to Arrays 255
Reserving Array Space 258
Parallel Arrays 260
Erasing Arrays 260
Introduction to Disk Files 262
Records and Fields 263
Types of Access 264
Closing Open Files 266
Creating Output Files 267
Reading the Disk File 271
Appending to a Data File 273
Two or More Files Open 274
Advanced Data Files 275
Chapter Highlights 276

11   Having Fun with QBasic **279**
Beeping the Speaker 280
The *SOUND* Command 281
The *PLAY* Command 285
Introduction to Graphics 286
The *SCREEN* Command 287
Turning Pixels On and Off 288
Drawing Lines and Boxes 293
Drawing Circles 297
Textual Graphs 298
Changing the *PRINT* Location 300
Chapter Highlights 302

12 Program Algorithms **305**
  Counters and Accumulators 307
  Swapping Values 310
  Sorting 312
  Searching Arrays 317
    The Sequential Search 319
    Improving the Sequential Search 320
    The Binary Search 324
  Subroutines 328
    The Need for Subroutines 329
  Chapter Highlights 335

13 How Companies Program **339**
  Data Processing and Other Departments 340
  Paying for the Data Processing Department 343
  Computer Jobs 346
  Job Titles 347
    Data Entry 348
    Programming 350
    The Analysis and Design Staff 353
    Management Possibilities 354
  The Standards Manual 356
  Structured Walkthroughs 357
  Putting a Program into Production 359
  The Data Processing Department's Equipment 362
  Consulting 363
  Chapter Highlights 364

14 The Future of Programming **369**
  Program Generators 370
  Program Development with CASE 372
  OOPs, It's Object-Oriented Programming 374
    Objects 375
    OOP and Non-OOP Programming 377
    Learning OOP 377
  OOP Languages 378
  Non-Traditional Programming Languages 379
    Macro Languages 379
    Database Languages 383
    DOS Programming 384

Your Training Needs 385
Chapter Highlights 387

A   Where Do You Go from Here? 389
Pascal 390
    Turbo Pascal Programming 101 390
    Turbo Pascal 6 Object-Oriented Programming 390
QBasic 391
    QBasic Programming 101 391
    Teach Yourself QBasic in 21 Days 391
Generic C 391
    Teach Yourself C in 21 Days 392
    C Programming Proverbs and Quick Reference 392
    Programming in ANSI C 392
    Advanced C 392
Generic C++ 393
    C++ Programming 101 393
    Tom Swan's C++ Primer 393
    Advanced C++ 393
Microsoft C++ 394
    Do-It-Yourself Microsoft C++ 7 394
    Microsoft C/C++ 7 Developer's Guide 394
Turbo C++ 394
    Do-It-Yourself Turbo C++ 394
    Turbo C++ Programming 101 394
    Turbo C++ for Windows Programming for Beginners 395
    Mastering Borland C++ 395
    Secrets of the Borland C++ Masters 395
    Borland C++ 3.1 Object-Oriented Programming,
        Third Edition 395
    Programming Windows Games with Borland C++ 396
Visual Basic 396
    Teach Yourself Visual Basic in 21 Days 396
    Do-It-Yourself Visual Basic for Windows,
        Second Edition 396
    Do-It-Yourself Visual Basic for MS-DOS 397
    Secrets of the Visual Basic Masters 397
    Extending Visual Basic 397
    Visual Basic for DOS Developer's Guide 397
    Visual Basic for Windows Developer's Guide 398
Moving... (Series) 398

Moving from C to C++ 398
Moving into Object-Oriented Programming with
   Turbo C++ 398
Moving from Turbo Pascal to Turbo C++ 399
Moving from Basic to C 399
DOS 399
1-800-HELP with DOS 399
Absolute Beginner's Guide to Memory Management 400
Alan Simpson's DOS Secrets Unleashed 400
Windows 400
1-800-HELP with Windows 400
Tricks of the Windows Masters, Deluxe Edition 401
Windows Revealed 401
Windows Resource and Memory Management 401
Absolute Beginner's Guide to DOS and Windows 401
Windows Programming 402
Teach Yourself Windows Programming in 21 Days 402
Uncharted Windows Programming 402
Windows Programmer's Guides 402
Windows NT 403
Migrating to Windows NT 403
UNIX 403
The Waite Group's UNIX System V Primer,
   Second Edition 403
C Programming for UNIX 404
Networking 404
Absolute Beginner's Guide to Networking 404
Technology 404
FractalVision: Put Fractals to Work for You 404
Multimedia Madness! 405
Creating Virtual Reality 405
Other Titles of Interest 405
Memory Management for All of Us,
   Deluxe Edition 405
Programming Sound with DOS and Windows.................406

B   ASCII Table 407

    Glossary 417

Index 431

XV

Acknowledgments

I want to thank Stacy Hiquet, *editor extraordinaire*, and the most important influence in my publishing life at this point. Thanks, Stacy, for letting me do what I feel is important, supplying what I need when I ask, and putting up with my complaints even when they are not justified.

My other editors and production staff, especially Tad Ringo and Rosemarie Graham, somehow shaped my writing into reading. Talking to a beginning audience without talking *down* to the audience is not easy. I want to thank the good people at Sams Publishing for caring enough about the reader to put clear writing before everything else.

My favorite people—my beautiful bride Jayne, my parents Glen and Bettye Perry, and friends Michael Stapp, Diane Moore, Rick and Ellen Burgess, Richard and Christine Chambers, and Luke the mutt with the most—keep me wanting to be the best I can. Thanks to all of you.

About the Author

Greg Perry has taught thousands of people how to program through his 14 computer books and his lectures at the college level. He has been a programmer and trainer for the past 14 years. He received his first degree in computer science and then a master's degree in corporate finance. He is currently a professor of computer science at Tulsa Junior College, teaching advanced programming courses while maintaining a full-time writing schedule and lecturing at programming conferences across the country. Some of his other book titles include *C++ Programming 101*, *Moving from C to C++*, *C By Example*, and *QBasic By Example*. In addition, he has published articles in several publications, including *PC World*, *Data Training*, and *Inside First Publisher*. He is fluent in nine computer languages and divides his time between Tulsa and travelling the rest of the country, with a hop to Italy each summer.

Introduction

Learning how to program computers would, some might think, make a South American jungle explorer cringe in fear. If you approach computers with hesitation, if you cannot even spell *PC*, if you have tried your best to avoid the subject altogether but can do so no longer, the book you now hold contains succor on which you can depend in troubled computing times.

This book does more than explain programming. This book does more than desribe the difference between BASIC, C, and Pascal. This book does more than teach you what programming is all about. This book is a *training tool* that you can use to develop proper programming skills. The aim of this book is to introduce you to programming using professionally recognized principles, while keeping things light and humorous at the same time. It is not this book's singular goal to teach you a programming language (although you will be writing programs before you finish it). This book's goal is to give you the foundation to make you the best programmer you can be.

This book delves into proper program design principles. You'll not only learn how to program, but how to *prepare* for programming. This book also teaches you how companies program and explains what you have to do to become a needed resource in a programming position. You'll learn all about programming job titles and what to expect if you want to write programs for others.

Who Should Read This Book

The title of this book says it all. If you have never programmed a computer, if you don't even like them at all, or if your VCR's timer throws you into fits, take three sighs of relief! This book was written for *you*.

This book is aimed at three different groups of people:

✖ Individuals who know nothing about programming, but who want to know what programming is all about.

✖ Companies that want to train non-programming computer users for programming careers.

✖ Schools—both for introductory language classes, and for systems analysis and design classes—that want to promote good coding design and style and that want to offer an overview of the life of a programmer.

Conventions Used in This Book

The following typographic conventions are used in this book:

✖ Code lines, variables, and any text you see on the screen appear in a `computer` typeface.

✖ New terms appear in *italics*.

✖ Pseudocode, a way of explaining in English what a program does, appears in *italics*.

Each chapter begins with a list of questions. These questions are designed to help you be alert for the important points you will encounter in that chapter.

Within each chapter you will encounter several icons that help you pinpoint the current topic's direction. Their meaning should be clear when you see them used in the context of the book. The next few paragraphs explain the meaning of each icon and its associated text.

Note: Notes are indicated by a scroll. Notes bring a particular topic to your attention when further thought is warranted. Often, the Note describes what others might do in the given situation.

Clue: Clues are indicated by a torn map. Clues are an insight into a certain topic. Clues often appear just after a subject is explained. The text of the Clue will provide a more detailed look and explanation of what is going on. If you skip a Clue, you will still be able to understand the material, but you won't have the extra insightful background that the Clue provides.

Pitfall: Pitfalls are indicated by the "BOTTOMLESS PIT" sign. Pitfalls focus your attention on a problem or side effect that can occur in a specific situation. Often, a Pitfall attempts to steer you away from the usual course of action that gives others trouble.

Warning: Warnings are indicated by a skull and crossbones. Warnings are more forceful than Pitfalls. When you see a Warning, read the text carefully—it will help you avoid possible problems.

Reward: Rewards are indicated by a treasure chest. Rewards show you an extra shortcut or advantage possible with the command or subject you just learned. A Reward is a tip that should help streamline your approach to the material being discussed.

Getting Started on Your Adventure

You do not have to be a wizard, or even an expert, to be proficient in computer programming. Without further ado, put on your thinking caps, set your learning mode to *enjoy*, and join adventurer Perilous Perry as you enter the world of programming.

Your Computer Is a Tool

1

Perilous Perry's trek through the jungle brought him to a clearing. There he saw it for the first time—the computer! The sight frightened him. Will Perilous Perry have the courage to tackle this unknown monster?

1. What does a computer do?

2. What is the difference between data and information?

3. What is a program?

4. What are the three most common misconceptions about computers?

5. How are computers used in the home?

6. How are computers used in business?

7. What makes a successful computer information system?

In your adventurous quest for computing knowledge, you may have decided to give up instead of giving in to all the technical manuals and error messages that invade the computer industry. Despite the widespread pronouncements of *user-friendly computing*, the mysteries of computers still elude many today. A visit to any bookstore verifies that lots of people are craving sincere help with computers. Look at your local community college's curriculum and you'll find class after class with titles such as "Introduction to Computers," "Computer Concepts," "PCs for Those Who Can't Even Spell PC," and maybe even "The Absolute Beginner's Guide to Programming."

The book you now hold promises you one thing above all else: to respect your ability to think and learn, but not teach above your head. This book shows that you don't have to be a wizard to become proficient (or even an expert) with computers. This chapter introduces you to the way computers are used in business and in the home. Without programs, computers would be nothing more than big calculators. Thanks to programs that programmers write, computers become tools that help you accomplish the work you need to do.

What a Computer Does

At its simplest level, a computer *processes data*. Many businesses call their computer departments *data processing departments*, because computers process data into meaningful information. You may not have considered the difference between the words *data* and *information* before, but there is a tremendous difference to a computer professional.

Data (plural for *datum*, although this book commonly uses *data* for both singular and plural) is made up of raw facts and figures. *Information*, on the other hand, is processed data. Information has meaning; data, in its raw form, does not. Figure 1.1 shows the fundamental data processing model. Notice that data goes into the computer, the computer processes that data, and meaningful information is the result.

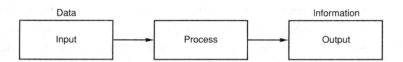

Figure 1.1. Data processing at its most fundamental level.

The data is generally input from some computer device such as a keyboard. The information generally comes from a computer device such as a screen or printer. As you will see throughout this book, the computer's input and output can come from many different types of devices.

Data by itself is not useful to people who need to make decisions with it. People need information—the processed data—to make decisions. Think for a moment of the president of a large company. The president is concerned about the payroll for the company's 1,500 workers. Times are good for the company, and the president is concerned about rewarding the employees accordingly. Therefore, the president wants to see the payroll figures for the last three months to analyze exactly where the company can direct more benefits.

Does that president need a list of every individual, down to the lowest paid part-time clerk? Does the president want the weekly payroll figures for 1,500 people for the last three months? Maybe, but that type of data would not be as useful as the total payroll per department, the payroll increases over this time last year, or the average payroll per employee compared to other companies in the same business. Such information, derived from data, is much more useful to the president. A computer with the right program can rapidly produce the kind of payroll figures the president needs.

The program is the driving force behind any job that any computer does. A *program* is a list of detailed instructions that the computer carries out. The computer cannot do anything without a program. It is the job of the programmer to design and write programs that direct the computer to take raw data and transform that data into meaningful information for the *end-user*. The end-user (or just *user*) of the computer is generally the non-technical, non-programming person who needs the results (the information) that the computer provides.

> **Note:** Data to one person might be information to someone else. To the clerk, the clerk's salary figure is vital and meaningful information; to the president, it might be just part of a pool of meaningless data. The president's perspective is different because the president makes different decisions concerning the payroll.

The programmer is most responsible for guiding the computer. Learning to program computers takes a while, but it is rewarding. Computer programming offers the advantage of instant feedback, unlike a lot of other jobs you can train for. Before you finish this book you will be writing your own programs and seeing the results. The Fortune 500 companies may or may not beat down your door for your skills after you master this book, but this book directs your programming path and explains what you can expect from programming like no other book does. So many people assume you already understand the background of computers and how they work, but this book guides you through the programming maze and directs you toward working as a programmer.

Common Misconceptions

It seems as though people who like computers love them, but people who don't like them absolutely abhor them. Most of the time, a person's dislike for computers directly reflects a lack of knowledge about computers. Despite worldwide usage of computers, many people still know very little about them. To those people, computers and the programs that drive them are nothing more than magic boxes that mere mortals need not understand.

This book aims directly at the heart of the matter: computers are easy to use and easy to program. A computer is nothing more than a dumb machine that "knows" absolutely nothing. A computer is like a blind slave that waits on your every command and acts out your instructions exactly as you give them. Of course, sometimes your instructions are incorrect. If they are, the computer goes right ahead and attempts them anyway.

> **Pitfall:** Don't fear computers. Computers are tools to help you get your job done.

You may have heard horror stories about a computer deleting someone's bank balance. You might believe that someday a computer is going to take over the world. People who often fear the worst with computers simply know little about them. These people fear that the computer somehow can do more than it really is capable of doing. A computer is just a machine, not a replica of a living human being's mind. A computer cannot take over the world any more than can a car, an electric drill, or a typewriter. (Remember, you can always pull the plug if it does...but it won't.)

Most of the misconceptions about computers stem from a lack of understanding how computers work and what computers are physically capable of doing. This book wants to shoot down the myths and improve your understanding of these machines. You'll be programming computers in no time. The computer is nothing more than a tool that helps you do certain types of work. The computer itself is not bad or good. A hammer is a tool you can use for good (to build houses) or for bad (to break things). A computer in the wrong hands can be used for bad, but that isn't the computer's fault any more than it is the hammer's fault if someone misuses it.

Computers are not only useful tools; they are required tools of companies today. Most businesses, schools, and banks would have to close their doors if computers disappeared. There is simply too much information moving from point to point to handle the numerous transactions manually. Consider how difficult and dangerous it would be to control airplanes around major airports without computerized assistance. Computers perform needed analysis for business, produce mailing labels for charities, forecast the weather, improve air traffic control, and keep the kids entertained while teaching them math, science, and reading skills.

The next few sections attack the three most popular computer myths. Have you heard any of them? Did you think some were true?

Myth 1: "Only Math Experts Can Program Computers"

Thank goodness this is a myth and not reality—thousands of people would be out of work (including me). Computers would be elitist machines used by engineers and scientists; the casual user could not master them. Computers would still be beneficial in some areas, but they would not provide the benefits that so many people can enjoy.

Not only can you be poor at math, but you don't have to like math or even have the desire to learn math to be a good computer programmer. The computer does all the math for you; that's one of its jobs. There are countless expert computer programmers in the world who cannot tell you the area of a circle or the square root of 64. Relax if you thought this myth was reality.

It turns out that, as you become a better programmer, you may find your math skills improving. Developing programming skills tends to improve your thinking on the left side of your brain (where psychologists believe that math and numeric skills reside). Therefore, being good in math might be a result of programming, but it's not a prerequisite.

People who favor logic puzzles, crosswords, anagrams, and word-search games seem to adapt well to programming, but again, liking these gaming activities is not a programming prerequisite. You will find that you can learn to program computers, and actually become extremely good at it, without liking math, being good at math, or having any flair at all for puzzles and word games.

Myth 2: "Computers Make Mistakes"

You might have heard the adage, "To err is human, but to *really* foul things up takes a computer!" This might be accurate, but only in that a computer is so very fast, it duplicates a person's mistakes rapidly.

Computers do not make mistakes—people make mistakes. If you have heard a bank teller tell you that $24 was incorrectly deleted from your savings account because "the computer made an error," the teller probably has no idea what really happened. People program computers, people run them, and people enter the data that the computer processes.

The odds of a computer randomly fouling up a customer's bank balance are minute. Computers simply do not make random mistakes unless they are programmed incorrectly. Computers are finite machines; when given the same input, they always produce the same output. That is, computers always do the same things under the same conditions.

Clue: You will know if a computer is broken.

When a computer malfunctions, it does not make a simple mistake; rather, it *really* messes things up. When a computer fails, it typically breaks down completely, or a storage device breaks down, or the power goes out. Whatever happens, computers go all out when they have a problem, and it is usually very obvious when they have a problem. The good news is that computers rarely have problems.

Before computers were invented, banks kept all their records on ledger cards. When a teller found a mistake (possibly one that teller had made), do you think the teller said, "The ledger card made a mistake"? Absolutely not. Computers can have mechanical problems, but the likelihood of small mistakes, such as an incorrect balance once in a while, are just too small to consider.

Myth 3: "Computers Are Difficult to Use"

Computers are getting easier to use every day. If you used a microwave or drove a car recently, the chances are good that you used a computer when you did. Yet, did you know you were using a computer? Probably not. The makers of computers have found ways to integrate computers into your everyday life to monitor and correct problems that might otherwise occur without them.

Of course, if you are reading this book, you want to learn enough about computers to write your own programs. Writing computer programs does take more work (notice that I did not say it takes smarter people) than using a microwave oven's computerized timer functions. The work, however, primarily involves getting down to the computer's level and learning what it expects.

Not only are computers getting easier to use every day, but you have better opportunities to learn about them than ever before. Cable television channels are loaded with educational shows about using and programming computers. Books and videos on the subject are all around you. There is probably a computer class now in session somewhere within 15 minutes of your house as you read this.

Think about the goals of the computer industry. Computer corporations want to make money. They want to make a lot of money, and the more money they make, the more people are buying their computers. When they make more money, they supply more jobs, increase the nation's tax base, and pump more money into the economy. Do you think the computer industry wants to *limit* the number of people who can learn to use computers? Not at all. When the computer manufacturers make computers easier to use, more people will use them, more people will buy them, and computers will help more people do their jobs better.

Some of this book explores the ways the computer industry is making computers easier to use and program. Operating environments such as *Windows* (see Chapter 2, "The Computer's Background") and word processors that make printing and proofing your letters as easy as pushing a button are only a couple of the thousands of programs on the market. Manufacturers try to produce programs that are easier to use than the competitions' so that you will purchase their product.

User-Friendly...NOT!

Too often, the term *user-friendly* appears in computer literature. In the 1960s and 1970s, when computers were selling like crazy but were still difficult to use, someone in marketing (isn't that always the case?) coined the phrase *user-friendly*. *User-friendly* meant that the programs were friendly to the computer user, as opposed to other programs that must have required heavy training and were hard to use (maybe *user-antagonistic* is the opposite of *user-friendly*).

The problem with the label *user-friendly* is that it seems every program ever written since is described as *user-friendly*. Nobody can measure whether a program is *user-friendly*, because people have different likes and dislikes, and people all learn skills differently.

Don't believe the cliché *user-friendly* unless it appears on the cover of this book!

Computers Benefit Many

Computers are wonderful tools that help make the world more productive. Our society is moving away from a primarily industrial one to more of an informational society. Information is considered a vital corporate asset. Today people have more information at their fingertips than ever before, thanks to computers.

There is no way to cover every use of computers in a single book, let alone a single chapter. Therefore, the following sections attempt to give you a glance at the ways computers are being used today in both business and personal computing. While reading through the information, keep one idea firmly planted in your mind: The reason computers are so beneficial is that someone took the time to learn how they work and how to write the programs that do the jobs at hand. A computer without a program is like a blank cassette; a computer is useless without its programs, because it is nothing more than a machine that you must direct every step of the way.

Computers in the Home

Walk into any computer store and the salespeople might say you can use the computer to balance your checkbook and keep your recipes. Although a computer can certainly do those things, it can do much more as well. Actually, keeping all your recipes on the computer can make for one messy machine during flour sifting, and you probably don't want to turn on your computer every time you write a check. Nevertheless, the computer's quick retrieval time makes storing records almost painless.

Don't try to do more with your computer than is practical. The computer is not a cure-all. If you don't keep up with your record keeping now, the computer may not be much help. The computer can, however, keep information organized in an orderly fashion as long as you routinely enter the necessary transactions. Using the computer for record keeping is a decision that only you can make. If you own a couple of rental properties, for instance, writing your own record-keeping system to organize payments and expenses makes a lot of sense. At the end of the year, you can press a key and print out all the records for your taxes.

One of the most beneficial uses of the home computer is for education. Adults as well as children are finding that computers can serve as teaching tutors, giving instant feedback on learning results. Complete computerized encyclopedias are commonplace today. If you have a *multimedia* computer (one that includes sound and graphics capabilities), you can hear and watch people and events as you read about them on the computerized encyclopedia screen (as Figure 1.2 shows).

Figure 1.2. Watching and hearing subjects on your computerized encyclopedia.

Children (and adults) play a much more active role in the learning process when a computer is involved. They view computerized learning tools as games, and people learn much more when they are having fun.

Clue: If you have children, you might want to develop some learning programs for them once you learn how to write programs. Instead of a store-bought program, you can design the program with your child's specific needs in mind.

More and more *online services* are offered today for home computer users. Online services are central computers that you can connect your computer to through the telephone lines. These services enable you to bank and shop from your own home. You can read thousands of magazines and books, search for investment information, and send electronic messages to anyone else on the online service no matter where they are in the world.

Probably the most common use of computers in the home today is word processing. As you may already know, a word processor is a computerized typewriter, but it is really much more. You can type, edit, move, copy, store, retrieve, and print text of any kind with an ease unmatched by yesterday's typewriters. Many of today's word processing programs are so powerful, you can integrate both text and pictures and create your own publications at your desk. Figure 1.3 shows a newsletter being created with Word for Windows, a popular word processor.

This book is not intended to be a descriptive text of the entire computing industry. This book is going to prepare you for programming computers. If you are reading this book, you probably already use a computer at home or at work, and you might already use a word processor. Nevertheless, it is important, even in a text such as this one, to remind you of that which drives all uses of computers today: computer programs.

This chapter shows you that the computer is nothing more than a tool, although it is a special kind of tool. It is one of the most general-purpose tools you will ever use in your life. One minute your kids are learning about the first moon walk and the next minute you're preparing a financial analysis for your office. You can use the computer to dial up an online banking service to transfer money from one account to another at 4:15 on a Sunday morning. You can store your family's genealogical history on the same disk that you keep your holiday mailing list.

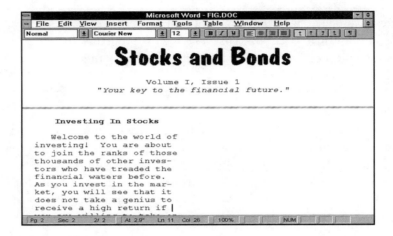

Figure 1.3. *Creating a publication at home.*

Although there are many programs already written for you to use, sometimes you need a program that fills a specific need and you cannot find one that does exactly what you want. When you are done with this book, you will know exactly what you need to design and write your own programs.

Computers in Business

Although word processors are the most-frequently used type of program in business as well as home, *electronic spreadsheets* come in a close second. An electronic spreadsheet is a program that acts like a word processor for numbers. Accountants, financial analysts, and other business people use spreadsheets to perform "what if" analysis, thereby looking at results given changing conditions.

Spreadsheets are useful for two reasons. First of all, spreadsheets are general-purpose programs that perform many different kinds of tasks. You might create one spreadsheet to compute business cycles and another to schedule employee lunch breaks. In effect, a spreadsheet is a program that non-programmers can direct to do a specific task.

Figure 1.4 shows a spreadsheet being used to calculate payroll amounts. Before spreadsheets became popular (in the early 1980s), business people would have to hire programmers to write programs that performed specific calculations. Now, a business person can develop his or her own spreadsheet applications. A spreadsheet eliminates the need for programming in one respect; that is, a skilled programmer does not have to get involved with the user of spreadsheets. A spreadsheet enables the non-programmer to program at a higher level—one that does not require knowledge of a computer programming language. By moving the cursor, defining rows and columns, entering calculations, and using the spreadsheet's built-in *macro language* (a simple and high-level set of spreadsheet programming commands), non-programmers can enjoy autonomy with their computers.

```
A:G20:                                                    READY

A     A        B        C         D        E       F       G      H
1
2                      * Payroll Amounts *
3                      --------------------
4
5  Department 1      Hrs. Wrked.        Total Gross Pay
6  ------------      -----------        ---------------
7  Smith, George         40                $1,432.34
8  Jones, Sally          41                $1,656.43
9  Wilbur, Michael       38                $1,213.60
10                      ----------         ----------
11     Totals:         119                $4,302.37
12
13
14 Department 2      Hrs. Wrked.        Total Gross Pay
15 ------------      -----------        ---------------
16 Linwood, Larry        43                $1,433.45
17 Abel, Laura           44                $1,329.45
18 Kinsley, Kerry        39                $1,090.34
19                      ----------         ----------
20     Totals:         126                $3,853.24
TOTAL.WK3
```

Figure 1.4. Spreadsheets can be programmed to take the place of some other programs.

Despite its power and programmability by non-programmers, a spreadsheet is a limited tool. It is great for analyzing numbers of all kinds, but there is an

15

abundance of jobs that spreadsheets are just too limited to handle. If the computer is to process transactions of any kind, such as printing payroll checks, or if the computer is to interact with the user from a focus point different from a grid of numbers and words (such as is done in educational programs), a spreadsheet just isn't enough.

> **Note:** Chapter 12 explains some of the basics of spreadsheet programming languages so that you will have an idea of how spreadsheet languages compare to regular programming languages.

Another popular business application is *database management*. One of the jobs that computers do best is process huge amounts of data. Companies can better manage that information when they organize it with a database program. Most database programs offer their own programming language that is generally more high-level (like the spreadsheet programming languages) than those used by programmers. By using the built-in programming languages of database programs, end-users (the non-programming users of computers) can develop simple applications that manage data in the way they prefer. Chapter 12 also explores some of the things a database programmer can do.

The *big three*—word processing, spreadsheets, and database management programs—comprise only a handful of the useful applications in business today. Businesses, non-profit organizations, churches, scientific laboratories, sporting groups, musicians, drafters, engineers, and governmental agencies use computers in their day-to-day processing and would likely have to cease their operations without them. The future of computers lies in the hands of programmers, not end-users, for it is the programmers who write the programs that people use.

Computers in the Job Market

Despite all the popular programs in use by business today, there are still a vast number of programs that businesses need. Programmers will have work for years to come. The transactions of business are too complex and change too rapidly for current programs to fill all the computer users' needs.

Computers do not replace people. If you ever had that notion, or heard some-one else say it, think again. The computer industry has created a tremendous number of new jobs. More and more people are needed to design computers, put them together, sell them, fix them, train people for them, and write the programs that drive them. That is where this book fits in; you have a challenging and fun career ahead of you if you want to program computers for a living.

Warning: Have you ever heard of a computer replacing someone's particular job? Despite the fact that computers generate more jobs than they replace, there may be specific instances where a person was replaced with a computer.

Be careful that you do not blame the computer for this, however. Almost every time, the person whose job was replaced by a computer was unwilling to change or learn more to use the computer. Companies know that people are much more reliable and important to their future than computers. Companies often attempt to find a way to integrate the computer into a person's job, letting the computer take over the tedious chores such as adding lists of numbers and typing lists of names and addresses. By replacing a person's tedious job with the computer, that person can then move into a more enriching job that requires intuitive thinking that computers aren't capable of doing.

The more people learn about computers, the more they can use the computer to enhance their jobs. Computers offer a positive impact on the job market. Rarely has there ever been a one-for-one replacement of an employee with a computer, except in the case where the employee did not want to adapt to the changing world as today's employees must do to remain with globally-competing firms. In that case, someone more open to learning new skills would be replacing the employee, not a machine.

Look in your Sunday newspaper's help-wanted professional section. You'll find that there is a severe shortage of computer programmers. Amidst the requests for C programmers, C++ programmers, COBOL programmers, systems analysts, senior systems analysts, object-oriented programmers, systems programmers, and application programmers, you may find yourself lost in a sea of uncertainty and *TLAs* (three-letter acronyms) that might, at first, seem hopeless. Do not fret; this book helps direct you toward areas of programming that might be right for you.

Chapter 13, "How Companies Program," explores the chain of computer jobs and describes what each type of programming job is all about. If you are just starting out, you probably won't be able to go to work as the most senior-level programmer, but you will be surprised at the salary your programming skills can bring you.

People and Computers

People and computers can work together very well. A person cannot add a list of 100 numbers in the blink of an eye, but a computer can. A person cannot print 1,000 names and addresses sorted by ZIP code in under a minute, but a computer can. People get bored doing the same jobs over and over, but computers never get bored. Computers can perform varied tasks, from graphic art to scientific calculations, while people are often really good at only a handful of different kinds of tasks.

The computer, however, is no match for a human being. People can think, whereas a computer can only blindly perform instructions line by line. Where do those instructions come from? They come from people who write the programs of instructions. People have insight into problems that computers can never achieve. People are intuitive and creative. People think. People can deal with ambiguities far superior to those that the most powerful computer in the world can. The computer is still years away that can understand a large vocabulary of human speech. Even then the computer will no doubt stumble between different accents and speaking patterns. Computers have no sense of the world around them except for some very limited devices that people attach to them.

It Takes More Than a Computer

So many people today buy a computer thinking that all of their problems are solved, only to find that the computer offers little or no help at all. Perhaps more computer buyers should be taught that the computer by itself is useless. As a programmer, it is incumbent upon you to teach others that a computer is useless, but a *computer information system* is useful. It is a computer information system that most people need when they purchase computers, but it is just a computer that they usually end up with.

A *system* is a collection of interrelated parts that work together for a common goal. The human body is a system; the hands, arms, legs, heart, ears, nose, and all the other parts work together to accomplish the common (and miraculous) goal of living. A computer is a system in that a computer's keyboard, printer, screen, and system unit work together to perform the needed task of computing.

A computer information system is more than just a computer. Buyers of computers are not fulfilled by the promise of computing unless they learn that a successful computer information system always consists of the following five components:

✖ Hardware

✖ Software

✖ People

✖ Data

✖ Procedures

The following sections look at each component of a computer information system and show you why all five components must be in place before a computer purchase is successful.

The Hardware

Hardware has been described as the parts of the computer you can kick. Although it is a sloppy definition, it does make the point that the *hardware* is the collection of physical components that make up the computer. The screen, printer, and system unit are hardware components. An analogy to stereo systems is useful here. Your stereo hardware is the tuner, amplifier, tape deck, and CD player. As stereo owners do not consider records, tapes, and CDs to be part of the hardware, neither do computer owners consider disks and programs to be hardware components. They fall into the category of *software*, which comes in the next section.

The falling prices of computers in the last few years have allowed more and more people to buy and use computers, but the falling prices have also led to many people buying a computer and then asking, "What now?" As mentioned in the previous section, a successful computer installation requires four more components than the hardware alone. Business owners often face a dilemma: only the hardware is affordable, but the hardware is just one-fifth of the equation that makes up a successful computer information system. When an accountant or attorney buys a $1,000 computer and gets it to the office, it is sad to note that the hardware is the least-expensive component of the computer information system.

Figure 1.5 shows a graph that might help illustrate this point. Even if you do not care for graphs, this one is easy to understand. You can see that time is going to the right and dollars are going up the left side of the graph. As time goes by, the cost of hardware steadily becomes cheaper. Today, you can buy more computing power than ever before. It seems that computers are obsolete almost as soon as you buy them because as soon as you do, another one takes its place that does a lot more for less money.

Pitfall: Some people fall into the trap of thinking they should wait to buy a computer and then never get one. If you need a computer, buy one knowing that it might be obsolete soon, but you can still get years of use out of the one you buy. If you keep waiting, you'll never have one. Too many months of waiting are wasted when you could have bought one and begun using it.

As long as you buy one that is fairly advanced at the time (you don't have to be on the *bleeding edge*—maybe just on the tail end of the *leading edge*), the computer you buy should fill your needs nicely for a long time to come.

There is an aftermarket for used computers, but you may get more from it if you donate it to a school when you buy your next one.

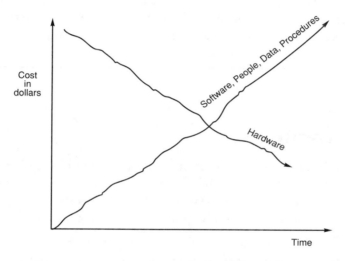

Figure 1.5. Hardware is going down in price while the cost of other computer information system components is going up.

Figure 1.5 also shows another phenomenon that you must consider. The other four components of a successful computer information system are going *up* in cost over time. Therefore, when businesses buy the hardware, they have shelled out only the beginning of their overall computer costs. The cost of the other components of the computer information system are not hidden from computer buyers, but buyers do not always know what is in store.

The next chapter explains the various components of hardware that make up most computers.

Clue: The cost of your computer hardware is analogous to the cost of your stereo. At first you might think you pay much more for your stereo than for your records and CDs, but if you had a fire tonight and only could save either your stereo equipment or your records and tapes, which would you choose? Almost everyone would save their records and tapes; they are much harder to replace and much more costly than the actual equipment. You can replace your equipment within a week (and probably with more modern equipment thanks to the computer components in most stereos), but it could take another lifetime to replace all your records and tapes.

The Software

While individual *software* (another term for the programs on computers) is going down in price, companies and individual computer owners invest more and more in software every year. Not only do people purchase new software as it comes out, but they update the older versions of programs they bought before.

Businesses and individuals must factor in the cost of software when making computer decisions. Whereas an individual usually buys a computer and is done with the hardware purchasing for a while, software purchasing never seems to end—software changes rapidly. As a future programmer, this is welcome news, because you have a secure career. For the uninformed computer purchaser, the cost of software can be staggering.

A business must also factor in the on-staff programmers and the time needed to write the programs it uses. More information on the programming and support staff appears in the next section.

When a company purchases software, they most often purchase a *software license*. If a company wants to buy a word processing program for 100 employees, legally it must purchase 100 copies of the program, or at least buy a *site license* that allows the company to use the software on more than one machine. When a company buys a program, it does not own the program. When you buy a record, you do not own the music; you have only purchased the rights to listen to the music.

You cannot legally alter the music, record it, give away recordings of it, and most importantly, you cannot sell recordings that you make of it. The same is true for software that you buy. The license for individual software grants you permission to use the software on one computer at any one time.

The People

If a company sells cars, that company's most important asset is not the cars, but its people (and not the customers, but the employees; the customers will come if the employees do their jobs). If a company sells insurance, the insurance is not the most important asset, but the company's people are.

When a company buys a computer, whether it's a desktop computer or a huge mainframe computer that fills an entire room, it must consider the cost of the people who will be a part of that computer information system. There will be costs associated with training, programming, and using the computer. There will have to be back-up personnel trained to take over the computer chores if someone else leaves. And as with software, the cost of personnel does not quit; it is an ongoing process. Often, a computer information system can save a company money in efficiency and processing power, but the company may have to hire additional staff, and people are expensive.

The Data

Look all the way back at Figure 1.1 for a moment and consider this: It is vital that the data going into the computer be as accurate as possible. If bad data comes in, almost assuredly bad information goes out. This is known as *GIGO*, or *garbage-in, garbage-out*. The programmer must constantly be on the look-out for better ways to get data so that it is accurate. The program cannot always determine if the data is bad.

If a company computerizes its payroll, someone must enter the weekly payroll figures, direct the payroll processing programs, and be there to put the checks in the printer. The payroll data that was previously recorded by hand and sent to an accountant must now be accurately entered into the computer.

23

Some larger companies have complete staffs of 20 or more people whose full-time job is to sit in front of a computer and enter data. Large companies have massive amounts of data. Computers can process that data, but only when it is entered properly and accurately. Oil companies must account for every drop of oil they refine and sell, accounts payable and accounts receivable must be updated every period, and records must be filed. The entry of this kind of data is tantamount to its processing and is a cost that must be factored into the price of a successful computer information system.

> **Note:** A company's data-entry department not only enters the data needed for its data processing, but it enters it *twice*. Typically, this is done by two different people. Because of the garbage-in, garbage-out phenomenon, companies help ensure that their data is accurate with double-entry. Once two different people enter the same data, a computer program compares the data for discrepancies. Although errors can still creep in, the chances are slim that any will.

The Procedures

Data processing procedures must be put into place soon after a computer is installed. These procedures generally include everything the user of the computer does on a daily basis to process the data needed. People change jobs, and the company must do what it can to provide adequate procedures in case someone else has to fill in.

Procedures also include computer security. Both physical security and data security must be maintained. Burglars won't touch desks and lamps, but they will take a computer. Whereas an office did not have to worry much about security before the computer, it now must maintain adequate protection of its computer systems. Although your job as a programmer may not include part-time deputy, you should be on the lookout for potential security problems. Make sure the computers are safely locked in their offices at night. Alarms and locks are now available that companies can install to make their computers more secure.

Most insurance companies now offer additional policies that specifically cover computer thefts.

If a phone line is connected to the computer, there is potential for unauthorized callers getting through to the system. Adequate passwords should be assigned.

Data protection is equally or more important than the hardware itself. Backup disks of all the data should be made each night and taken *off-site* (the backups would not be much use if a fire destroyed both the computer files and the backup disks sitting next to the computer).

Data privacy should also be maintained. Although most employees are honest, important company figures such as payroll amounts should be guarded. Don't let employees have direct access to their payroll files, and make sure the person who runs the payroll programs knows the importance of privacy.

Spread the Word

As you go through your programming career, keep in mind that all five components must be in place before a computer information system is successful. Although some companies cannot adapt overnight, most will make an honest effort to put all five components into place, but you must let them know how important the five components are. Your job as a programmer will be more vital to the companies you program for if you can do more than just program; you must learn to be their overall computer consultant, helping them sometimes to see the big picture.

Chapter Highlights

You now have an understanding of what computers do and how they are used. Many people who are unaccustomed to computers have fears that are not justifiable. You can now help alleviate their fears that are based on computer myths and show them where computers help streamline what we do today.

✖ You now understand that computers are not magic machines; they are only machines that perform the tasks they are given.

25

✖ The computer is a tool to help you and others do the work you normally do without computers. If the computer is working properly and the programs are in place, the computer can increase efficiency and effectiveness.

✖ At its most fundamental level, the computer takes input data, processes it, and turns the data into a meaningful output of information.

✖ Computers enjoy a wide range of uses at home. Word processing is the most common application, although education and personal finance play important roles as well.

✖ Without computers, many businesses would shut down; there is just too much data to process in this changing, global economy.

✖ To successfully use a computer, people must understand that a successful computer information system is more than just the hardware. To be successful, the hardware, software, people, data, and procedures must be in place.

The Computer's Background

Perilous Perry stood at the foot of the mountain. He knew that to find out where he was headed, he had to understand the path others had taken to get there. Will Perilous Perry scale this mountain? Will our hero reach the dizzying heights that await him in the realm of computers?

1. What was the first generation of computers?

2. What was the second generation of computers?

3. What was the third generation of computers?

4. What is an integrated circuit?

5. What is the history of computers?

6. What is a supercomputer?

7. How does a supercomputer compare to a mainframe?

8. Why are minicomputers not as popular as they once were?

9. How can businesses use microcomputers and mainframes at the same time?

10. What are the parts of a computer called?

11. What is DOS?

The computer industry is one of the newest in existence. Medicine, mathematics, and engineering all date back to the early ages, but the first real computer was invented in the 1940s. Although the roots of computing go all the way back to the *abacus* (a mechanical calculating contraption used for addition and subtraction), the first electronic computers are around 50 years old. This chapter tells you a little about the roots of computers and describes some of their history. As a new programmer, you need to understand the trends of the industry to know where it is heading. You must understand the past to understand the future, because there are some very obvious trends that have been going on since the first computer was invented. Primarily, computers are getting smaller, cheaper, and faster.

This chapter's computer background was written with the programmer in mind. The facts presented here help guide you to an understanding of how these machines matured through the years and what your role can be in their future. Once you learn about where these machines have been and where they are heading, you will learn a little more about the hardware and software that make up computers.

A Quick Overview

The following sections take you on a journey through the young roots of the computer industry. A different approach is taken from that of a lot of historical computing textbooks. Instead of concentrating on the facts and dates, the patterns of the evolving computer are presented with an emphasis on the three distinct periods of computers: first generation, second generation, and third generation computers.

The First Generation

The early computers were huge. They were known as *first generation* computers. The first generation computers, developed in the late 1940s, were *tube-based*. If you have ever looked inside an old television set, you may have seen lots of components that look like little light bulbs. These are tubes—also known as vacuum tubes—and they were the storage and computing mechanisms used in the early computers.

The first generation computers were so massive, they took up several rooms—almost an entire building. Actually, the computers took up much of the space, and the gigantic air conditioning needed to keep the huge machines cool took the rest. Large power plants were needed to supply the power to the thousands of tubes inside these machines.

The first generation computers were so massive and took so much energy to run that only one organization, the United States government, had the funds to buy one and keep the early ones running. The military used these early computers for their calculations and projections.

Note: The first generation computers were incredibly powerful...well, they were not quite as powerful as today's solar-powered pocket calculators, but for their time, they were a needed invention. Until electronic computers came along, there was simply no way to compute and process large amounts of data.

Although they were great for their time, the first generation computers had lots of drawbacks. The vacuum tubes were not as reliable as more modern electronic components. Although a tube, on the average, might last five or more years, when there are several thousands of tubes in the same location, the odds are good that any one of them might go out and bring the entire system down. There were actually people whose full-time jobs were to run up and down the aisles of these machines with milk crates of tubes, replacing them as they went out. How would you like to have *that* job?

The cost, size, and energy requirements kept the first generation computers out of the hands of most organizations. It was not until the second generation came along that many more people began using them and learning more about computing possibilities.

The Second Generation

The first generation computers were replaced by the second generation in the late 1950s. Second generation computers were composed of *transistors*. If you have ever seen the inside of a transistor radio, you may have seen the little colored parts, which are transistors. Transistors were the smaller replacements for vacuum tubes in electronic computers, immediately increasing computers' power, decreasing their size, and lowering their cost. Hundreds of transistors fit in the size of a single vacuum tube. Transistors are also much more reliable than tubes. If a transistor works the first time power is supplied to it, it will usually work for 20 years or more.

Transistors also take much less power to use and run much cooler than vacuum tubes. Also, instead of taking up an entire building, the second generation computers took only a large room or two. What was even more important than their size was that now businesses and schools could finally afford these computing machines. The costs of first generation computers kept people away from them.

Clue: Do you see the benefits of lower-cost computing? Because more organizations could afford computers, more people had access to computers. A synergy took place, because not only was the computer hardware being fine-tuned by leaps and bounds, but advances in computer software were also taking place at unbelievable rates.

It was primarily during the second generation of computers that programming languages, such as those you are learning about in this book, were developed.

Thanks to the second generation computers, computing technology—both the hardware and software—grew by leaps and bounds. Computers became a tool of business, and the 1960s saw an unbelievable growth of computer uses and jobs. More companies got into the computer business, science fiction stories and movies were produced that showed these computing machines in both good and bad light, and everybody knew that the computer was here to stay.

The Third Generation

In the 1960s, NASA decided they wanted to send people to the moon. Imagine that! They had a realistic problem, however. Computers were needed to send people to the moon, and the lightning-fast calculations of computers were needed during the flight. Computers had to be in control of a lot of the operations.

Note: Be aware of how seriously NASA had to take the computers in space missions. Split-second calculations are necessary or the rockets could end up on the sun, and *that* wouldn't be good (unless they went at night, of course).

The problems that NASA faced were not programming problems, because there were enough programmers around to take care of the software. The problem was the distance from the earth to the moon. Even though the computers down on earth could control the rocket ship by radio signals, radio signals take time to travel through space. It takes about 3.5 seconds for a radio signal to make the trip from the earth to the moon. By that time (3 seconds is almost an eternity to a computer) the rocket could be in danger if course corrections were required.

NASA could not send rockets into space without on-board computers to control the rockets. Even though the second generation computers were much smaller and lighter than the first, they were still too large to fit into a rocket ship. Therefore, NASA either had to design smaller computer components or shelve major space projects until they could.

Some NASA genius developed a component, still used today, called the *integrated circuit*. The integrated circuit (also called an *IC* or *chip*) is about the size of a matchbook, black in color, and has silver connections that usually run along two sides, making the IC look like a high-tech black beetle. Whereas the transistor replaced vacuum tubes one-for-one, integrated circuits replaced thousands of transistors. The entire circuitry of a second generation computer could be squeezed into the space of a matchbook. Computers instantly got dramatically smaller, NASA got to the moon and back with their on-board computers, we got desktop computers, a computer was now available to every person, and the *third generation* computers were born and have thrived ever since.

An integrated circuit is an almost magical device. Its designers use laser tools to install and connect the thousands of miniature components onto its wafer body. Integrated circuits are also known as *microprocessors*. Because of the microprocessor's widespread use in today's desktop computers, the term *microcomputer* was coined and the name stuck. Most people who read this book probably are using a microcomputer as their primary computing machine.

> **Note:** The term *machine* is used in the computer industry to mean *computer*. Unlike most other devices called *machines*, computers have relatively few moving parts. The printer and disk drives have moving parts, but there are few others.

The True Beginnings

There is not a lot of advantage into going into the details, dates, and facts of the history of the computer. The previous discussions attempt to give you a feel for where computer technology has come from so you can have a better idea of where it is heading. Nevertheless, you might be interested in a brief summary of some of the milestones in the computing industry. Table 2.1 offers a glimpse into the computing timeline in case you are interested in further details.

Table 2.1. A brief history of computers.

Approximate Date	Description of Event
3000 B.C.	The abacus was invented and used for quick, manual addition and subtraction calculations.

Approximate Date	Description of Event
1645 A.D.	A mechanical adding and subtracting machine called the *Pascaline* (after its inventor, the French mathematician Blaise Pascal) was invented.
1830	Charles Babbage, the *father of computers*, designed the first electronic computer called the *difference engine*. Unfortunately, the difference engine was never actually made, but today's computers are based on the difference engine.
1890	The 1890 census was predicted to be so vast that people-power alone could not tabulate it. Therefore, an inventor named Herman Hollerith invented the *punch card*. Census data was punched onto these cards, and tabulating machines churned through them computing the totals. The punch card was the primary input device for 20th century computers through the 1960s.
1937	An electromechanical calculator was built with the help of IBM. Although not truly an electronic computer because all of its parts were mechanical and moving, this *Mark I computer* (as it was named) proved that the theory of computing machines could be a reality and not only theory.
1939	The first vacuum tube calculating machine was invented.
1946	The first true general-purpose, vacuum-tube, first generation computer, named the *ENIAC*, was invented.

continues

35

Table 2.1. continued

Approximate Date	Description of Event
1945-1952	Computers named the *EDSAV* and *EDVAC* were developed that had electronic memories that held both data and programs.
1957	FORTRAN, one of the oldest programming languages still in use today, was developed to aid scientific and mathematical programmers.
1959	The second generation computers came on the scene.
1960	COBOL was developed as a programming language that gave business programmers the language they needed to write programs.
1964	The first version of BASIC, the most important language for start-up programmers, was written.
1965	The third generation computers were perfected.
1976	BASIC was ported to the early microcomputers by Microsoft, a company formed and run by two teenagers out of their garage (one of whom, Bill Gates, still keeps his hand in the computer industry by running Microsoft, Inc., and accepting credit for being America's richest living person in the early 1990s).
1976-1978	Two of the most important microcomputers that started the true trend of home computing, the Apple computer and Radio Shack's TRS-80, were invented and sold for a few hundred dollars each. Their low cost and widespread availability probably did more for the microcomputer industry than any other single accomplishment.

Approximate Date	Description of Event
1981	The introduction of IBM's first microcomputer, the IBM PC, finally added stability to microcomputers. Until the PC was invented, lots of companies were making lots of incompatible machines. As the IBM PC sold more computers than anybody (including IBM) had predicted, more and more people saw the benefits of sticking to one kind of machine. Programs, data, and add-on parts could be used interchangeably as long as you had an IBM or an IBM-compatible computer.
1982	The American National Standards Institute (ANSI) agreed to a universally accepted standard for the C programming language. C would prove to be the most important computer language of the 1980s, spreading to larger computers and slipping into industry previously owned by the COBOL language stronghold.
1989	The C++ programming language was made available for a wide variety of microcomputers, helping spearhead the *object-oriented programming* (*OOP*) movement that promises to change the way programmers write programs.

Pitfall: The information in Table 2.1 is meant to give you an overview only. Don't waste your time learning dates and all the ins and outs of the computer's past.

continues

37

continued

There are expert programmers who have fantastic programming jobs who know less about the history of computers than you know now. You can probably jump right in and begin programming without knowing much about the background of the computing industry. However, there is so much literature that refers to the computer's background and to the different generations of computers that you will only benefit from having a cursory understanding of the computer's short history.

Think about how lost you might be, however, if you jumped right in and started learning about what a program is if you had no idea what the computer itself was all about. It is the opinion of the author and most computer school instructors that a brief background is vital for new programmers so that they can appreciate the efforts made by those before them and better understand the needs of the industry today.

Today's Computers

If you read many texts on today's computers, you will see the terms *fourth generation* and *fifth generation* computers used sometimes. Most computer pundits agree that the distinction between generations after the third is nothing more than opinion. There has not been as obvious and distinct a separation of technology since the third generation as there were with the first three. Nevertheless, every day it seems that computer manufacturers are finding ways to squeeze more parts onto smaller integrated circuits at a fraction of the previous technology's cost.

The future of computer technology seems intent on repeating the previous 50 years. It appears that more and more computing power will be squeezed into smaller, more reliable, faster, and cheaper boxes. More and more people will use computers for more and more uses.

What this means to the programmer is twofold. First, as more people use computers, more programmers are needed to write the programs for the computers. Second, as computers get more powerful and faster, older uses of computers (and therefore, older programs) have to be updated to take advantage of the new hardware.

Clue: How fast is "fast enough"? Will there be a day when computers do not have to go any faster? Have we already reached that point?

Think about this for a moment: If computers were several times faster than today's machines, forecasters could predict the weather with stunning accuracy—much more accurately than today. "So what?" you might still ask. Think about how many lives could be saved if the exact pattern and severity of every hurricane, tornado, and flood could be tracked weeks in advance. The advantages of working until computers are fast enough to predict the weather perfectly are recordable in human lives. Completely accurate weather predictions are just one of the many areas, along with space exploration, statistics, economic policy planning, and scientific research, where computers much faster than today's versions would benefit society.

The Types of Computers

Computers come in all shapes and sizes, but they primarily fall within four broad categories: *supercomputers, mainframes, minicomputers,* and *microcomputers.* Before delving into the hardware specifics of computers, it will be helpful to define what the four types of computers are all about.

Pitfall: Don't fall into the trap of thinking that small desktop computers will someday replace larger ones. It looks as if that will never happen. What some people forget is that as desktop computers become faster and more powerful, larger computers become faster and more powerful, too. The largest computers of today, called *supercomputers*, are four times as fast as the supercomputers of two years ago.

Despite the fact that computers are getting smaller, there is still need for large computers. Businesses, banks, universities, and other large organizations need the power that larger computers bring. Although desktop computers are getting more powerful every day, the larger machines still produce hundreds of times more computing power than smaller ones do.

One thing to note before looking at the specific types of computers is that all types but the microcomputer are designed to be multi-user computers. That is, even though computers can perform only one instruction at a time, they do it so very fast that more than one person can share the computer and each person thinks he or she is the only person on that computer at the time. Today's microcomputers are beginning to show multi-user capabilities, but they are still used primarily as single-user machines.

Supercomputers

The most expensive and fastest computers in existence are supercomputers. Supercomputers are so fast that they are best used for scientific applications where heavy mathematical calculations must be swift. The expense of supercomputers and their lack of availability (there are only a few hundred in existence) cause most businesses to turn to the other kinds of computers mentioned in subsequent sections.

The name most associated with supercomputers is *Cray*. The *Cray Research Company*, the largest (and first) maker of supercomputers, founded by Seymour

Cray, is the company known for continually perfecting and improving super-computers with each version they release. IBM, Burroughs, and some Asian firms are competing for dominance in the supercomputer field, but Cray has sold more and is currently known for being the primary supplier of supercomputers for the world.

Supercomputers run at speeds up to 75,000 times that of the fastest micro-computers. Supercomputers generally take a large staff to run and maintain. The physical size of a supercomputer is generally not as large as that of mainframes (the next level of computers). What makes supercomputers different from main-frame computers is that they are supercooled (hence, the name *super*computer). Hydrogen, helium, or other gases are cooled down to tremendous levels so they form a liquid. This supercooled liquid is then run throughout the circuits of the supercomputer. When computer components are cooled, they run faster because there is less resistance (heat increases electronic resistance) on the circuits.

Not only is the inside of a supercomputer different from the other types of computers, but the outward appearance also is different. Supercomputers often come in strange shapes, such as semicircles and ovals (the standard shape of other kinds of computers is a square or rectangle). The designers of supercomputers shape the enclosures so that the internal wires have less distance to travel. With shorter distances come faster speeds. The shape and super cooling properties of super-computers help make them the fastest type of computer.

Mainframes

Mainframe computers are the cornerstone of modern-day business data process-ing. When heavy processing and several thousand users must be handled at once, a mainframe is the primary choice for businesses.

Mainframe computers require large staffs of maintenance personnel, operators, programmers, and data-entry clerks. They run around the clock, and any *downtime* (machine failure) is costly to the companies that rely on them. Mainframe computers require a large room or two to house because of their large system units and the numerous storage devices attached to them. These rooms are

41

often environmentally controlled, being cooled to keep the computer running at a comfortable level, and the air is filtered to keep as much dust out of the system as possible.

Some companies have two or more mainframe computers connected to each other, as well as networked also to minicomputers and microcomputers. The smaller computers offload some of the workload from the mainframe, leaving the mainframe to handle the more calculation-intensive tasks.

Minicomputers

The minicomputer is generally a multi-user computer that can handle up to 300 users at the same time. A minicomputer typically is no larger than a refrigerator. Small businesses that cannot afford the cost of mainframes can buy one or two minicomputers to do the data processing that is still too heavy for microcomputers. The minicomputer is not as fast as a mainframe, but it does not cost as much, either. These smaller computers rarely require the special environmentally controlled rooms that mainframes do.

If any computer is phased out over the coming years, it will be the minicomputer. The microcomputer is getting more powerful and is becoming fast enough to handle more than one user seamlessly. Today's microcomputer storage capacities rival that of minicomputers, and the cost of the microcomputer is much less than that of the minicomputer.

During the 1970s and 1980s, the minicomputer filled a niche that the microcomputer was not capable of filling at the time. Mainframes were out of reach to a lot of companies, and the microcomputer was not powerful enough for serious multi-user business data processing.

The most popular operating system on minicomputers is the *UNIX* operating system. The growth of UNIX popularity appears to have peaked in the last couple of years. Many people feel that businesses are buying several microcomputers and networking them together in place of using a more costly minicomputer.

"The Operating System" section later in this chapter explains what operating systems are all about in case you are unfamiliar with them.

> **Note:** A company can purchase much more computing power for less money if it buys lots of microcomputers instead of a single minicomputer. There is an advantage to having all of the processing on a single machine, because there is less maintenance and more uniformity among users and programs. However, there are more long-run advantages to networking microcomputers together. By networking them, the individual computers can share data, and if one breaks down, the others can continue processing.

Microcomputers

The microcomputer is the smallest, least expensive, and most popular computer in existence today. Often called *desktop computers*, *PCs*, and *personal computers*, the microcomputer has seen a tremendous growth in popularity since the late 1970s and its fast-paced growth seems to be continuing into the future.

The most popular type of microcomputer is the IBM-compatible computer. The line of IBM-compatibles includes a microprocessor from the 80X86 family of processors. Intel is the company that developed the original 8088 (the chip on which the first IBM PC was based) and has since improved the chip. The improved versions of the chip are named 80286, 80386, 80486, and the naming trend continues.

The microcomputer second in popularity is Apple's line known as the Macintosh. Although the Macintosh computers have always taken the lead in graphics and musical capabilities, the IBM-compatibles are never far behind. Because businesses originally adopted the IBM PC en masse instead of Apple's original line of computers named the Apple II, no Apple computer since the IBM PC was introduced has enjoyed as big a sales share as the IBM-compatibles.

PCs are taken very seriously in the world of business. "A PC on every desktop" seems to be the objective of today's management. PCs are now small enough to fit in a briefcase, and fewer business travelers are without their PCs. It is also common to see at least one microcomputer in most homes—something almost unheard of a decade ago.

The most commonly used operating system used on PCs is MS-DOS, an operating system written by Microsoft for IBM-compatible computers. (IBM brand computers use the PC DOS operating system, which is the IBM version of MS-DOS and fully compatible in every way.)

Because of the wide availability and low cost of microcomputers, most programmers learn programming on them. The focus of this book is programming on the PC, although some attention is devoted to programming on the larger computers. This book assumes that you are learning to program on a PC, but as your skills progress, you someday may be programming in a larger organization. You will not only learn to write programs, but you will also learn how a company goes about designing and writing programs.

The Computer's Hardware

This section of the chapter gives you a brief overview of computer hardware and how the programmer can direct that hardware in programs. The PC is the primary focus of this discussion. If you will be programming a larger computer, such as a mainframe, all of the same information applies on a much larger scale. All computers, from supercomputers to the smallest PCs, have the same primary components; they all have memory, a processor, and input and output devices.

Figure 2.1 shows you what a typical PC looks like today. Almost every PC has a system unit, monitor, keyboard, and printer. Long-term storage is achieved through the disk drives. Earlier microcomputers used a cassette tape for data and program storage, but disk drives are more reliable and offer faster retrieval. Larger computers have the same parts, although they usually have more of each and are scattered over a larger area. Some mainframes have as many as 1,000 keyboards, 50 disk drives, and 50 printers attached to them.

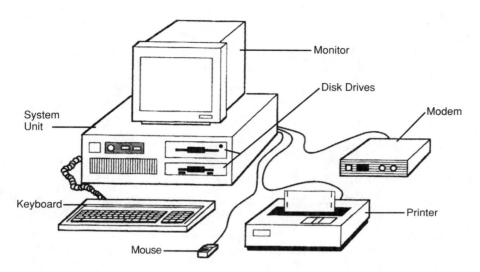

Figure 2.1. The typical parts of a microcomputer.

The System Unit

The primary component of a PC is the system unit. It is in the system unit where the primary memory, power supply, disk drives, and, most importantly, the microprocessor are located. The microprocessor is often called the *CPU* (for *central processing unit*). The CPU is the true computer as it does all the work of processing the data and producing the information needed.

Figure 2.2 shows you what the inside of a typical system unit looks like. The power supply steps down the wall outlet's voltage from 110 volts to around 5 volts. The circuitry inside the computer needs very little voltage to run. A fan next to the power supply keeps the air circulating enough to keep the temperature down.

Clue: Remember that only a few years earlier, much of an entire building was devoted to the power supply and air conditioning of the computer? Can you see that they've come a long way?

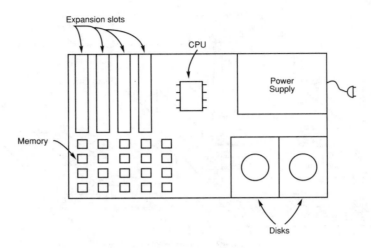

Figure 2.2. *The inside of a PC's system unit.*

In the back of the system unit resides a set of expansion slots that hold electronic circuit cards. These slots enable you to expand the capability of your computer so that you can add storage and additional devices to the computer later. It is in these expansion slots that you can add an expansion card for a *modem*, which lets your computer communicate with other computers via the telephone lines.

> **Note:** The devices inside and outside the system unit are often called *peripheral devices.* A device is either an *input device, output device,* or both *input/output device* (*I/O device* for short). To know which is which, picture yourself inside the CPU. If data is coming *in* to you, such as that from a keyboard, the device is an input device. If you are sending information *out* of the computer, such as to the printer, you are writing to an output device.

The memory of the PC generally resides inside the system unit as well. Memory is housed in small integrated circuit chips (generally smaller than the CPU) inside the computer. The important memory is known as *RAM,* which stands for *random access memory.* When you execute the programs you write, the computer stores those programs in RAM during the programs' execution. RAM is volatile; that is, when you turn the computer off, the contents of RAM are automatically erased.

Another type of memory, called *ROM* (for *read-only memory*), is not very important to programmers. You cannot change the contents of ROM. ROM is used to store the self-test procedure that runs when you turn on the computer, and it also loads DOS from the disk drive into memory.

Clue: If the different memory measurements such as *640K* confuse you, don't be alarmed, because there is an easy-to-understand explanation. In computer terminology, *K* means 1,024 kilobytes, although most computer people round the number down to an even 1,000 when discussing memory. (A *byte* is any single character in the computer.) Therefore, *640K* means approximately 640,000 bytes of storage. An *M* after a number means *megabyte. Mega* is computer lingo for *million. 20M* means approximately 20 million bytes of storage.

Disks

Disks hold the long-term storage of your programs and data. Like cassette tapes, disks hold data until you erase or change that data. Disks are non-volatile; that is, they retain their memory after the power is turned off because data is stored on them magnetically.

The *disk drive* is the box connected to the computer that holds the disk. There are two primary types of disks: *hard disks* and *floppy disks* (also known as *diskettes*). The hard disk is sealed inside the disk drive and is usually located inside the system unit. Hard disks are faster and have much more storage capacity than floppy disks. Floppy disks offer the advantage of portable storage; you can save data on a floppy disk and transfer that data to any other computer with a floppy disk drive compatible with yours.

> **Note:** Because you can store information on and read data from a disk, it is known as an *I/O device*.

The Keyboard

As you probably already know, the keyboard is the typewriter-like set of keys attached to your computer. The computer's keyboard includes both alphabetic and numeric keys. Often, the keyboard includes a *numeric keypad*, a calculator-style set of number keys that makes entering numeric data easier than using the numbers across the top of your alphabetic keys.

The Enter key is also known as the *carriage return* key. You often press Enter when you want to end a line of input. If you have used a word processor before, you may be used to the *word wrap* feature available on most word processors. As you get to the end of a line of text, the word processor automatically wraps down to the next line without requiring you to press Enter as you would on a typewriter. As a programmer, you rarely want to use word wrap because you need to control exactly how the lines end in your programs.

There are several other keys important to the programmer. The Alt and Ctrl keys work like a second and third set of Shift keys; that is, you hold down Ctrl or Alt, press another key while still holding down Ctrl or Alt, and then let up on both. The arrows move the *cursor* (the blinking line that shows where on the screen the next typed character will appear) around the screen in some programs. The Esc key generally acts like a back-up key, letting you quit, or *escape* early from a command that you have started.

The keys labeled F1 through F10 (some keyboards go as high as F12) are called *function keys*. The function keys are shortcut keys for other tasks. Each program you use maps different functions to the function keys, so you will have to learn the many uses of them as you learn more about your programs.

The Monitor

The monitor is the television-like device on which you view computer output. The monitor is also called a *video screen* and *CRT* (for *cathode ray tube*). Monitors are either color or *monochrome* (one-color text on a black background). The price difference between color and monochrome is so little these days that most people go ahead and purchase a color monitor when they buy a computer system. Graphics are much more useful when you can view them in color.

The monitor plugs into a card that is located in one of your system unit's expansion slots.

The Printer

The printed output from programs goes to the printer. The printer prints to paper whatever your programs send to it. The printer's output is often called *hard copy*. When you produce a hard copy listing of a program, you are printing a listing of the program on paper.

There are many kinds of printers, but they primarily fall into two categories: dot matrix and laser printers. A dot matrix printer forms its characters with a series of small dots that strike the paper through the ribbon. A laser printer uses a laser beam to burn toner dust onto the paper. A laser printer is much faster and produces better output than a dot matrix. If cost is an issue, however, an inexpensive dot matrix printer will last for years and works well in all computer environments.

The Operating System

The hardware is useless without an operating system. The operating system is the go-between for the hardware and the programs and data. When a program issues a command to write to or read from a device, the operating system carries out the work. Figure 2.3 shows the logical view of the operating system and the rest of the computer's hardware and software.

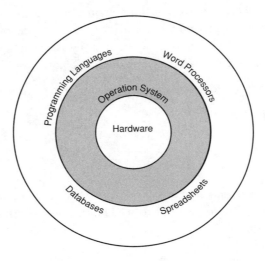

Figure 2.3. *The operating system helps the software communicate with the hardware.*

The operating system forms a common interface for programs. Instead of your having to include all the specifics of writing to the disk, moving the read/write disk head, spinning the disk platter, and so on, the operating system makes sure all these tedious chores are done for you.

Although the operating system is often called *DOS* for *disk operating system*, DOS handles more than just the disks. DOS controls all the peripheral devices on the inside and outside of your computer. Most programmers take the time to learn a little about the operating system on which they program. You should plan to learn a few DOS commands along with learning a programming language. If you do, you will be able to take control of your computer instead of it taking control of you.

Warning: The make-up of operating systems is changing rapidly. You should keep your learning hat on and your eyes open for changes in the way your operating system works throughout its future versions. Some computer professionals feel that the MS-DOS environment is headed for an early grave, but there are still hundreds of thousands of MS-DOS users who might argue the point.

It is almost certain that graphical user interfaces (*GUIs*) will continue to dominate more of the operating system environment in the future because they streamline the use of the operating system; instead of having to learn a bunch of operating system commands, you can select from icons (little pictures on the screen) that represent what you want to do. Microsoft Windows is currently the most popular GUI, and the Windows NT promises to become a dominate player in the GUI market. The Apple Macintosh interface is also an integrated GUI environment. Learn about both DOS and GUI environments, because GUI is here to stay. Don't let GUIs sneak up on you before you learn something about them in advance.

Chapter Highlights

Now that you know where the computer industry has been, you will have a good idea of where it is heading. The computers of tomorrow will be faster, cheaper, and smaller than today's, and more people will be needed to program them.

✖ The computer industry is one of the newest industries.

✖ The first electronic computer was developed in the late 1940s.

✖ Computers have gone through three stages: First generation computers were tube-based, second generation computers were transistor-based, and third generation computers contain integrated circuits that hold all of their components.

✖ Computers keep getting cheaper, smaller, and more powerful over time.

✖ The most powerful computers in the world are supercomputers. They are supercooled and built in various shapes to eke out more speed.

✖ Mainframes are the most commonly used computers in business today. Thousands of users can use a mainframe at the same time. A large support staff is generally on hand to care for and operate the mainframe.

✖ Minicomputers are smaller computers popular for businesses throughout the 1970s and 1980s. Their popularity is waning as microcomputers become more powerful and less expensive.

✖ The microcomputer is the least expensive and least powerful of the four types of computers. Because microcomputers are getting more powerful every day, businesses and individuals are integrating them into day-to-day work. Many businesses let their employees connect microcomputers to the company's mainframe to share the computing power and workload.

✖ The parts of a computer are similar whether it is a supercomputer or a microcomputer. All computers have CPUs, memory, disk drives, printers, and keyboards.

✖ The operating system is the go-between that lets your programs work with your computer's hardware. The operating system is nothing more than a big program that always runs under your own programs.

✖ There are several graphical-oriented operating systems being developed that make using computers easier.

What Is a Program?

3

Perilous Perry was lost. Our hero was uncomfortable with such an involved and detailed map. Will Perilous Perry make sense of all the directions?

1. Why are programs like directions to the computer?

2. Why do programs have to be so detailed?

3. Why must programs reside in memory instead of remaining on the disk drive when you execute them?

4. Is programming considered an art or a science?

5. What are some of the more common programming languages?

6. Why do computers not yet understand a human language?

7. What are the two types of errors that can occur in programs?

The words *program* and *programmer* are mentioned throughout this book, and you've undoubtedly heard them before you picked up this tome. Before delving into the specifics of programming languages, this chapter attempts to explain what a program really is. A firm grasp of this chapter's material is a prerequisite for moving on to the programming languages later in this book.

As you read this chapter, keep in mind that programming is rewarding, not only financially, but also mentally and emotionally. Programmers often feel the same sense of creative rush that artists and skilled craftspeople feel while honing their projects. Writing a program, however, can be tedious. It is often a detailed task, and ample frustration comes with the territory. If you are not a "details person," don't fret—the tedium of programming does not really translate into the same tedium that other types of jobs generate. The computer's quick feedback on your mistakes often provides a sense of accomplishment that keeps you programming until you get it right.

The Need for Programs

When individuals and companies need a program, there are three ways they can obtain it.

✖ They can buy one that's already written.

✖ They can buy one and modify it.

✖ They can write their own.

There are advantages and disadvantages to each option, which Table 3.1 lists. The first two options are much quicker than the third, and also much less expensive.

Table 3.1. The advantages and disadvantages of the three software options.

Option	Advantages and Disadvantages
Buy one	**Advantage:** The program can be obtained quickly and inexpensively. **Disadvantage:** The program may not be exactly what is needed.
Buy and modify one	**Advantage:** A usable program that does what is needed can be obtained fairly quickly. Also, the program is relatively inexpensive, depending on the changes needed. **Disadvantage:** It isn't always possible to modify the program.
Write one	**Advantage:** The program (after proper design and debugging) does exactly what you want it to do. **Disadvantage:** This option is very expensive and takes a lot longer than the other options.

Most microcomputer users choose the first option because the programs are fairly inexpensive given their power. Because companies such as Borland, Microsoft, and Lotus sell so many of the same versions of programs, they can do so at fairly inexpensive prices. Individual microcomputer users simply do not have the resources that companies have to write every program they need.

Companies, on the other hand, do not always choose the first option, although you may question why. Companies spend many years developing products and services that distinguish themselves from other companies. When a company computerizes any of its record keeping, it is vital that the programs reflect exactly what the company does already. The company should not have to change the way it does business just so it can use programs it buys. Purchased programs have to be generic so the producers of the programs can sell them to more than one customer.

57

The second option might then seem like the smartest, but it is chosen least often. If companies could buy a program that is already written, they would have a framework in which to quickly adapt it to their specific needs. The problem is that software is rarely sold; rather, it is *licensed*. When you buy a program, you do not own the program, you only own the right to use it. You cannot legally change it, sell it, or copy it (except for backup purposes). Not only are there legalities involved, but sometimes you cannot physically change the software either. As you will learn later in this chapter, once a program is written, it is translated to a compressed format that programmers can no longer modify.

Note: There are some reverse-engineering methods, such as programs called *disassemblers*, that can take the translated code and offer clues as to how the original program looked. These programs are, at best, only guessing as to what the original programmers did, and they offer little help in finding what went on before the program was translated into its compressed, machine-readable format.

Therefore, although it is expensive and time-consuming to write programs from scratch, most businesses prefer to do so, keeping large programming departments on hand to handle the programming load. A company might have several members of its data processing staff spend a full year writing a program that is a lot like one the company could buy, but not exactly like any they could purchase. Despite the cost and effort involved, it is worth it to the company not to have to conform to a program they buy from someone else.

Reward: Some companies have found that they can sell programs they develop to *other* firms doing similar business, thereby recapturing some of their development costs.

Companies often measure the amount of time it takes to write programs in *people years*. If it takes two people years to write a single program, it is estimated that two people could write it in a single year, or one person would take two years.

A 20-people-year project would take 20 people one year, or one person 20 years, or ten people two years, and so forth. This measurement is only an estimate, but it gives management an idea of how it should allocate people and time for programming projects.

Programs, Programs, Everywhere

Why aren't all the programs needed already written? Walk into any software store today and you'll see hundreds of programs for sale. There are programs for everything: word processing, accounting, drawing, playing games, designing homes, and planning trip itineraries. It seems as if any program you need is within reach. Because computers have been around for 50 years, you would think we'd be about done with all the programming anyone would need for a long time.

If all the programs needed were already written, you would not see the large listings of "Programmer Wanted" ads in today's newspapers. The fact is, the world is changing every day, and businesses and people must change with it. Programs written ten years ago are simply not up-to-date with today's practices. They were also written on computers much slower and more limited than today's machines. As hardware advances are made, the software must advance with it.

There is a tremendous need for programmers out there, today more than ever. As computers get easier to use, some people believe that programmers will become relics of the past. What they fail to realize is that it takes top-notch programmers to produce those easy-to-use programs.

Programs As Directions

If you have followed a map into unfamiliar territory, you know what it is like for your computer to follow a program's instructions. With only the map, you feel blind as you move from place to place, turning left and right, until you reach your destination or find that you made a wrong turn somewhere. Your computer, as the previous chapters explain, is a blind and dumb machine waiting for you to

59

give it directions. When you do, the computer acts out the instructions you give it without second-guessing your desires. If you tell it to do something incorrectly, it does its best to do so. Recall this definition of a program (from Chapter 1):

A program is a list of detailed instructions that the computer carries out.

The term *detailed* is vital to making a machine follow out your orders. Actually, the job of programming is not difficult; what is difficult is breaking the computer's job into simple and detailed steps that assume nothing.

To get an idea of the thinking involved in programming, have some fun thinking about how you would describe starting a car to someone from the past. Suppose a cowboy from the old west named Heath appears at your doorstep, bewildered by the sights around him. After getting over the future shock, Heath wants to adapt to this new world. Before learning to drive a car, Heath must learn to start it. Once he is comfortable doing that, you will teach him to drive. Unlike a 16-year-old learning to drive, Heath has not grown up seeing adults starting cars, so he really needs to master this process before going any further. Being the busy programmer you are, you leave him the following set of instructions:

1. Use this key.

2. Start the car.

How far would Heath get? Not very far. You gave correct instructions for starting a car, but you assumed too much knowledge on his part. You must remember that he knows nothing about these contraptions called automobiles and that he is relying on you to give him instructions that he can understand. Instead of assuming so much, these might be better instructions:

1. Attached is the key to the car. You need it to start the car.

2. With the key in hand, go to the car door that is closest to the front door of the house.

3. Under the door's handle, you will see a round silver-dollar-sized metal part in which you can insert the key (with its rough side pointing down).

4. After sticking the key into the hole as far as it goes, turn it to the right until you hear a click.

5. Turn the key back to the left until it faces the same way as it did when you inserted it and remove the key.

6. Open the door and get into the car. Be sure to sit in front of the round wheel on the left-hand side of the front seat.

7. Close the door.

8. On the right side of the column holding the big round wheel (called a *steering wheel*), you will see a slot in which you can put the key.

Are you beginning to get the idea? This list of eight items is very detailed, and Heath hasn't even started the car yet. You still have to describe the gas pedal that he must press while he turns the key (in the correct direction, of course), and you don't want to assume that Heath will turn *off* the car when he is done practicing, so you have to give him those directions as well.

If you are beginning to think this car-starting analogy is going a little too far, consider what you must do to tell a nonthinking piece of electronic equipment to perform your company's payroll. A payroll program cannot just consist of the following steps:

1. Get the payroll data.

2. Calculate the payroll and taxes.

3. Print the checks.

To the computer, these instructions lack thousands of details that you might take for granted. It is the detailing of the program's instructions that provides for the tedium and occasional frustration of programming. Programming computers isn't difficult, but breaking down real-world problems into lots of detailed steps that a computer can understand is hard.

Clue: A typical payroll program might contain 20,000 or more lines of instructions. Don't let this deter you, however. Most company's large programming projects are written by teams of programmers; you will have plenty of help if you ever write such programs for a living. Also, new programming techniques and programming environments for today's computer languages make programming, even for the individual programmer working alone, much easier than ever before.

There are many design tools that help you take large problems and break them down into detailed components that translate into programming elements. Chapter 4, "Designing the Program," explains many of the methods that programmers use to get to a program's needed details. Therefore, instead of jumping ship amid this chapter's seemingly horrendous descriptions of the details of programs, keep a stiff upper lip because help is on the way. Also consider this: If programming were truly difficult, there is no way so many computer advances could have been made over the last 50 years.

> **Warning:** Not only are the programming instructions themselves important, but so is their order. When writing a program, you must think through the exact order necessary to perform the job at hand. The computer executes a program in the order that your commands dictate. You cannot print bills before calculating how much the customers owe.
>
> The detailed nature of programming makes putting programming statements in the right order even more difficult. It's not always an easy job breaking a problem into details and then ordering them correctly so that each step can rely on the preceding steps. Luckily, there are design tools to help you get the program's sequence in order. You will learn about some of them in the next chapter.

Programs Are Saved Instructions

The nice thing about programs you write is that you save them to disk after you write them. As with word-processed text, store the programs you write in disk files. A program is to a computer like a recipe is to a cook. When a cook wants to make a certain dish, he or she finds the correct recipe and follows the instructions. When someone wants to execute a program, she or he instructs the computer to load the program from disk into memory and then run the program's instructions.

The computer's internal RAM is vital for program execution. Your computer's CPU cannot execute a program's instructions on the disk. Just as you cannot know what is in a book lying on a table until you read the book's contents into your memory (using your own CPU, your mind), your CPU cannot process a program's instructions until it loads the program from disk into main memory. Figure 3.1 shows the process of loading a program from the computer's disk into memory. As the figure shows, the CPU has direct access to memory, but has no access to the disk drive. The disk is the long-term storage, and the memory is the short-term storage where programs temporarily reside while the CPU executes them.

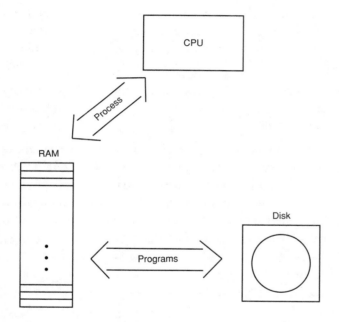

Figure 3.1. *A program must be in memory before the CPU can execute the program's instructions.*

Keep in mind the difference between the program and its output. The program is a set of instructions, and the output is the *result* of those instructions. A recipe's output is the finished dish, and the program's output is the printed output once the instructions are running.

If you use a word processor, you probably follow these steps:

1. You load the word processing program from the disk into the computer's main memory. Before now, you may not have even realized you were doing this. When you type the word processing program's name at the DOS prompt (or when you select the program from a menu or from within a windows environment), you are instructing the computer to search the disk drive for the program and load it into main memory.

2. The word processor's main menu or editing window appears on your screen. What you see on the screen is output from the program. Even though you can produce more output by typing in text and printing it on the printer, the screen's information is program output as well.

3. When you exit the word processor, your operating system regains control. The word processing program is no longer in memory, but it is still safely tucked away on disk.

As you can see, the results of a program's execution make up the output. The instructions themselves are what produce those results. Figure 3.2 gives an overview of the program/output process. Modern-day programs produce output in many different ways. Programs play music, talk to other computers over the phone lines, and control external devices. Output sent to the screen and printer still makes up the majority of today's program output.

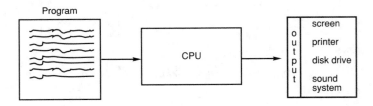

Figure 3.2. *The program comes from disk, executes, and then sends its results to any of the many output devices such as the disk, screen, or printer (or more than one of them from within the same program).*

When a program is in memory, it is not there alone. Your operating system always resides in memory. If it did not, you could neither load a program from disk nor run one. Limited memory often poses a problem for larger programs. You should recall that a program processes data, and the data must be in memory as well as the program before the program can process it easily.

Figure 3.3 shows what a typical computer installation's memory looks like when a program is running. The operating system takes a big chunk, the program must be there too, and, finally, there must be room for data.

Figure 3.3. *A typical memory layout.*

Art or Science?

A debate that you often see in computer literature is whether programming is an art or a science. Throughout the years, there have been advances made in programming that, if followed, improve a program's accuracy, readability, and maintainability (the process of changing the program later to perform a different or additional set of tasks). Most of these advancements are nothing more than suggestions; that is, programmers do not have to use them to write programs that work.

Two of the most important advances in programming are more philosophically based than engineered. They are *structured programming* and *object-oriented programming*. This book explores these two programming advances thoroughly in the chapters that follow. They both offer suggested ways that a programmer can write a program to make it better. Again, though, these are just suggested approaches to programming that programmers can (and many do) ignore.

Pitfall: There is no one correct way to write a program, but there are a lot of *wrong* ways!

There are many ways to write even the smallest and simplest programs. Just as authors write differently and musicians play differently, programmers each have their own style. Therefore, you would think that programming is more of an art than a science. On the continuum of science to art, you would be closer to being correct than those few who argue that programming is more of a science.

Nevertheless, as more advances are made into developing programming approaches such as structured programming and object-oriented programming, you should see a shift in thinking. With the proliferation of computers in today's world, there is a massive education in process to train tomorrow's programmers. Because the programming industry is young (as is the entire computer industry), there are a lot of advancements left to make.

Some of the biggest proponents of moving away from the artful approach to a more scientific approach, using structured and object-oriented programming, are the companies paying the programmers. Companies need to react quickly to changing business conditions, and they need programs written as quickly and as accurately as possible. As advances in computer programming are discovered, more companies are going to adopt policies that require their programmers to use more scientific and proven methods of writing better programs.

Speak the Language

The instructions you give in your programs must be in a language the computer understands. At its lowest level, a computer is nothing more than thousands of switches, flipping on and off lightning fast. A switch can have only two states; it can be *on* or *off*. Because either of these two states of electricity can be controlled easily with electronic switches, many thousands of them control what your computer does from one microsecond to another.

If it were up to your computer, you would have to give it instructions using switches that represent on and off states of electricity. Actually, that is exactly the way the early computers were programmed. A panel of switches, such as the one shown in Figure 3.4, had to be used to enter all programs and data. The next time you find yourself cursing your programs, think of what it would have been like programming 45 years ago.

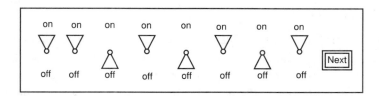

Figure 3.4. *A panel of switches programmed early computers.*

The on and off states of electricity are represented as 1s and 0s at the computer's lowest level. You can control what your computer does if you know the correct pattern of 1s and 0s required to give it commands. Of course, programming in 1s and 0s is not much better than the switch panel, so there has to be a better way.

Pitfall: Computers are not going to learn English any time soon, despite what you might see in science fiction movies. You have to learn a programming language if you want the computer to do what you want.

English and all the other spoken languages are too ambiguous to computers. People's brains can decipher sentences intuitively, something a nonthinking machine cannot do. There are some inroads being made into *artificial intelligence*, which is the science of programming computers so they can learn on their own. It also includes programming them to understand a spoken language such as English. Despite recent advancements, artificial intelligence is many years away (if it is even possible for computers to understand simple English).

Consider the following sentence:

Time flies like an arrow.

Your mind has no trouble understanding the parts of this sentence. You know that it is an analogy, and the parts of speech make total sense to you. *Time* is a noun that performs an action, it *flies*, and it does so *like an arrow*. If you teach the computer to accept these descriptions of this sentence, it will work fine until it runs into something like this:

Fruit flies like an orange.

Think about this for a moment. Again, you have no problem understanding this sentence, even though it is completely different in every way from the other one. The computer taught to decipher the first sentence, however, is going to throw its cables up in frustration at the second sentence because none of the parts of the sentence are the same. The word *flies* is now a noun and not an action verb. The phrase *like an orange* is no longer a description of the action, but rather both the verb (*like*) and the object receiving the action (*an orange*). As you can see from these two sentences alone, understanding simple sentences that most people take for granted poses a tremendous problem for programmers trying to "teach" a computer to understand English.

Therefore, computers and people are at opposite ends of the spectrum. People want to speak their own language, but so do computers that only really understand 1s and 0s. There has to be some kind of go-between, so programming languages were created to try and appease both the computer and the person programming the computer. Programming languages use words similar to those that people use, but they have a highly specific *syntax* (ordering, grammar, and spelling) that allows little room for the ambiguity so prevalent in spoken languages. The computer can take a programming language and translate it down to its machine language of 1s and 0s; the human programmer can learn, remember, and use the programming languages more effectively than 1s and 0s because they appear similar to spoken languages.

You are going to learn a lot about different programming languages in this book. You may have heard of some of them before, and you might not have heard of others. Over the years since the first computer language was invented, many hundreds of programming languages have been written, but there are a handful that have prevailed to dominate the rest. The following is a list of several programming languages that gained more than obscure notoriety through the years:

Machine Language *	Assembler *
Algol *	PL/I *
PROLOG *	LISP
COBOL *	Forth *
RPG *	RPG II *
Pascal *	Object Pascal *
SNOBOL	Ada *
C *	C++ *
Objective C	FORTRAN *
SmallTalk *	Eiffel
BASIC *	Visual BASIC *
APL *	

* These languages achieved dominance through either sheer numbers of usage, or in their specific area of expertise. For example, PROLOG is rarely used outside the artificial intelligence field, but has been the language of choice there.

Each programming language has its own dialects. BASIC is tremendously popular in all of the following varieties:

GW-BASIC
Quick BASIC
QBasic
BASICA
Visual BASIC

Before you finish this book, you will be writing programs in BASIC. Chapters 8, 9, and 10 teach you QBasic (one of today's most popular versions of the original BASIC language) and show you how to write complete programs that do what you want them to do.

Clue: Don't get frantic about the prospects of learning a new language. Learning a foreign language is much more difficult than learning a programming language for several reasons. The vocabularies of foreign languages are much larger, and the ambiguity of the languages stumps many students (just as it stumps the computer).

Most of a programming language is made up of words you already know, such as *while, if, then, for, let,* and so on. The computer's strict nature dictates very specific uses of these words, but the similarity of the words' meanings to that of their English usage makes programming languages easy for you to learn and remember.

The computer is like a tower of Babel, indirectly responsible for more programming languages than are probably needed. Most people considered to be "computer experts" might only know a handful of programming languages—from three to six—and they probably only know one or two very well. Therefore, don't let the large number of them deter you from wanting to learn to program.

There are lots of reasons why there are so many programming languages. Different people have different preferences, some languages are better than others depending on the tasks, and some people only have access to one or two of the languages.

Note: The program that you write is called a *source program* (or *source code*). Throughout this book, when you see the term *source program*, that text is referring to your program before it is compiled.

The Language Translator

Your computer cannot actually understand BASIC, C, Pascal, or any of the other programming languages. "Wait!" you might yell. "The previous section explained that computer languages are important because the computer cannot understand English, or any other languages that people speak, because there is too much ambiguity in speech." Even so, the computer cannot understand BASIC either, but it is easy for a program to translate BASIC to the actual 1s and 0s that the computer *does* understand.

There are two kinds of language translators: *compilers* and *interpreters*. Both take programming languages such as Pascal and translate them into a form readable by the computer. Each takes a different approach, but their end results are the same; both take programs and convert them into 1s and 0s (called *machine language*), as Figure 3.5 shows.

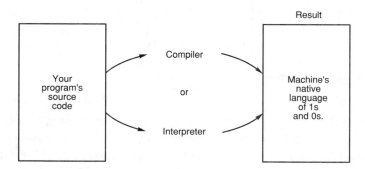

Figure 3.5. *Both interpreters and compilers translate source code into low-level machine language that the computer can understand.*

Interpreters

Some programming languages, such as APL and BASIC, come as interpreters (there are also BASIC compilers available). Interpreters translate one line at a time, executing each line as it is translated. The name *interpreter* is very descriptive. You are familiar with the way computer interpreters work because you already understand the way human interpreters work.

Suppose someone gives you a book written in a foreign language that you do not understand. In order to understand the book, you could hire a human interpreter to read the book to you. The interpreter reads a line, translates it, and then reads the next line to you. The only drawback to interpretation (as opposed to compilation, which the next section describes) is that the interpreter must reinterpret lines that you want read again. Interpretation is slower than compilation. Figure 3.6 shows the position of the human interpreter between you and the book. Keep this in mind as you read about the computer interpreters.

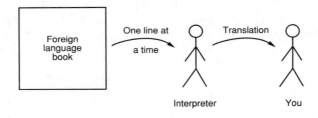

Figure 3.6. *An interpreter translates one line at a time.*

A programming language interpreter acts like the human interpreter in that it can be a slow process, interpreting one line at a time. Computers often perform repetitive tasks, such as printing several hundred payroll checks. If you have an interpreted programming language, the interpreter takes each line of the program, translates it, and then executes it. This process makes repetitive tasks run very slowly.

Here is a section from a BASIC program. You will learn more about the BASIC language specifics later in the book, but for now all you need to know is that these three lines repeat 50 times:

```
FOR i = 1 TO 50
  PRINT i
NEXT i
```

The reason the interpreter is slow is that every time it repeats a line, it must first interpret the line again. Therefore, these three lines of code are interpreted 50 times as well as run 50 times.

Interpreters do offer some advantages over compilers. Interpreted languages are a little easier to learn for beginning programmers. The process of compiling programs is historically more difficult than interpreting them (although many of today's compilers are almost as easy as to use as interpreters). The time from running the program to seeing the results is quicker when you use an interpreter. This quick feedback is helpful for beginners learning to program.

Compilers

Instead of hiring an interpreter to read the foreign language book to you, you might be better off asking the translator to *compile* the book for you. The translator can sit down and write out all the interpretation for you, without reading it to you while doing so. Although it takes much longer to prepare, you then can read the compiled version and refer to it as often as you need it.

Figure 3.7 shows the process of compiling the volume. The nice thing about having the compiled book is that you don't need the interpreter once the book is compiled.

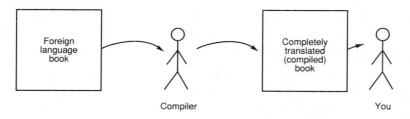

Figure 3.7. After compiling the book, you no longer need the translator.

Compiling a program takes an extra step over interpreting a program. You must request the compiler to compile the program and then wait for the results. Only after fully compiling the program will any of it work. Most beginning programmers have a difficult enough time learning about the hardware, operating system, and programming language, without having to learn compiler commands as well.

Most businesses prefer compiled programming languages because, once compiled, the programs run much faster than they would if they were interpreted. In the previous three-line BASIC example, the three lines only have to be compiled into machine language one time. Once the compiler is finished, the code executes the 50 repetitions without any translation at all.

Clue: Businesses prefer compiled programs over interpreted ones for security as well. Once compiled, a program cannot easily be changed. When you buy a program that is already written, the chances are good that it is compiled. You can run it, but you cannot see the source program itself.

Accuracy Is Everything

You now are well aware that the computer is a machine that cannot deal well with ambiguity. A programmer's plague is the collection of errors that show up in code. Programmers must ensure that they do not write programs that contain errors, although this is not always as easy as it might seem.

In computer terminology, a program error is known as a *bug*. When breaking the programming problem into detailed instructions, programmers often leave things out or code the wrong thing. When the program runs, errors creep up due to the bugs in the code.

Note: The term *bug* has an interesting origin. The late Naval Admiral, Grace Hopper, one of the early pioneers of computer hardware and software (she helped write the first COBOL compiler), was working on a military computer system in the early 1950s. While printing a report, the printer stopped working. Admiral Hopper and her coworkers set out to find the problem.

After spending lots of time without finding any problems in the program or data, Admiral Hopper looked in the printer and noticed that a moth had lodged itself in the wires of the printer, keeping the printer from operating properly. As soon as the *bug* (get it?) was removed, the printer worked perfectly. The moth did not fare as well, but it did go down in computer history as the first computer bug.

Debugging is the process a programmer goes through to exterminate the bugs from a program. As a programmer writes a program, he or she often runs the program in its unfinished state (as much as can be run) to catch as many bugs as possible and keep them out of the finished program. Often, the majority of the bugs can only be found after the program is completely written.

Absolute beginning programmers often fail to realize how easy it is for bugs to creep into code. Expect them and you will not be surprised. Many early programming students have taken a program into the instructor crying, "the computer doesn't work right," when in reality, the program has a bug or two. When you begin to write your first programs, expect to have to correct some problems. Nobody writes a perfect program every time.

Depending on the length of a program, the time it takes the programmer (or programmers) to correct the problems is often almost as long as the time taken to write the program originally. Some errors are very difficult to find.

There are two categories of computer bugs: *syntax errors* and *logic errors*. To learn the difference, take a few moments to find the two errors in the following statement:

There are two errrors in this sentence.

Clue: Need a clue? Not yet; look again for the two errors before going further.

75

The first error is obvious. The word *errrors* is misspelled. It should be *errors.* The second problem is much more difficult to find. The second problem with the statement is that the entire premise of the statement is incorrect. There is only *one* error in the statement, and that error is the misspelled word *errrors.* Therefore, the statement itself is in error.

This problem demonstrates the difference between a syntax error and a logic error. The syntax error is much easier to find. Syntax errors are commonly misspelled programming language commands and grammatical problems with the way you used the programming language. Logic errors occur when your program is syntactically correct, but you told it to do something that is not what should really be done.

Compilers and interpreters locate your program's syntax errors when you try to compile or run it. This is another reason why syntax errors are easier to spot: Your computer tells you where they are. When a computer runs into a syntax error, it halts and refuses to analyze the program further until you correct the syntax error. Figure 3.8 shows a QBasic program that stopped because of a syntax error. The QBasic interpreter stops and tells you the exact line where the error occurred.

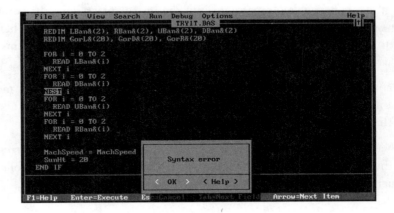

Figure 3.8. *QBasic finds a syntax error and refuses to continue.*

Suppose you're writing a program to print invoices for your company's accounts receivable. Because of an error, the computer prints all the invoices with a balance due of –$1,000. In other words, according to the invoice, every customer has a $1,000 credit. Your computer did its job, acting out your program's instructions. The program obviously contained no syntax errors because it ran without stopping. The logic errors, however, kept it from working properly.

Extensive testing is critical. The programmer wants to get all the errors out so the program will work correctly when the user finally uses it. The larger the program, the more difficult this is. Exterminating program bugs is just part of the daily job programmers tackle.

Chapter Highlights

There are several ways to get programs for computers, but to really make computers do what you want, you have to write the programs yourself. The programs direct the processing of data. You have to learn a programming language before you can write a program that the computer will understand.

✖ If you want your computer to do something, you must use a program. You can either buy one and use it, buy one and modify it before using it, or write one yourself.

✖ You do not really buy programs; you buy licenses to use programs. Therefore, you cannot always legally change them if you buy them.

✖ Most companies find they have to write programs they need. This explains the large programming staffs many companies hire.

✖ A program is a set of detailed instructions that the computer follows. Those instructions must be detailed for a machine to carry them out properly.

✖ Writing programs requires learning a programming language.

✖ There are many programming languages, but most programmers only know a handful, and they are a master of only one or two.

✖ There are some programming techniques that help streamline the programming process and move it from a pure art into a mixture of art and skilled science.

✖ Programs must be loaded from disk into the main memory before they can execute.

✖ Programs and output are different things. The programs create the output you see.

✖ Programming languages are needed as a stop gap measure between the low-level computer's 1s and 0s and the high-level human programmer who speaks in ambiguous speech.

✖ A translator, either an *interpreter* or *compiler*, must be used to translate the programming language into the machine's language.

✖ A *bug* is a program error.

✖ There are two kinds of program bugs: *syntax errors* and *logic errors*.

✖ Syntax errors are easy to spot. Generally, your compiler will tell you if there is a syntax error in your program.

✖ Logic errors are not usually found until you run your programs. Some logic errors are so obscure that it takes a long time to find them.

Designing the Program 4

Perilous Perry knew what he wanted. He had the necessary resources, but he couldn't seem to figure out where to begin. How will our hero solve this dilemma? What will Perilous Perry do first?

1. Why is program design so important?

2. What are the three steps required when writing a program?

3. What is meant by "output definition"?

4. Why is top-down design better than bottom-up design?

5. What is a flowchart?

6. What do the symbols in a flowchart mean?

7. Does pseudocode have advantages over flowcharts?

8. What is the last step in the programming process?

Programmers learn to develop patience early in their programming careers. They learn that proper design is critical to a successful program. Perhaps you have heard the term *systems analysis and design*. This is the name given to the practice of analyzing the problem to be programmed and then designing the program from that analysis. Complete books and college courses have been written about systems analysis and design. This chapter attempts to cover the highlights of systems analysis and design, letting you see what mainstream computer programmers go through before writing programs.

The Need for Design

When a builder begins to build a house, that builder does not pick up a hammer and begin on the kitchen's frame. The builder must go through many steps before the hammering starts. The house must be properly designed before anything can happen. As you will soon see, a program must also be designed before it is written. I'll continue with the house-building analogy a little further to acclimate you to the need for proper design.

The first thing the builder must do is find out what the purchaser of the house wants. Nothing can be built unless the builder has an end result in mind. (This isn't abstract art, you know.) Therefore, the buyers of the house must get with an architect. They tell the architect what they want the house to look like. The architect helps the buyers decide by telling them what is possible and what isn't.

Once the plans for the house are drawn, the builder must plan the resources needed to build the house. The builder must file the proper permits, get financing, gather the materials, and gather the workers. The builder must also decide on some kind of time frame and determine a proper schedule for completing each part of the building (the roof cannot go up before the foundation).

Only after the design of the house is finished, the permits filed, the money in place, the materials purchased, and the laborers hired, can any physical building be done. As a matter of fact, the more effort the builder puts into these preliminary requirements, the faster the house can actually be built.

The problem with building a house before it is properly designed is that the eventual owners may want changes made after it is too late to change them. It is very difficult to add a bathroom in the middle of two bedrooms *after* the house is completed. The primary idea is to get the owners of the house to agree with the builder on the final house. Once the specifications are agreed to by all the parties involved, there is little room for disagreement later.

Program Design

Sure, this is not a book on house construction, but you should always keep the similarities in mind before writing a program of any great length. You should not go to the keyboard and start typing instructions into the program before designing it any more than a builder should pick up a hammer before the house plans are determined.

Clue: As you will see throughout this chapter, the more up-front design you do, the faster you will finish the final program. Resist the temptation to start typing without having a firm idea of what your program should do.

Thanks to computer technology, a computer program is easier to modify than a house. If you leave out a routine that a user wanted, you can add it later more easily than a builder can add a room to a finished house. Nevertheless, adding something to a program is not ever as easy as designing the program correctly the first time.

Program maintenance is one of the most time-consuming parts of the programming process. Programs are continually updated to reflect new user needs. Sometimes, if the program is not designed properly before it is written, the user will not want the program until it does exactly what the user wants it to do.

83

Computer consultants learn early to get the user's acceptance, and even the user's signature, on a program's design before the programming begins. If both the user and the programmers agree on what to do, there is little room for argument when the final program is presented. Companies with internal data processing departments also require that their programming staffs come to a written agreement with the users who want them to write the programs. Company resources are limited; there is no time to add something later that should have been in the system all along.

Pitfall: Because computer programs must be extremely detailed, you have to follow some tried and tested procedures for breaking down problems into their detailed components. This chapter helps show you how to do this. Only after you understand that a program's details are critical can you begin to write programs with any success.

There are three steps you should perform when you have a program to write:

1. Define the output.

2. Develop the logic to get to that output.

3. Write the program.

Notice that writing the program is the last step in writing the program. This is not as silly as it sounds. Remember that physically building the house is the last stage of building the house; proper planning is critical before any actual building can start. You will find that actually writing and typing in the lines of the program is one of the easiest parts of the programming process. If your design is well thought out, the program practically writes itself; typing it in becomes almost an afterthought to the whole process.

The rest of this chapter explores these three components of program design.

> **Note:** You will write small programs that don't require these steps, but programs of any significant size at all deserve the respect of proper design. You end up with a program much faster if you design it first rather than if you blindly take off and begin typing lines of code. You also receive the benefit of fewer bugs in the programs that you think through before beginning them.

Step 1: Define the Output

Before beginning a program, you must have a firm idea of what the program should produce. Looking back at the fundamental model of programming (repeated in Figure 4.1), you see that the output is the last thing produced, but it is the *first thing you must design.* Just as a builder must know what the house should look like before beginning to build it, a programmer must know what the output is going to be before writing the program.

Figure 4.1. Data processing at its most fundamental level.

A program's output consists of more than just printed information. Anything that the program produces and the user sees is considered output that you must define. You must know what every screen in the program should look like and what will be on every page of every printed report.

The output definition is more than a preliminary output design. It gives you insight into what data elements the program should track, compute, and produce. Defining the output also helps you gather all the input you need to produce the output.

> **Warning:** Some programs produce a huge amount of output. Do not skip this first all-important step in the design process just because there is a lot of output. Quite the contrary, because there is more output, it becomes more important for you to define it. Defining the output is relatively easy—sometimes even downright boring and time-consuming. The time you need to define the output can take as long as the third step, typing in the program (the second step is the most time-consuming). You will be out that time and more, however, if you shrug off the output definition at the beginning.

The output definition consists of many pages of details. You must be able to specify all the details of a problem before you know what output you need. One of the best approaches for specifying the details of a problem is *top-down design*.

Top-Down Program Design

The most important design tool available is *top-down design*. It is with top-down design that you produce the details needed to accomplish a programming task. Top-down design is the process of taking the overall problem to program and breaking it down into more and more detail until you finalize all the details.

The problem with top-down design is that programmers tend not to use it. They tend to design from the opposite direction (called *bottom-up design*). When you ignore top-down design, you impose a heavy burden on yourself to remember every detail that will be needed; with top-down design, the details fall out on their own. You do not have to worry about the petty details if you follow a strict top-down design because the process of top-down design takes care of producing the details.

> **Clue:** One of the keys to top-down design is that it forces you to put off the details until later. Top-down design forces you to think in terms of the overall problem for as long as possible. Top-down design keeps you focused. If you use bottom-up design, it is too easy to lose sight of the forest for the trees. You get to the details too fast and lose sight of your program's primary objectives.

You can learn about top-down design more easily by relating it to a common real-world problem before looking at a computer problem. Top-down design is not just for programming problems. Once you master top-down design, you can apply it to any part of your life that you must plan in detail. Perhaps the most detailed event that a person can plan is a wedding. Therefore, a wedding is the perfect place to see top-down design in action.

What is the first thing you must do to have a wedding? First, find a spouse, but that is a different book. The top-down design is a good thing to develop first. The way to *not* plan a wedding is to worry about the details first, yet this is the way most people plan them. They start thinking about the dresses, the organist, the flowers, and the nuts to serve at the reception. The biggest problem with trying to cover all these details from the beginning is that you lose sight of so much; it is too easy to forget a detail until it is too late. The details of bottom-up design get in your way.

Here is the three-step process necessary for top-down design:

1. Determine the overall goal.

2. Break that goal into two, three, or four or more detailed parts. Too many more details make you leave out things.

3. Put off the details as long as possible. Keep repeating steps 1 and 2 until you cannot reasonably break down the problem any further.

What is the overall goal of a wedding? Thinking in the most general terms possible, "Have a wedding" is about as general as it can get. Therefore, if you were in charge of planning a wedding, the general goal of "Have a wedding" would put you right on target. Assume that "Have a wedding" is the highest-level goal.

> **Note:** The overall goal keeps you focused. Despite its redundant nature, "Have a wedding" keeps out details such as planning the honeymoon. If you don't put a fence around the exact problem you are working on, you'll get mixed up with details and, more importantly, you'll forget some details. If you're planning both a wedding and a honeymoon, you should do two top-down designs, or include the honeymoon trip in the general goal. The wedding being planned here includes the event of the wedding itself—the ceremony and reception—but does not include any honeymoon details. (It's up to your spouse-to-be to do that anyway, right?)

Now that you know where you're heading, begin breaking down the overall goal into two or three details. For instance, what about the colors of the wedding, what about the guest list, what about paying the minister... *oops,* too many details. The idea of top-down design is to put off the details for as long as possible. Don't get in any hurry. When you find yourself breaking the current problem into more than two or four parts, you are rushing the top-down design. Put off the details. Basically, you can break down "Have a wedding" into the following two components: the ceremony and the reception.

The next step of top-down design is to take those components and do the same for each of them. What makes up the ceremony are the people and the location. The reception includes the food, the people, and the location. The ceremony's people include the guests, the wedding party, and the workers (minister, organist, and so on, but those details come a little later).

The top-down design naturally produces a triangular result, the first part of which appears in Figure 4.2. There are a lot of details left to put in, but that is just the point; you should put off the details as long as possible. The details fall out on their own as you divide the tasks into more parts. By making sure your overall goal includes the general idea of where you want to head, the details will eventually come.

Soon, you will run out of room on the page. That's okay; use more sheets of paper. You can number the sheets and put the page number of each in the box "above" that page in the top-down design. Actually, keeping track of the pages is not as important as you might think. The first page is your focus page that makes sure you are working toward the goal you really want. Keep breaking down each of the succeeding detail pages until you can go no further. You will find that no detail is left out at the end.

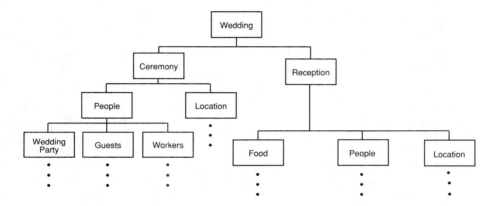

Figure 4.2. *The early part of planning a wedding using top-down design.*

Clue: Don't worry about the time-order of the details that you eventually get. The top-down design's goal is to produce every detail you need (eventually), not to put those details into any order. You must know where you are heading and exactly what is required before considering how those details relate to each other and which come first.

Eventually, you will have several pages of details that cannot be broken down any further. For instance, you'll probably end up with the details of the reception food, such as peanuts for snacking. (If you start out listing those details, however, you probably would forget many of them.)

Moving to a more "computerized" problem, what if you were assigned the task of writing a payroll program for a company. What would that payroll program require? You might begin to list the payroll program's details, such as this:

1. Print payroll checks.

2. Calculate federal taxes.

3. Calculate state taxes.

What is wrong with this approach? If you said that the details were coming too early, you are correct. The perfect place to start is at the top. The most general goal of a payroll program might be "Perform the payroll." Despite this obvious statement, the overall goal keeps other details out of this program (no general ledger processing will be included, unless part of the payroll system updates a general ledger file) and keeps you focused on the problem at hand.

Consider Figure 4.3. This might be the first page of the payroll's top-down design. Any payroll program has to include some mechanism for entering, deleting, and changing employee information such as address, city, state, ZIP code, number of exemptions, and so on. What other details about the employees do you need? At this point, don't ask. The design is not ready for all those details.

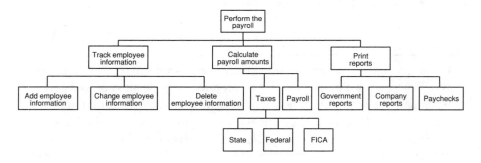

Figure 4.3. The first page of the payroll program's top-down design.

There is a long way to go before you finish with the payroll top-down design, but Figure 4.3 is the first step. You must keep breaking down each of the components until the details finally appear. Only after you have all the details ready can you begin to decide what the program is going to produce.

Reward: Work with the user when doing the top-down design. There are many advantages to working with the user early in the program's design. The user feels more involved with the finished product and is more willing to adapt to your system instead of fighting "that computer contraption."

Only when you and the user gather all the necessary details through top-down design can you decide what is going to comprise those details.

Tools for Output Definition

The details stemming from the top-down design are not all output. Many of the details are procedures the final program must perform. For instance, one of the details of a payroll program would probably be "Compute net pay." Computing net pay causes no output to appear. Elsewhere in the top-down design, somewhere under payroll reports, would be the "print net pay on the paycheck" detail. That detail would be output.

You must make sure that the output consists of and looks exactly like what the user wants to see in the final program. It is your job to get with the user and define every single element of the program's output. This is called *output definition.*

There are several things that can help you define the output. Graph paper is useful for sketching out the details of each screen and report. Consider Figure 4.4. From this figure, you can determine how many lines and spaces separate the elements on the screen. The form also shows the maximum width of each printed number and name to help you plan disk storage requirements for the data.

Reward: You can purchase pads of *printer spacing charts* and *CRT Display Layout Forms* at a local office supply store. Unlike graph paper, these forms map directly to a typical 80-column screen and 132-column printer.

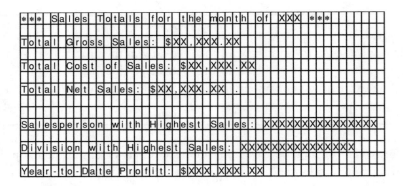

Figure 4.4. Graphing the output elements helps indicate their final placement in the program.

Given the flexibility of today's word processors, you can design your screens on the computer. The word processor helps you move titles and data around. When the screen is completed, you can print it. There are even some programs available today called *screen-generators* that convert screen images from a word-processed text file into final program code.

Be sure to include data-entry screens as part of your output definition. This may seem contradictory, but input screens require that your program place *prompts* (questions and titles of the data required) on the screen, and you should plan where these input screen elements go. Figure 4.5 shows a data-entry screen for a retail store. Although the end-user will enter the required data elements (called *fields*), defining the screen's layout before writing the program that produces the screen greatly speeds the completion of your program.

In conclusion, all output screens, printed reports, and data-entry screens must be defined in advance so you know exactly what is required of your programs. You also must decide what data to keep in files and the format of your data files. As you progress in your programming education, you will learn ways to lay out disk files in formats they require.

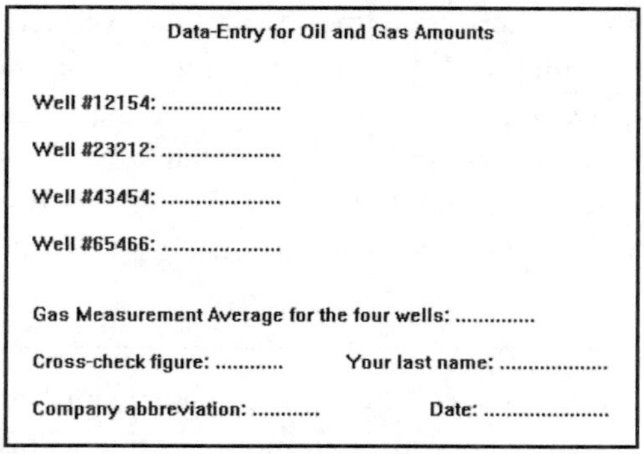

```
┌──────────────────────────────────────────────┐
│         Data-Entry for Oil and Gas Amounts     │
│                                                │
│  Well #12154: ....................             │
│                                                │
│  Well #23212: ...................              │
│                                                │
│  Well #43454: ...................              │
│                                                │
│  Well #65466: ...................              │
│                                                │
│                                                │
│  Gas Measurement Average for the four wells: ............. │
│                                                │
│  Cross-check figure: ...........    Your last name: .................. │
│                                                │
│  Company abbreviation: ............       Date: ..................... │
└──────────────────────────────────────────────┘
```

Figure 4.5. You must define all data-entry screens as well as output screens.

Working with Users

Unless you will be the final user of your program, you have to get with the users and define the output with them. Often, users have only a vague idea of what they want the program to do. You have to help them define what it is the program will do and what the output is going to be as well.

Some end-users who want programs written have no idea what the computer is capable of doing. You'll learn to develop some professional guidance counseling skills as you design programs for them. You must be able to hone the user's overall program requests into meaningful and concrete pieces.

The output definition is one of the best tools you can use to define the user's program requests. Continually show the user your output designs and ask questions such as, "Is this what you wanted?" and "Does this report contain everything you need?" If you are writing programs for a company, the company often has strict requirements as to what each report should contain. For instance, in some companies, every page of every computer-generated report is to contain the date and time the report was printed. You have to delve into the output standards within a company to find out what they require.

When working with users, it is often helpful to give them *prototypes* to work with. A prototype is a model of the final program. For instance, you could write a program that displays output and data-entry screens and lets the user fill in the blanks with the keyboard. The underlying program doesn't do anything with the data entered by the user, but the user will have a very good idea whether or not the program will have all the necessary elements.

> **Warning:** Be sure to get some final written agreement from the user, even an informal one, that the output definition is correct. This vital step, required before starting the logic development, contractually binds the user (and you) to the output definition. When you present the final program later, the user won't be able to argue that it does not produce the results he or she wanted.

There are now programs, often called *demonstration and prototyping* programs, that do nothing more than let you design data-entry and output screens for users to try. If you do a lot of programming for an organization or for a large number of clients, you will want to invest in such a program. Your local computer software store can help you find the latest versions of some prototyping programs.

What do you do with all the details of the top-down design and output definition? You must now move them into some kind of time-order logic that your program can follow to produce the details. That is where design tools such as flowcharts and pseudocode come in.

Step 2: Develop the Logic

Once you and the user agree to the goals and output of the program, the rest is up to you. It is now your job to take that output definition and decide how to make a computer produce the output. You have taken the overall problem and broken it down into detailed instructions that the computer can carry out. This does not mean that you are ready to write the program—quite the contrary. You are now ready to develop the logic that produces that output.

The output definition goes a long way toward describing *what* the program is supposed to do. Now you must decide *how* to accomplish the job. You must order the details that you have so they operate in a time-ordered fashion. You must also decide which decisions your program must make and the actions produced by each of those decisions.

Flowcharts

Flowcharts and related logic-development tools are the staple item of computer professionals. The complexity of programs requires that you somehow find a way to depict the logic of a program before writing it. It is said that a picture is worth a thousand words, and the flowchart provides a pictorial representation of program logic. The flowchart provides the logic for the final program. If your flowchart is correctly drawn, writing the actual program becomes a matter of rote. After the final program is completed, the flowchart can act as documentation to the program itself.

> **Note:** The flowchart describes the middle box of the input-processing-output model for computer programs.

Flowcharts are made up of industry-standard symbols. You can buy plastic flowchart symbol outlines, called *flowchart templates*, at an office supply store to help you draw better-looking flowcharts instead of relying on freehand drawing. Figure 4.6 shows you a typical flowcharting template. There are also some programs that guide you through a flowchart's creation and print flowcharts on your printer.

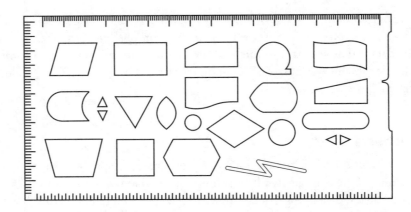

Figure 4.6. You can purchase a plastic flowchart template to draw better-looking flowcharts.

Warning: There is no way that one section in a book can teach you how to flowchart. However, after finishing here you will know what flowcharting is all about and be able to read and follow them yourself. Only after learning to program can you learn to flowchart a program, yet you must flowchart (or use one of the other kinds of related logic development tools) before writing programs. This "chicken before the egg" syndrome is common for beginning programmers. Once you begin to write your own programs, you'll have a much better understanding of the need for flowcharts.

As you can see from the flowchart template, there are many flowcharting symbols possible. Nevertheless, only a handful are used a lot. This chapter teaches you about the most common flowcharting symbols. With the ones you learn about here, you can write any flowchart that you'll ever need. The remaining symbols are simply refinements of those you learn here.

Figure 4.7 describes the flowcharting symbols used in this chapter. You should take the time to learn these symbols because they are extremely common in the programming literature that you will come across. As with top-down design, you can use flowcharts to help map out any event, not just computer programs. There are many noncomputer "how-to" books on the market that use these very same flowcharting symbols.

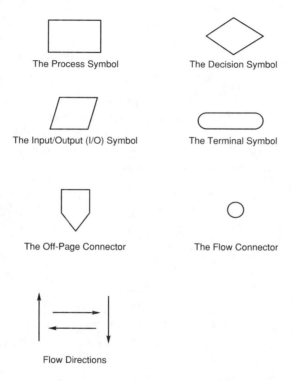

The Process Symbol   The Decision Symbol

The Input/Output (I/O) Symbol   The Terminal Symbol

The Off-Page Connector   The Flow Connector

Flow Directions

Figure 4.7. The common flowcharting symbols and their meanings.

Note: The flowcharting symbols have nothing to do with the top-down design's boxes. Remember that the top-down design was the tool you used to produce the program's needed details. Flowcharts provide the logic needed to produce those details.

Table 4.1 describes each of these symbols and how to use them.

Table 4.1. The flowcharting symbols and their usage.

Symbol	Description
Process	Contains a description of what is being done. Use a process symbol when straight processing of data is taking place, such as a calculation or program initialization.
Decision	Use when the program must make a decision based on two outcomes, such as printing either to the screen or to the printer, depending on where the user requested the printing.
Input/Output	Use for any input or output the program does, such as asking the user a question, or printing a report. (The slanted shape of the I/O symbol gives you a clue as to what it means; the slash in *I/O* slants the same way.)
Terminal	A terminal symbol with the word *Begin* or *Start* written in it always begins every flowchart. A terminal symbol with the word *End* or *Finish* written in it always ends every flowchart. When you refer to the flowchart later, there will be no question where it begins or ends.
Off-page	Put an off-page connector at the bottom of any flowchart that is continued to another page. Put the next page's page number inside the off-page connector. Put an off-page connector at the beginning of each page that concludes a previous page's flowchart. Put the previous page's number inside the off-page connector that begins the new page of the flowchart.

Symbol	Description
Flow connector	Use when one logic flow of the flowchart is to merge with existing logic. You typically see an alphabetic letter inside the flow connectors. A matching flow connector (one with the same letter) indicates the reentry point to the existing logic.
Flow direction	These arrows connect every symbol in the flow-chart and indicate the direction of the program flow.

The Rules of Flowcharting

Although every programmer draws flowcharts differently, there are some distinct rules that you should acquaint yourself with before going further. These rules are almost universally followed, and therefore you should understand them so the flow-charts you write will be readable by others. With each rule, you will see an ex-ample that both follows and breaks the rule so you can get an idea of how to use the rule.

> **Rule #1:** *Use standard flowcharting symbols.* If you stick to the conven-tional symbols, others can understand your flowchart's meaning, and you can understand theirs. Figure 4.8 shows the right and wrong ways of following this rule.

> **Rule #2:** *The flowchart's logic should generally flow from the top of the page to the bottom of the page, and from left to right.* If your flowcharts do not follow this standard, they could become disorganized and hard to follow. Figure 4.9 illustrates the proper flow direction of flowcharts. Notice that the flow direction arrows point in the direction that the logic follows.

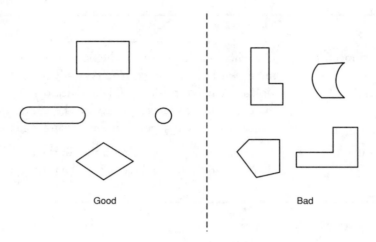

Figure 4.8. Use standard, conventional flowcharting symbols.

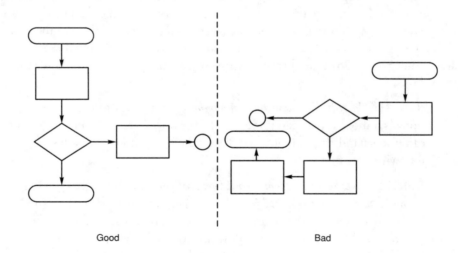

Figure 4.9. Flowchart logic should flow from top to bottom and from left to right.

Some flowcharts have no need to move to the right because they describe sequential program logic, but most have some kind of flow going in either of the two recommended directions. There might be times when a proper flowchart seemingly breaks this rule; you will see one shortly. Because of repetition in logic, the flowchart might have areas that go back up and to the left to repeat sections of the logic, but eventually the logic must continue in the preferred directions. The *overall* logic must flow from top to bottom and from left to right.

> **Rule #3:** *The decision symbol is the only symbol that can have more than one exit point, and it always has two.* Most flowcharting symbols have one entry point and one exit point. The direction flow arrows indicate the entry and exit points. The decision symbol always has two exit points because, at that place in the logic, one of two things takes place, and the next flow of logic is determined by the result of that decision. Figure 4.10 illustrates this rule.

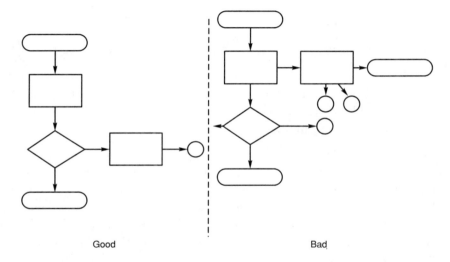

Good   Bad

Figure 4.10. Only the decision symbol can have more than one exit point, and it has exactly two.

> **Rule #4:** *A decision symbol should always ask a yes or no question.* A flowchart's decision should always have two and only two outcomes (hence, Rule #3's two-exit reasoning). You will see the decision in the symbol itself. Most flowcharting symbols have words in them that describe what is taking place at that point in the flowchart. Figure 4.11 illustrates this rule.

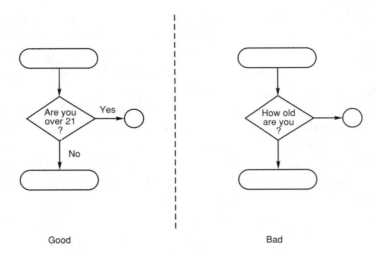

Good   Bad

Figure 4.11. *A decision symbol should always ask a yes or no question.*

You should clearly label the exits of each decision symbol as well. Because the exits are the result of a yes or no question, label the exit *Yes* or *Y* and *No* or *N* so you know what the exits indicate.

You might wonder if it is reasonable to expect all decisions to have only two possible results. There are times when your program must choose between one of many values, based on the data it receives. However, multiple decision symbols will take care of any number of possibilities. When you were a child, you may have played Twenty Questions, a game in which someone thinks of an object or person, and you can only ask yes or no questions to determine what the object is. Ask enough yes or no questions, and you can determine anything. The same concept applies to decisions in a program. In the chapters on QBasic programming, you will see how to direct programs to handle more than two possibilities.

> **Rule #5:** *Instructions inside the symbols should be clear English descriptions, not* computerese *or programming language statements.* You should develop a flowchart before you write a program. You should not include programming statements inside flowcharting symbols. If you were ready for the programming language at this point, you wouldn't need to take the time flowcharting.

The flowchart is your own development of the logic. You will eventually convert the flowchart into programming language statements, but only after you are clear that the flowchart performs the logic you need, and not before.

A Real-World Flowchart

As with the top-down design wedding plans, it may be helpful to see a common everyday problem described with a flowchart before seeing a more traditional flowchart for a computer program. Always keep in mind that the logic dictates what the machine does, so you cannot leave out any details.

Figure 4.12 shows the flowchart for calling a friend on the telephone. To keep the example reasonable, the flowchart includes the important aspects of the problem, but there are many other ways to write the same flowchart. See if you can follow the flowchart. The direction arrows show you how to do it. Follow the flowchart several times, from start to finish, given each of these conditions:

1. Assume your phone is dead when you begin the call.

2. Assume your friend is home and answers the phone.

3. Assume your friend's phone is busy.

4. Assume nobody is home at your friend's house.

5. Assume your friend is not home, but her roommate answers.

Notice that the flowchart does not leave out the details of an actual phone call. It tries not to assume too much either. Calling a friend, to you, might just mean picking up the phone and calling, but when you flowchart the details, you begin to see how much you take for granted.

Notice also how the connector symbols work to keep the flowchart clean and tidy. There are several places where parts of the flowchart repeat. For example, if the friend's phone is busy, the connector circle with the *A* directs the flow back up to the top of the flowchart. Repetitive logic such as this might appear to go up the flowchart, breaking the second flowcharting rule, but it does not because the repeating logic eventually continues down and to the right when the friend's phone is finally answered.

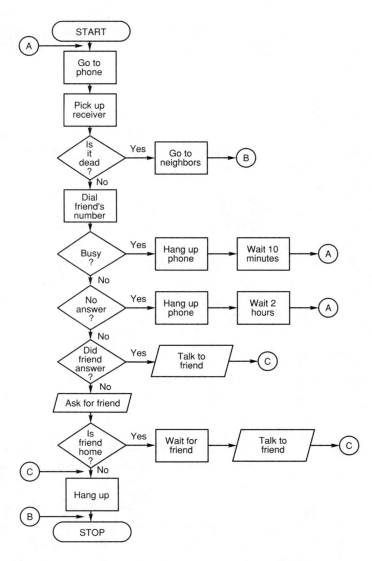

Figure 4.12. One possible flowchart for calling a friend on the telephone.

Moving to a problem that uses a computerized solution, suppose you have to flowchart the logic of many payroll systems with overtime. You have to detail the procedure necessary to compute net pay given the possibility of time-and-a-half and double overtime. Before getting the flowchart, try to decipher these details:

1. If an employee works 40 hours or less, the employee gets paid an hourly rate times the number of hours worked.

2. If an employee works between 40 and 50 hours, the employee gets paid the regular pay rate times 40 hours, plus time-and-a-half (1.5 times the hourly rate) for those hours between 40 and 50.

3. If an employee works more than 50 hours, the employee gets double time (2 times the hourly rate), plus 10 hours of time and a half (for those hours between 40 and 50), and 40 times the regular hourly rate for the first 40 hours.

Even though you can follow these details if you had to, the flowchart provides a much easier way of depicting the logic. Follow the flowchart in Figure 4.13. Take any number of hours worked and follow those hours through the flowchart. The flowchart keeps you on the right path of logic flow without the details that don't apply getting in the way. Trying to write a program from the previous three-point list is much more difficult than writing a program from the flowchart.

Pseudocode

Despite the power and ease of flowcharting, some companies prefer another method for logic description called *pseudocode*. Pseudocode, sometimes called *structured English*, is a method of writing logic using sentences of text instead of the diagrams necessary for flowcharting.

Flowcharts take a long time to draw and a lot of paper doing so. Even though you can buy flowcharting programs, they are often limited and do not offer the flexibility that a lot of programming logic needs. Therefore, you must often resort to drawing flowcharts by hand. When you finish a flowchart and realize that you left out two critical symbols, you have to redraw much of the flowchart. Because of their nature, flowcharts take lots of time to draw, and some companies do not want their programmers taking the time to flowchart when pseudocode can take its place and is more time efficient.

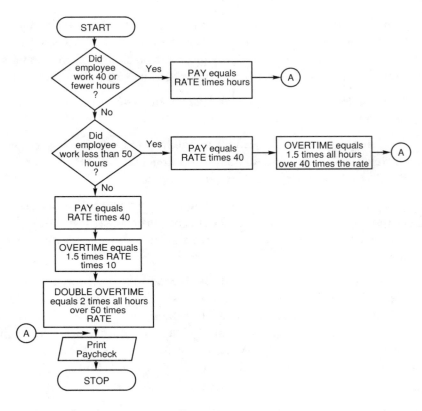

Figure 4.13. *Flowcharting a payroll routine.*

The only tool you need for pseudocode is a word processor. Word processors offer the power to insert, move, and delete text. Because pseudocode requires no drawing, it is faster than flowcharting and easier to maintain.

As with flowcharts, there is no way to teach some pseudocode techniques unless you have been programming for a while. The term *pseudo* means false; therefore, pseudocode literally means *false code*. The more you know about programming languages, the more you will adapt to pseudocode, so just read the next example and try to get a feel for pseudocode.

Pseudocode does not have any programming language statements in it, but it also is not free-flowing English. It is a set of rigid English words that allow for the depiction of logic you see so often in flowcharts and programming languages. As with flowcharts, you can write pseudocode for anything, not just computer programs. A lot of instruction manuals use a form of pseudocode to illustrate the steps needed to assemble parts. Pseudocode offers a rigid description of logic that tries to leave little room for ambiguity.

Here is the flowchart for the payroll problem, presented earlier in the chapter, in pseudocode form. Notice that you can read the text, yet it is not a programming language. The indention helps keep track of which sentences go together. The pseudocode is readable by anyone, even by people unfamiliar with flowcharting symbols.

For each employee:
> *If the employee worked 0 to 40 hours then*
>> *net pay equals hours worked times rate.*
> *Otherwise,*
>> *if the employee worked between 40 and 50 hours then*
>>> *net pay equals 40 times the rate;*
>>> *add to that (hours worked – 40) times the rate times 1.5.*
>> *Otherwise,*
>>> *net pay equals 40 times the rate;*
>>> *add to that 10 times the rate times 1.5;*
>>> *add to that (hours worked – 50) times twice the rate.*
> *Deduct taxes from the net pay.*
> *Print the paycheck.*
End the problem.

Step 3: Write the Program

Now for the big finale! Once the output is defined and the logic determined to get that output, you must go to the computer and generate the code—the programming language statements—you need to get there. This means that you must learn a programming language first. As mentioned earlier, there are many programming languages, and writing programs is no easy task for beginners, but you will soon be writing them with skill and expertise.

The program writing takes the longest to learn. Once you learn to program, however, the actual programming process takes less time than the design if your design is accurate and complete. The nature of programming requires that you learn some new skills. The next few chapters describe the programming process and give you the background of many of the popular programming languages available today.

Chapter Highlights

A builder does not build a house before designing it, and a programmer should not write a program without designing it as well. Too often, programmers rush to the keyboard without thinking through the logic. The result of a badly designed program is lots of bugs and later maintenance.

✖ You must design a program before writing it.

✖ Proper design ensures a quicker programming process and fewer errors.

✖ The first step in the design process is to define the output.

✖ Top-down design helps you get to the details in a program.

✖ Top-down design forces you to put off details and lets them appear on their own.

✖ You can apply top-down design to any task you are assigned that involves lots of details.

✖ The second step in the design process is to develop the logic that helps you get the output you have defined.

✖ Flowcharts help you develop a program's logic by visually demonstrating the logic.

✖ You only need to learn a handful of the flowcharting symbols to write any flowchart.

✖ Pseudocode offers some advantages over flowcharts. It is easier to write and change but does not have the visual appeal of flowcharts.

✖ The last step in the programming process is to physically write the program and type it into the computer.

The Programming Process

5

Perilous Perry held the bubbling potion. He was awestruck. This would be another step in Perilous Perry's journey. What metamorphosis will our hero undergo when he drinks from the Programmer's Grail?

1. What does it take to write a program?

2. What is an editor?

3. What is the difference between a line editor and a full-screen editor?

4. Why is structured programming important?

5. What is a programming construct?

6. What are the three structured programming constructs?

7. What are the steps for testing a program?

8. Is there a difference between desk checking and beta testing?

9. Why is parallel testing critical for a user?

Now you are familiar with the steps to take before programming. In this chapter, you begin the programming process, starting to learn about specific languages and to write your own programs. You now know that two steps must always precede writing the program—defining the output and developing the logic. After you develop the logic, you can write the program using one of the many available programming languages.

To finish the programming process, you must do the following:

1. Write the program.

2. Test the program.

3. Distribute the program.

Of course, all three steps assume you know a programming language. The rest of this book completes the programming process that began with the design of the program output and the development of the logic.

The Editor

An *editor* is the tool you use to type programs into your computer. An editor is like a word processor in that it enables you to type lines of code, edit them, move and copy them, and save them to the disk. For this reason, editors are often referred to as *text editors*. An editor is unlike a word processor, however, in that it doesn't perform *word wrapping*. When you get to the end of a line in a word processor, the word processor moves the cursor and the partial word at the end of the line to the next line. Word wrap would be detrimental to computer programs. Remember that programming languages must be concise. Programming statements can't run together like printed speech can. Using some programming languages you can put more than one programming statement on a single line, but this isn't recommended because it makes reading the program more difficult for you and others.

Editors fall into the following two categories: *line editors* and *full-screen editors*. The next two sections describe each one.

> **Note:** Programmers are sometimes fanatical about their editors, often thinking the editor they use is the only one anyone should consider when doing *serious* programming. Generally, whatever editor you get comfortable with is the one you should use. Get used to both kinds of editors, as each offers advantages over the other in certain situations.

Line Editors

Many programmers feel that line editors are an ancient relic of the past, useful only for those old teletype terminals that were considered the cutting edge in 1965. There is another group of programmers, however, who say that they are more productive using a line editor than any other kind.

Using a line editor, you can enter and edit program text. What differentiates a line editor from a full-screen editor is that the line editor lets you work on only a single line at a time. Line editors don't let you use the cursor-movement keys (generally the Up, Down, Left, and Right arrow keys), to move around the screen making changes to several lines one after the other, as does a full-screen editor. Instead, you must specifically tell the editor which line you want to change. You can make changes to that line only. Then you must designate another line you want to edit.

The two most popular line editors in use today are the UNIX-based version called *vi* (for *visual*) and the MS-DOS-based *Edlin* (for *edit lines*). Vi is available for microcomputers and is used by many UNIX programmers who have moved to the microcomputer environment. Edlin is available for all versions of MS-DOS. Some programmers are so used to this editor that they copy their older version's DOS Edlin editor to their newer version that doesn't have it.

Figure 5.1 shows a sample session from an Edlin editing session. Study the figure and read the following table to understand what is happening. As you will see, you must be specific about what line you want to edit. Those of you who have never used a line editor before, but have used a word processor, may wonder how programs ever got written before full-screen editing!

```
C:\>edlin test.ed
New file
*1i
        1:*These will become
        2:*the first four lines
        3:*in a final program file
        4:*after you save the file.
        5:*^Z
*1,2d
*1
        1:*in a final program file
        2: after you save the file.
*e

C:\>type test.ed
in a final program file
after you save the file.

C:\>
```

Figure 5.1. *Using the Edlin program editor.*

The first line of the figure starts the Edlin editor and displays a file named *test.ed*. Because the computer responds with New file, you know that test.ed didn't exist, so this editing session will create it.

The asterisk (*) is the Edlin *prompt*. Just as the DOS prompt (typically, something like c:>) lets you know that DOS is ready, the Edlin prompt lets you know Edlin is ready for you to issue a command. You need to know only a handful of Edlin commands. They are summarized in Table 5.1.

Clue: This section isn't trying to teach you everything there is to learn about Edlin. Edlin may not be your editor of choice. Please follow the example, however, because you may someday have to use a line editor and this example will help you get a feel for how line editors work.

Table 5.1. Common Edlin commands you can issue at the Edlin prompt.

Command*	Description and Example
i	Insert lines of text. 3i means that you want to insert a new line of text before line 3.
d	Delete lines of text. 2d means that you want to delete the second line. Line numbers are relative, not absolute. Therefore, when you delete line 2, line 3 "moves up" to become the new line 2. (This is common with most line editors.)
l	List the lines of text in the file. For example, to list lines 1 through 25, type 1,25l.
q	Quit the editing session and return to DOS without saving the text file.
e	Quit the editing session, save the file, and return to DOS.

Any command can be entered in upper- or lowercase letters.

The first thing to do is enter text, so the insert command is used next in Figure 5.1. Even though the figure shows 1i, meaning *insert before line 1*, the 1 is optional in this instance because there is no other line to insert before.

Edlin supplies the line number and moves the prompt (the asterisk) to the next line. You can begin typing. The text you type after the asterisk prompt appears in column one of the file you are creating. Figure 5.1 shows four lines being typed.

If you keep typing, Edlin keeps adding your lines to the file. There has to be some way of getting out of the text insert mode. To return to Edlin's command prompt, press the F6 function key. This performs the equivalent of pressing Ctrl-Z, which means *end of file* on PCs. (You could also have pressed Ctrl-Z.) The ^z on the screen indicates that is where you pressed F6. (There is nothing special about F6 to make it the end-of-file function key. Edlin and DOS programmers selected that key to indicate the end of a file.)

The first two lines of text are deleted. As in the figure, a range of lines (more than one line) of text can be deleted as long as you put the starting line and ending line numbers before the d command with a comma between the numbers. Therefore, this Edlin command

```
1,2d
```

tells Edlin to delete lines 1 through 2. You can see the resulting file with the list command, which is performed next in Figure 5.1. The figure then shows the e command, which saves the file and returns the screen to the DOS prompt. The file is then displayed on-screen (using the DOS TYPE command, which displays text files) to show you that the Edlin session did as described.

Warning: Even those programmers who prefer line editors over full-screen editors have to agree that more and more programmers are moving to full-screen editors (described in the next section). Full-screen editors are considered easier to learn and use, especially because they mirror the actions of many word processors.

Be careful that you don't dismiss line editors as something you can ignore, however. The advantage of line editors is that they are almost always available, no matter what computer you use. Some dial-up computer systems don't allow full-screen editors because the modem connection doesn't permit full-screen control from a remote site (although even modem connections that don't permit full-screen control are becoming less common). Therefore, even if you don't master a line editor fully, you should spend some time learning a few commands from one so that you can use one quickly if you ever need to.

Full-Screen Editor

The tedium of line editors causes many programmers to switch to a full-screen editor and stay there. Many of today's full-screen editors have pull-down menus and mouse capabilities. If you've used a word processor, you may not need to learn any editor commands to use a full-screen editor. As long as you can use the menus and find the Help key, you can do almost anything you want with a program file.

Figure 5.2 shows a QBasic program being entered. Many programming languages today come with their own full-screen editors. Because QBasic has been supplied with every version of DOS since Version 5.0's release, you can write QBasic programs if you have a PC.

```
   File   Edit  View  Search  Run  Debug  Options                    Help
                                QB.BAS
' Program without subroutines
PRINT "Welcome to the label printing program!"
PRINT
PRINT "This program prints mailing labels"
PRINT "on your printer, three at a time."

LINE INPUT "What is your name? "; nm$
LINE INPUT "What is your address? "; ad$
LINE INPUT "What is your city? "; ct$
LINE INPUT "What is your state? "; st$
LINE INPUT "What is your zip code? "; zp$

PRINT "Get the printer ready, and press Enter when "
INPUT "you want me to begin printing..."; en$

LPRINT nm$      ' Print first label
LPRINT ad$
LPRINT ct$; ", "; st$; SPC(5); zp$
LPRINT
                              Immediate
<Shift+F1=Help> <F6=Window> <F2=Subs> <F5=Run> <F8=Step>          00001:001
```

Figure 5.2. *Using the QBasic full-screen editor.*

Note: If you want to practice a little with the QBasic editor, type QBASIC at the DOS prompt. If you get an error, try changing to your DOS subdirectory with CD \DOS first, and then type QBASIC. As with all DOS commands, you can use uppercase or lowercase letters.

In Figure 5.2, you see many elements common to most full-screen editors. The large editing window in the middle of the screen is where you enter and make edits to the program. Across the top of the screen is a row of menu options. Unlike a line editor, such as Edlin, you don't have to memorize a bunch of commands to use a full-screen editor; you only have to select from menus.

Most of the time when you are in an editor, you are typing and changing the program's text. With full-screen editors, you can use the arrow keys to move the cursor around the screen, inserting and deleting text as you would with a word processor. When you want to perform more than typing and changing characters and words, you can resort to the menu, which has commands for saving and loading programs to and from the disk, searching and replacing text, and moving and copying blocks of text (a block is one or more characters).

Clue: Program menus offer the same help for computer people that restaurant menus offer for customers. When you walk into a restaurant that you have never been in, you have no idea what they serve. The restaurant gives you a menu of choices so that you can order. You don't have to memorize what every restaurant serves.

A program such as a full-screen editor supplies a menu to list the options from which you can order. Instead of memorizing commands, you order from the menu what you want the computer to do next.

Most of today's full-screen editors offer *pull-down menus*. Figure 5.3 shows the File pull-down menu. When you select File (by selecting with the mouse, if you have one, or pressing Alt-F), QBasic brings down a list of all the File menu's options (sometimes called a *submenu* because it's a menu produced from the main menu). When you see a pull-down menu, you can either select one of its options (by moving the menu highlight with the arrow keys or selecting with the mouse) or you can get rid of the menu altogether by pressing the Esc key.

One of the biggest advantages of integrating program editors with program interpreters and compilers is their ease of use. Before integration (back when line editors were the *only* kind of editors available), you had to start an editor, enter the program, save the file, exit the editor, compile the program you just typed (which means learning another set of commands), and if the program had errors, you had to go back into the editor and correct the errors.

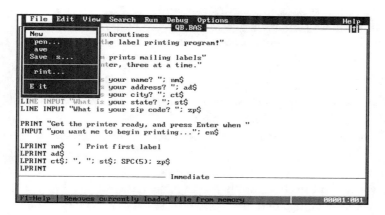

Figure 5.3. Most full-screen editors come with helpful pull-down menus.

With an integrated editor and programming language, you can use the same set of menu commands and a common environment to enter the program, interpret it (or compile it), and run it, all from within the same place. This simplicity means that beginners can concentrate more on the program's contents and less on all the other commands needed to get the program working. Once you enter the program, you can use the menus to translate the program into machine language and run it without leaving the full screen environment. You can view the program output and instantly switch with one keystroke back to the program that produced the output. (You can continue switching back and forth as many times as you like.) If the output has errors, you can easily find the errors and change the source code.

Some of the most powerful integrated full-screen editors and programming languages are Borland's C and C++, and similar compilers from other companies such as Microsoft. These full-screen editors and compilers offer the usual fare of powerful editing and compiling menu options and advanced programming tools such as *debuggers* and *profilers*.

With a debugger you can run a program one line at a time, inspecting pieces as it runs, looking at the output being generated at your own pace instead of trying to figure out what's wrong at the lightning-fast execution speed at which programs normally run. When you begin to write long programs, you will appreciate the debugger even more because it makes the chore of exterminating program bugs less painful.

A profiler is a program that monitors the execution of your program, looking for sluggish code that might be optimized for either speed or size. Many of today's compilers are *optimizing compilers* that try to take your code and turn it into the fastest possible machine code, but there is always room for improvement. On average, 5 percent of a program takes 95 percent of the program's execution time. The profiler can help you find that most critical and slow 5 percent of your program so that you can have the chance to make changes that improve the speed and efficiency of your program.

Borland's integrated full-screen editor, compiler, debugger, and profiler comes in two versions. One is a DOS-based version, shown in Figure 5.4. The other is a Microsoft Windows-based version, shown in Figure 5.5. If you are writing programs for the Windows environment, it helps to perform the program writing, testing, and debugging from within Windows.

Figure 5.4. The DOS-based Borland C++ full-screen editor.

```
Borland C++ - [j:\borlandc\bin\design2.c]
 File  Edit  Search  Run  Compile  Project  Browse  Options  Window        Help
 ?

    /*  scrn  = fopen("CON", "w"); */        /*  Open screen device */

    for (wid_ctr=0; wid_ctr<num_widths; wid_ctr++)
      {
        for (thick_ctr=0; thick_ctr<num_thicks; thick_ctr++)
          {
            fscanf(fp_si," %f %f %f %f %f %f %f %f",
               &sizes[wid_ctr][thick_ctr].nominal_width,
               &sizes[wid_ctr][thick_ctr].width_tole_max,
               &sizes[wid_ctr][thick_ctr].nominal_thick,
               &sizes[wid_ctr][thick_ctr].cross_sec_area,
               &sizes[wid_ctr][thick_ctr].weight_per_len,
               &sizes[wid_ctr][thick_ctr].moment_inertia,
               &sizes[wid_ctr][thick_ctr].thick_tole_max,
               &sizes[wid_ctr][thick_ctr].thick_diff_max);
/* Print just for testing... */
printf("  %5.2f   %5.3f %9.2f %9.2f %9.2f %9.3f %9.3f %9.3f\n",
          sizes[wid_ctr][thick_ctr].nominal_width,
          sizes[wid_ctr][thick_ctr].width_tole_max,
          sizes[wid_ctr][thick_ctr].nominal_thick,
          sizes[wid_ctr][thick_ctr].cross_sec_area,
          sizes[wid_ctr][thick_ctr].weight_per_len,
          sizes[wid_ctr][thick_ctr].moment_inertia,
          sizes[wid_ctr][thick_ctr].thick_tole_max,
          sizes[wid_ctr][thick_ctr].thick_diff_max);
getch();   /* pauses after each line */
          }
      }

    /*  fclose(scrn); */
      fclose(fp_si);

 94:52           Insert
```

Figure 5.5. *The Windows-based Borland C++ full-screen editor.*

Structured Programming

In the late 1960s, programming departments began to wallow in programming backlogs that built at tremendous rates. More people were writing more programs than ever, but many programmers had to be hired to maintain the previously written programs.

Reward: It has been said that a program is written only once, but read and changed numerous times. Learn to write readable and maintainable programs. By using a conscientious approach (instead of the old "throw a program together" approach that some programmers use), you help ensure your future as a programmer for many years. Companies save money when a programmer writes code that is maintained easily.

121

When you finish a program, you are finished only for the time being. That program's "assumptions" about the job it performs will change over time. Businesses never remain constant in this global economy. Data processing managers began recognizing that the programming maintenance backlog was beginning to take its toll on development. Programmers were pulled away from new projects and placed on updating older projects. The maintenance was taking too long.

It was during the maintenance crisis of the 1960s that data processing people began looking for new ways to program. They weren't interested in new languages necessarily but were interested in new ways to write programs that would make them work better, faster, and most importantly, that would make them readable so that others could maintain the program without too much trouble. *Structured programming* techniques were developed during this time.

Structured programming is a philosophy stating that programs should be written in an orderly fashion without a lot of jumping to and fro. If programs were made easier to read while they are being written, the program could be changed more easily. People have known for many years that clear writing styles are important, but it became obvious to computer people only after about 20 years of using nonstructured techniques.

Clue: You don't write well-written code just for others to read. As you begin to write more and more programs, you tend to forget exactly what you did in earlier programs. Often, programmers go back to code they wrote months earlier, and the code is as foreign as it would have been if someone else had written it. Therefore, you help yourself as much as anybody when you write easy-to-read, well-written programs.

There is some debate as to exactly when beginning programmers should be introduced to structured programming. Some people feel that programmers should know no differently, so they should be trained in structured programming from the beginning. Others feel beginners should learn to program using any way that gets the job done, and then they should adapt to structured programming only after being comfortable in a programming language.

The problem, the people for the latter group argue, is that a beginning programmer doesn't even know any programming languages to which to relate structured programming techniques. They say a beginning programmer doesn't know enough to understand structured programming. However, because you now understand flowcharts and pseudocode, you can see what structured programming is all about with those tools. Then, when you learn a programming language in the last half of this book, you will be thinking in the structured programming mode and will naturally fall into a structured programming pattern from the beginning.

To give you a feel for the need for structured programs, consider the following list of directions given to you when you ask how to get to the library:

1. First, go to steps 8 and 9.

2. Drive one mile straight.

3. Drive one mile straight again.

4. Drive one mile straight again. You will see the branch library on your right.

5. If the branch library is closed for repairs, go to step 11.

6. Stop at the branch library.

7. Go to step 13.

8. Drive straight to Harvard Avenue.

9. Turn right at 51st Street.

10. Go to step 2.

11. Turn left on Yale Street.

12. Go four miles straight and you will see the main library branch on your left.

13. Go in library to return your books.

There is nothing wrong with this list of directions to get to the library. Nevertheless, aren't directions supposed to be a little more organized? Do you think a total stranger to your town, following these directions, would think they were good directions? Probably you wouldn't think so. The problem is that this list of directions seems to have been thrown together, and even though one could follow them, one couldn't do so without a little frustration and slowdown.

The following list contains the same directions. You can see that it makes more sense.

1. Drive straight to Harvard Avenue.

2. Turn right at 51st Street.

3. For the next three miles, keep driving straight. You will see the branch library on your right.

4. If the branch is open, go inside.

5. Otherwise, if the branch is closed, turn left on Yale Street. Go four miles straight and you will see the main library branch on your left.

6. Go inside whichever library is open and return your books.

The second list of instructions gives the same directions for returning library books, but it uses fewer than half the statements of the first list. The smaller size isn't the primary advantage of the second list; its advantage is that it is much better thought out and written down. Anyone would find the second list easier to follow than the first.

> **Note:** Keep the importance of program size in perspective as you learn to program. Better-written, well-documented, well-structured programs often take longer to type and consume more disk space. Remember, though, that a program is written once but read and changed many times. Put some effort into writing readable code. Disk space is cheaper these days than ever, and file size shouldn't be a prime consideration when writing programs.

A well-written and easily read program doesn't necessarily mean it's structured. Structured programming is a specific approach to programming that generally produces well-written and easily read programs. Nothing can make up for a programmer rushing to get a program finished by what he thinks is the fastest way. The following is heard a lot, "Later, I'll make it structured, but for now, I'll leave it as it is." "Later" never comes, and people begin to use the program until one day when changes have to be made, and the changes take as long as or longer than they would have if the entire program were scrapped and rewritten from scratch.

Structured programming includes the following three *constructs*:

* ✖ Sequence

* ✖ Decision (also called Selection)

* ✖ Looping (also called Repetition or Iteration)

A construct (from the word *construction*) is a building block of a language and one of the language's fundamental operations. As long as a programming language supports these three constructs (most do), you can write structured programs. The opposite of a structured program is known as *spaghetti code.* Like spaghetti that flows and swirls all over the plate, an unstructured program—one full of spaghetti code—flows all over the place with little or no structure. An unstructured program contains lots of *branching.* A branch occurs when a program goes this way and that with no order. The first list of directions to the library branches on its very first statement.

Note: Most programming languages enable you to branch with a GOTO statement. The GOTO works as it sounds; it tells the computer to *go to* another place in the program and continue execution there. Having to search down in a program for the next instruction to execute makes you break your train of thought.

Some programmers and programming textbooks warn you to stay away from the GOTO statement completely. The GOTO statement, by itself, isn't a bad statement when used conservatively, but it can wreak havoc on a program's readability if you overuse it.

The three structured programming constructs aren't just for programs. You will find that you can use them for flowcharts, pseudocode, and any other set of instructions you write for others. The three structured programming constructs ensure that a program doesn't branch all over the place but any execution is controlled and easily followed.

The following three sections explain each of the three structured programming constructs. Read them carefully and you'll see that the concept of a structured program is easy to understand. Learning about structure before learning a language should help you think of structure as you develop your programming skills.

Sequence

Sequence is nothing more than two or more instructions one after the other. The sequential instructions are the easiest of the three structured programming constructs because you can follow the program from the first statement to the last within the sequence. Figure 5.6 shows a flowchart that illustrates sequence.

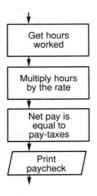

Figure 5.6. *The sequence structured programming construct.*

Here is pseudocode that matches the sequence of the previous flowchart:

Get the hours worked.
Multiply the hours by the rate.
Subtract taxes to compute net pay.
Print paycheck.

Because computers must be able to make decisions and perform repetitive tasks, not all of your programs can consist of straight sequential logic. When sequence is available, however, it makes for straightforward program logic.

Decision (Selection)

You have seen the decision construct before. The decision symbol in a flowchart is the point at which a decision is made. Anytime a program makes a decision, it must take off in one of two directions. Obviously, a decision is a break from the sequential program flow, but it is a controlled break.

By its nature, a branch must be performed based on the result of a decision (in effect, the code must skip the code that is not to execute). A decision, however, as opposed to a straight branch, ensures that you don't have to worry about the code not performed. You won't have to go back and read the part of the program skipped by the decision. (Based on new data, the program might repeat a decision and take a different route the second time, but again, you can always assume that the decision code not being executed at the time is meaningless to the current loop.)

Figure 5.7 shows a flowchart that contains part of a teacher's grading program logic.

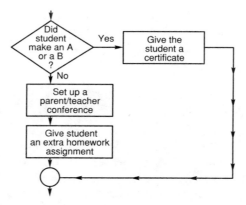

Figure 5.7. *The decision structured programming construct.*

Here is the pseudocode for the decision shown in the flowchart:

If the student makes an A or B,
> *give the student an achievement certificate.*

Otherwise:
> *set up a parent-teacher conference;*
> *give the student extra homework.*

Looping (Repetition and Iteration)

Perhaps the most important task done by computers is *looping* (the computerist's term for repeating or iterating through lines of program code). Computers repeat sections of a program millions of times and never get bored. Computers make the perfect companions for workers who have lots of data to process, because the computer can process the data, repeating the common calculations needed throughout all the data, and the person can analyze the results.

Looping is prevalent in almost every program written. Rarely do you write a program that is a straight sequence of instructions. The time it takes to design and write a program isn't always worth the effort when a straight series of tasks are involved. Programs are most powerful when they can repeat a series of sequential statements or decisions.

Figure 5.8 shows a flowchart that repeats a section in a loop. Loops only temporarily break the rule that says flowcharts should flow down and to the right. Loops within a flowchart are fine because eventually the logic will stop looping.

Pitfall: Be aware of the dreaded *infinite loop*. An infinite loop is a never-ending loop. If your computer gets into an infinite loop, it continues looping, never finishing, and it is sometimes difficult to regain control of the program without rebooting the computer. Loops should always be prefaced with a decision statement so that, eventually, the decision triggers the end of the loop and the rest of the program can finish.

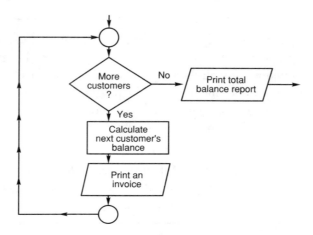

Figure 5.8. *The looping structured programming construct.*

Here is the pseudocode for the flowchart you just saw:

If there are more customers,
> *do the following:*
> > *calculate the next customer's balance;*
> > *print an invoice.*

Otherwise,
> *print the total balance report.*

As you can see, eventually there won't be any customers and the loop (beginning with *do*) will stop looping so that the rest of the logic can take over.

None of these structured programming constructs should be new to you because you saw them used in the last chapter. As long as you keep these three constructs in mind as you write flowcharts, pseudocode, and the eventual program, and as long as you resist the temptation to start branching all over the program, you will write well-structured, easy-to-maintain programs and ensure your position as a programmer for many years.

> **Reward:** Spaghetti code often results when a programmer doesn't design the program properly. If you go straight to the keyboard and begin typing code before thinking through the program and developing its logic, you are almost sure to leave elements out of the program. When you add them, it is too easy to stick them "wherever it works," and branch back and forth to the new code instead of integrating the new code into the existing logic.
>
> Proper planning helps ensure that when you get to the programming step, the program will be well thought-out and your structured programming techniques will be included in the final code.

Testing the Program

When you finish writing the actual program code, you aren't completely done with the program. You must now turn to the task of debugging the program. You want to get as many bugs out of the program as possible. For obvious reasons, you don't want the user to do this. You don't want the user of your program finding all kinds of mistakes that you made. Therefore, you must thoroughly test the program. Here are the typical testing steps that programmers should follow before distributing a final version of the program to users.

1. Perform desk checking.

2. Perform a beta test.

3. Compare results of the beta test against the old system's parallel test results.

Most programmers go through a series of *desk checks* on their programs. Desk checking is the process of sitting in front of a computer checking the program using as many different scenarios of data as possible, trying to find weak spots and errors in the code. During desk checking, programmers should try extreme values, type bad input, and generally try their best to make the program fail.

Programmers should also try every option available in the program, using different combinations to see what happens in all situations.

Once desk checking is completed and programmers are as confident as they can be about the program's correctness, programmers should set up a series of users to try the program. This is known in the industry as the *beta testing* stage. The more beta testers (test users of the program) you find to test the program, the better the chance that errors will be found. Users often try things the programmer never thought of while writing the program.

The user should never abandon an old system and switch to the new program right away. A period of *parallel testing* should be performed. For instance, if you write a payroll program that's going to replace the manual payroll system for a dry cleaner, the dry cleaner shouldn't get a copy of your program and use only that. Instead, the dry cleaner should continue using its manual payroll system and your program at the same time. Although this means payroll takes a little longer each pay period, the results of the program can be compared against the manual systems to see that they match.

Only after several pay periods of well-matched parallel testing should the user feel confident enough to use the program without the manual backup.

During this testing period, programmers may have to make several changes to the program. Expect that changes will be necessary, and you won't feel disappointed or lose your programming confidence. Programmers rarely write a program correctly the first time. It usually takes many attempts to get programs correct. The thorough testing described in this section doesn't ensure a perfect program. Somes errors might appear only after the program is used for a while. The more testing you do, the less likely that errors will creep up later.

The Program Language

One important step has been left out of this book so far. That is the step of learning the language itself. The rest of this book is devoted to describing the various programming languages available. It also introduces you to a popular programming language named QBasic.

131

Most programming books jump right in and start teaching a language in the first chapter. There is nothing wrong with this approach, but somewhere along the way, you need to learn to design programs, and that is the purpose of this book. At this point, you have a good grasp of programming fundamentals, and you understand more about what professional programmers do in their programming environments.

It is now time for you to take the plunge into the world of programming languages and begin to see what you will face as you learn a programming language.

Chapter Highlights

The programming process requires more than sitting at the keyboard. Proper design is important, as are structured programming techniques and proper testing.

* ✖ The program-writing process takes three steps. You must write a program, test it, and distribute it to the end user.

* ✖ An editor is the tool you use to type your programs into the computer.

* ✖ Program editors are a lot like word processors. With these editors, you can enter, change, delete, move, copy, and save (to disk) program text.

* ✖ There are two kinds of editors: line and full-screen.

* ✖ A line editor generally isn't as easy to use as a full-screen editor, especially for beginners. You must learn editing commands, and you can edit only a single line of text at a time.

* ✖ Line editors have the advantage, however, of being available in almost any computing environment. Some dial-up computer systems have only line editors available.

* ✖ A full-screen editor enables you to move the cursor around the screen and throughout the file, as you locate the text to change.

* ✖ Many of today's programming languages come with their own editor built into the compiler. They make editing and compiling programs easier than using a separate editor and compiler.

✖ You and others can maintain a well-written program. Because of the changing world and the high maintenance of programs, you should attempt to learn structured programming techniques that help clarify programs.

✖ The three structured programming constructs are sequence, decision, and looping.

✖ The opposite of structured programming is spaghetti code. In spaghetti code, the program's logic branches all over the place without any order.

✖ Thorough testing is critical to ensure program correctness.

✖ The first test a programmer should perform is a desk check to get as many bugs out of the program as possible.

✖ The next step of program testing is the beta test. In a beta test, users get an early copy of the program to try on their own.

✖ Users should never switch "cold turkey" to a beta test program. They should run the program in parallel with their current procedures to ensure that the results match.

Programming Languages: The Early Years

Perilous Perry unrolled his map and charted his course. Where will his route take him? What have other adventurous programmers discovered along this route? What discoveries lay ahead for Perilous Perry?

1. What is a bit?

2. How many bits are in a byte?

3. What is the ASCII table used for?

4. How does the computer perform mathematical calculations?

5. What is a 2's complement?

6. What kinds of programs are best suited to FORTRAN?

7. Why is COBOL still used today?

8. Why would a company adopt FORTRAN over COBOL?

9. Why would a company adopt COBOL over FORTRAN?

10. Why did PL/I not succeed as its designers had hoped?

11. Why is APL not used much?

12. Why would someone want to learn ADA?

Ith this chapter, you can step into the ranks of the few, the proud, the people of tomorrow, by developing an understanding of several programming languages. This chapter focuses on the earlier programming languages, many of which are still in use today. You will learn how programming languages began and how they have evolved over the years.

To understand how programming languages work, you must learn how computers store programs and data at the machine's lowest level. This chapter teaches you a little *binary representation* (with which you can impress your friends at the next cocktail party you attend). Once you see how computers actually do things at their lowest level, you'll move up to learn about some of the many high-level programming languages.

Storage of Programs and Data

While typing away in your program editor, what do you think happens when you press the keys? Does a letter *A* go somewhere inside the computer's memory when you press the *A* key? It must, or else the computer could never remember your program's contents. The computer does store the *A*, but not in the format you might first expect. The computer only stores a representation of the letter *A*. For all intents, the *A* is in memory, but it does not look like you think it should.

Your computer's memory is made up of many characters of storage. As you learned in Chapter 2, "The Computer's Background," when you purchase a computer with 640K of memory, you get a computer with a little more than 640,000 characters of storage. That means that you can store approximately 640,000 characters—not 700,000 characters. Think of the cassette tape analogy; a 60-minute tape cannot hold 90 minutes of music no matter how hard you try to squeeze 90 minutes of music on it.

Remember that your computer is nothing more, at its lowest level, than thousands of switches turning electricity on and off. Each character in your computer is represented by a combination of on and off switches. Programmers generally refer to an on switch as a *1* and an off switch as a *0*. Since these switches have only two values, programmers call the 0s and 1s *binary digits*, or *bits* for short. There is a total of eight bits for every character in your computer, and eight bits are known as a *byte*. Therefore, every character of storage takes eight bits to represent (eight on and off switches), and therefore, a character is a byte.

Clue: The reason it takes eight switches is that if there were fewer, there wouldn't be enough combinations of on and off states to represent all the characters possible (uppercase, lowercase, digits, and special characters such as %, ^, and *).

Years ago, somebody wrote the various combinations of eight 1s and 0s, from 00000000 to 11111111 and assigned a unique character to each one. The table of characters was standardized and is known today as the *ASCII table* (pronounced *ask-ee*, so if you don't *know-ee*, you can ASCII...). Table 6.1 shows a partial listing of the ASCII table. ASCII stands for *American Standards Code for Information Interchange*. Some ASCII tables use only the last seven bits (called the *7-bit ASCII table*) and they keep the far left-hand bit off. 7-bit ASCII tables cannot represent as many different characters as can today's 8-bit ASCII tables.

Table 6.1. Some ASCII values.

Character	ASCII Code	Decimal Equivalent
Space	00100000	32
0	00110000	48
1	00110001	49
2	00110010	50
3	00110011	51
9	00111001	57
?	00111111	63
A	01000001	65

continues

Table 6.1. continued

Character	ASCII Code	Decimal Equivalent
B	01000010	66
C	01000011	67
a	01100001	97
b	01100010	98

Each of the ASCII values has a corresponding decimal number associated with it. These values are shown at the right of the eight-bit values in Table 6.1. Therefore, even though the computer represents the character *?* as 00111111 (two off switches with six on switches), you can refer, through programming, to that ASCII value as 63 and your computer will know you mean 00111111. One of the advantages of high-level programming languages is that they often let you use the easier (for people) decimal values and the programming language converts the value to the eight-bit binary value used inside the computer.

Note: As you can tell from the ASCII values in Table 6.1, every character in the computer, both uppercase and lowercase letters, and even the space, has its own unique ASCII value. The unique ASCII code is the only way the computer has to differentiate characters.

Every microcomputer, and many minicomputers, use the ASCII table. (Mainframes use a similar table called the *EBCDIC table*, pronounced *eb-se-dik*.) The ASCII table is the fundamental storage representation of all data and programs that your computer manages.

Reward: You can find a complete ASCII table in Appendix B.

Think back to the internal storage of single characters described earlier in this section. When you press the letter *A*, that *A* is not stored in your computer; rather, the ASCII value of the *A* is stored. As you can see from the ASCII values in the previous table, the letter *A* is represented as 01000001 (all of the eight switches except two are off in every byte of memory that holds a letter *A*).

Clue: The ASCII table is not very different from another type of coded table you may have heard of. Morse code is a table of representations for letters of the alphabet. Instead of 1s and 0s, the code uses combinations of dashes and dots to represent characters. The dashes and dots represent the length of radio signals people send or receive. The letters *SOS* are represented by DOT-DOT-DOT DASH-DASH-DASH DOT-DOT-DOT.

As Figure 6.1 shows, when you press the letter *A* on your keyboard, the *A* does not go into memory, but the ASCII value of 01000001 does. The computer keeps that pattern of on and off switches in that memory location as long as the *A* is to remain there. As far as you are concerned, the *A* is in memory as the letter *A*, but now you know exactly what happens. If you print the program you just typed, and the computer is ready to print the "character" stored in that memory location, the computer's CPU sends the ASCII code for the *A* to the printer. Just before printing, the printer knows that it must make its output readable to people, so it looks up 01000001 in its own ASCII table and prints the *A* to paper. From the time the *A* left the keyboard until right before it printed, it was not an *A* at all, but just a combination of eight 1s and 0s that represent an *A*.

Binary Arithmetic

At their lowest level, computers cannot subtract, multiply, or divide. Neither can calculators. The world's largest and fastest supercomputers can only add—that's it. It performs the addition at the bit level. Binary arithmetic is the only means by which any electronic digital computing machine can perform arithmetic.

139

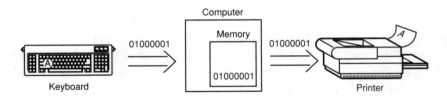

Figure 6.1. The A *is not an* A *once it leaves the keyboard.*

The computer makes you think it can perform all sorts of fancy calculations because it is lightning-fast. The computer can only add, but it can do so very quickly.

Suppose you want the computer to add seven 6s together. If you asked the computer (through programming) to perform the calculation

$$6 + 6 + 6 + 6 + 6 + 6 + 6$$

the computer would zing the answer, 42, back to you before you could say *bit bucket.* The computer has no problem performing addition. The problems arise when you request that the computer perform another type of calculation, such as this one:

$$42 - 6 - 6 - 6 - 6 - 6 - 6 - 6$$

Because the computer can only add, it cannot do the subtraction. However (and this is where the "catch" comes in), the computer can *negate* numbers. That is, the computer can take the negative of a number. Therefore, it can take the negative of 6 and represent (at the bit level) negative 6. Once it has done that, it can *add* –6 to 42 and continue doing so for seven times. In effect, the internal calculation becomes this:

$$42 + (-6) + (-6) + (-6) + (-6) + (-6) + (-6) + (-6)$$

Adding seven –6s produces the correct result of 0. This may seem like a cop-out to you. After all, the computer is really subtracting, right? In reality, the computer is not subtracting. At its bit level, the computer can convert a number to its negative through a process known as *2's complement*. A number's 2's complement is the negative of its original value at the bit level. The computer has in its internal logic circuits the ability to rapidly convert a number to its 2's complement and then carry out the addition of negatives, thereby seemingly performing subtraction.

> **Pitfall:** Surely, you wouldn't fall for the old computer joke about the 2's complement being "Oh, that's a very fine TWO you have there." That might be the 2's *compliment*, but not the 2's complement.

Once the computer can add and simulate subtraction (through successive adding of negatives), it can simulate multiplying and dividing. To multiply 6 times 7, the computer actually adds 6 together seven times and produces 42. Therefore,

$$6 \times 7$$

becomes this:

$$6 + 6 + 6 + 6 + 6 + 6 + 6$$

To divide 42 by 7, the computer subtracts 7 from 42 (well, it adds the *negative* of 7 to 42) until it reaches zero and counts the number of times (6) it took to reach zero, like this:

$$42 + (-7) + (-7) + (-7) + (-7) + (-7) + (-7)$$

The computer represents numbers in a manner similar to characters. As Table 6.2 shows, numbers are easy to represent at the binary level. Once numbers reach a certain limit (256 to be exact), the computer will use more than one byte to represent the number, taking as many memory locations as it needs to represent the extent of the number. The computer, once it is taught to add, subtract, multiply, and divide, can then perform any math necessary as long as a program is supplied to direct it.

Table 6.2. The first 20 binary numbers.

Number	Binary Equivalent
0	00000000
1	00000001
2	00000010
3	00000011
4	00000100
5	00000101
6	00000110
7	00000111
8	00001000
9	00001001
10	00001010
11	00001011
12	00001100
13	00001101
14	00001110
15	00001111
16	00010000
17	00010001
18	00010010
19	00010011
20	00010100

Clue: The first 255 binary numbers overlap the ASCII table values. That is, the binary representation for the letter *A* is 01000001, and the binary number for *65* is also 01000001. The computer knows by the context of how your programs use the memory location whether the value is the letter *A* or the number *65*.

   To see an example of what goes on at the bit level, follow this example to see what happens when you ask the computer to subtract 65 from 65. The result should be zero, and as you can see from the steps below, that is exactly what the result is at the binary level.

1. Suppose you want the computer to calculate the following:

```
  65
- 65
```

2. The binary representation for 65 is 01000001 and the 2's complement for 65 is 10111111 (which is –65 in *computerese*). Therefore, you are requesting that the computer perform this calculation:

```
 01000001
+10111111
```

3. Because a binary number cannot have the digit *2* (there are only 0s and 1s in binary), the computer carries 1 anytime a calculation results in a value of 2; 1 + 1 equals 10 in binary. Although this can be confusing, you can make an analogy with decimal arithmetic. People work in a base-10 numbering system. (Binary is known as base 2.) There is no single digit to represent ten; we have to reuse two digits already used to form ten, namely *1* and *0*. In base 10, 9 + 1 is 10. Therefore, the result of 1 + 1 in binary is 10 or "0 and carry 1 to the next column."

```
 01000001
+10111111
─────────
100000000
```

4. Because the answer should fit within the same number of bits as the two original numbers (at least for this example—your computer may use more bits to represent numbers), the ninth bit is discarded, leaving the zero result. This example shows that binary 65 plus binary negative 65 equals zero as it should.

Reward: The good thing about all this binary arithmetic is that you don't have to understand a *bit* of it (pun intended) to be an expert programmer. Nevertheless, the more you know about what is going on under the hood, the better you will understand how programming languages work and the faster you will master new ones by seeing similarities between them.

The First Programs

The earliest computers were not programmed in the same way as today's computers. It took much more effort to program them. The early computers' memories held only data and not programs. The concept of programming those early computers was vastly different because the programs were *hard-wired* into the machine. The programs were physically wired by experts to generate and process the data. The first computer programmers had never heard of using a keyboard, editor, and compiler; the first programmers were hardware experts, not software experts.

Programming these computers was very difficult. To make a change, the hardware programmer had to reroute the wires that made the program do its thing. It wasn't long before a man by the name of John von Neumann invented the *shared-program* concept. He demonstrated that a program could be stored in memory along with the data. Once the programs were in memory and out of the wired hardware, the programs were much easier to change. John von Neumann's breakthrough was one of the most important and lasting advances in the entire computing history; we still use his shared-program concept in today's machines.

Those early programmers used the switch panel described in Chapter 3 to enter the programs into the computer's shared memory. Although it was fantastic for its time, programming these computers took a tremendous effort because they had to be programmed in the machine's native 1s and 0s. Therefore, the first few instructions to a computer might look like this:

```
01000110
11000100
10111011
00011101
    .
    .
    .
```

Whenever a programmer wanted to add two numbers, move values in memory, or whatever, the programmer had to refer to a table that described the proper patterns of 1s and 0s for the desired instructions. Flipping the switches and programming the machine took hours, but it was a giant leap forward from hardwired computer programming.

Enter the Keyboard

Someone watching over the programming process got the brilliant, but today seemingly obvious, idea of attaching a keyboard to the computer. Instead of typing those 1s and 0s, the programmer could type names associated with each instruction in the machine language. Therefore, the previous few instructions might look something like this:

```
ADD A, 6
MOV A, OUT
LOAD B
SUB B, A
    :
```

These commands are cryptic, but they are a lot easier to remember than the 1s and 0s. The words are called *mnemonics*, which means the words are easy-to-remember abbreviations for the instructions. ADD A, 6 is a lot easier to remember when you need to add 6 to the value of a memory location named *A* than is 01000110.

Of course, the computer could not understand the mnemonics, but a translator program called an *assembler* was written to be the go-between for the programmer's mnemonics and the 1s and 0s to which they were translated. Figure 6.2 shows how the assembler acts as the go-between for the human programmer at the keyboard and the machine. A huge leap forward was made when the assembler language became the primary means by which programmers entered instructions into the computer. This second programming language (the first was the native 1s and 0s machine language) allowed for much faster program development. The software revolution was begun just a few years after the computer hardware was born.

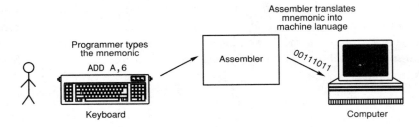

Figure 6.2. The assembler translates mnemonics into 1s and 0s.

Note: The keyboards used with the early computers were not attached to the machines as directly as they are today. Often, programmers would use a card-punch machine. These machines had keyboards, but the typing produced punched holes in computer cards. Then the cards were read into the computer's memory. You may have seen these punched cards, but they are rarely used today. Online terminals (screen and keyboard combinations) are much more efficient than card-punch machines, and you won't rearrange a thousand-line program on a terminal as easily as you would if you dropped a box of punched cards.

These first two programming languages—machine language and assembler language—are called *low-level* programming languages. The computer doesn't need to translate much to convert assembler to machine language because each assembler instruction has a one-to-one correlation with a machine-language instruction (a machine-language instruction may take more than one byte of memory, though). Although low-level languages are not used as much today as the high-level programming languages (BASIC, C, and Pascal, for example), you can still program today's computers using low-level languages. For instance, if you have a PC, you can use a program called DEBUG to enter machine language code directly into the computer's memory locations.

Figure 6.3 shows a machine language program being entered using DEBUG. Notice that machine language programming is cryptic, although it is less so today than the machine language of the early computers. Today's machine-level code is more powerful than before. For instance, there are machine-language instructions to perform multiplication and division, whereas computers of the first and second generation rarely had that power at the machine level. Programmers had to write machine language programs to perform such mathematical feats.

```
C:\DOS>DEBUG
-d cs:0000
21A2:0000  CD 20 00 A0 00 9A EE FE-1D F0 4F 03 06 1C 8A 03    .........O.....
21A2:0010  06 1C 17 03 06 1C BF 06-01 01 01 00 02 FF FF FF    ................
21A2:0020  FF FF FF FF FF FF FF FF-FF FF FF FF E1 1B 4E 01    ..............N.
21A2:0030  C6 20 14 00 18 00 A2 21-FF FF FF FF 00 00 00 00    . .....!........
21A2:0040  05 00 00 00 00 00 00 00-00 00 00 00 00 00 00 00    ................
21A2:0050  CD 21 CB 00 00 00 00 00-00 00 00 00 20 20 20 20    .!..........
21A2:0060  20 20 20 20 20 20 20 20-00 00 00 00 20 20 20 20         ....
21A2:0070  20 20 20 20 20 20 20 20-00 00 00 00 EE 10 00 00        .......
-r
AX=0000  BX=0000  CX=0000  DX=0000  SP=FFEE  BP=0000  SI=0000  DI=0000
DS=21A2  ES=21A2  SS=21A2  CS=21A2  IP=0100   NV UP EI PL NZ NA PO NC
21A2:0100 40            INC     AX
-E 21A2:0050 29
-E 21A2:0051 1C
-E 21A2:0052
21A2:0052  CB.7F    00.00    00.34    00.13    00.DE    00.0D
-E 21A2:0070
21A2:0070  20.12    20.43    20.45    20.FF    20.E2    20.00
-
```

Figure 6.3. A sample DEBUG programming session.

Clue: Today's machine language programmers do not use binary 1s and 0s, but what they do use is almost as cryptic, especially to the uninitiated in the ways of low-level languages. By converting the binary values to *hexadecimal* values (also known as *base 16*), machine language programs are slightly easier to work with. (Figure 6.3 uses hexadecimal instead of binary values.) Of course, "slightly easier" is a strictly relative term here.

There are several modern assembler language translators on the market today. The most common is Microsoft's Macro Assembler, shown in Figure 6.4. Borland's Turbo Assembler (which comes with most of Borland's C++ compilers) is also gaining popularity. Each of these products offers a slightly easier programming environment than machine language programs, but they still offer complexity that most programmers never have to master.

```
 1:*BEGIN:    INT     20
 2:          ADD     [BX+SI+9A00],AH
 3:          OUT     DX,AL
 4:          CALL    FAR CalcInt        ; Perform Math routine

 5:          LOCK
 6:          DEC     DI
 7:          ADD     AX,[8A1C]          ; Compute offset
 8:          ADD     AX,[171C]
 9:          ADD     AX,[BF1C]
10:          PUSH    ES                 ; Save the pointer to the data

11:          ADD     [SI],AX
12:          ADD     [BX+SI],AX
13:          ADD     BH,BH              ; Double age value
14:          INC     DX
15:          ADD     SP,SI
16:          PUSH    ES                 ; Save the pointer again

17:          JO      Speaker
18:          PUSH    SS
19:          ADD     [DI+06],AL
20:          HLT                        ; Halt if not in system
```

Figure 6.4. A sample assembler language programming session.

Clue: When a program's speed and low overhead is critical, there are no better programming tools than assembler and machine language. It is more difficult to learn a low-level language than a high-level language, and it takes longer to program in the low-level languages, but for some applications the assembler level is the only place to be.

Quite often, programmers combine a high-level programming language, such as C, with some assembler language routines, speeding up the critical processes while keeping the more readable (and maintainable) high-level language for the majority of the program.

Getting Closer to English

High-level programming languages evolved from the complexity of the low-level languages. Once assembler language was made available, more companies began using computers. With the beginning of widespread use of computers came the need to write more complex software applications to support those companies. The low-level machine and assembler language were too inefficient for the quick turnaround that the companies needed. Therefore, high-level languages were developed to add one more layer between the programmer and the hardware. That extra layer meant that more work was required by the computer to translate a high-level language into machine language, but the programmers were free from the job of low-level coding. Two of the earliest high-level programming compilers were FORTRAN and COBOL. Both of these languages are still in widespread use today.

Note: The fact that these early programming languages are still being used says a lot for their capabilities and the foresight of their authors. There have been many languages developed since, most of which are touted as being the "best ever," yet companies still use the two old workhorses, FORTRAN and COBOL, for many tasks.

The FORTRAN Language

FORTRAN stands for *FORmula TRANslator*. As its name implies, it is used for mathematical and scientific applications. FORTRAN works very well with

149

high-precision numbers and offers an excellent library of built-in trigonometric routines that aid the scientific developer.

Over the years, programmers have added to the FORTRAN language, giving it more character-manipulation capabilities. The early versions of FORTRAN existed to solve mathematical computations without much regard for the cosmetics of how the results looked. Today's FORTRAN compilers work better with character data (often called *character string* data because strings of characters make up words and sentences) than the older versions did, but they still retain their mathematical capabilities.

Listing 6.1 shows you a sample FORTRAN program. It is not the goal of this chapter, or of this book, to teach you FORTRAN. FORTRAN is not regarded as a beginner's language (although it is not as difficult as many of the others; once you learn BASIC, you can pick up FORTRAN relatively easily, because BASIC was originally based on FORTRAN). The program in Listing 6.1 is an example of a payroll computation that you can study.

Listing 6.1. A sample FORTRAN program.

```
*
* Calculate payroll amounts and print the net pay
*
* Print a title
      WRITE(6,10)
   10 FORMAT(1H1, 2X, '** PAYROLL COMPUTATION **'//)
*
* Initialize overtime to 0
*
      TOVRTM = 0.0
*
* Get hours worked and other pay data from user
*
      WRITE(6, 20)
   20 FORMAT('WHAT WERE THE HOURS WORKED? ')
      READ(5, 21) HRS
   21 FORMAT(F4.1)
      WRITE(6, 22)
   22 FORMAT(/'WHAT IS THE HOURLY RATE? ')
```

```
      READ(5, 23) RATE
   23 FORMAT(F7.2)
      WRITE(6, 24)
   24 FORMAT(/'WHAT IS THE TAX RATE? ')
      READ(6, 25) TAXRTE
   25 FORMAT(F7.2)
*
* Calculate the results
*
* Overtime is left at 0.0 or is double pay
* depending on the hours the employee worked
      IF (HRS .LT. 40.0) GOTO 100
      TOVRTM = (HRS - 40.0) * RATE * 2.0
      GROSS = 40.0 * RATE
      GOTO 200
  100 GROSS = HRS * RATE
  200 GROSS = GROSS + TOVRTM
      TNET = GROSS * (1.0 - TAXRTE)
*
* PRINT THE RESULTS
*
      WRITE(6, 300) HRS, RATE, TAXRTE, GROSS, TNET
  300 FORMAT(//'Hours: ', F4.1, 2X, 'Rate: ', F7.2,
     1    2x, 'Tax rate: ', F7.2, 2x, 'Gross: $', F10.2,
     2    2x, 'Net: $', F10.2)
      END
```

Notice that FORTRAN is a high-level language, easier to read than its assembler language precursor shown earlier, but still not extremely obvious to non-programmers. Although you may not understand everything in the program, you can see some words you recognize such as WRITE and FORMAT. You should begin to see that high-level programming languages are closer to spoken language than either the 1s and 0s or the mnemonics of the low-level languages.

FORTRAN is not known as a large language. It has relatively few commands (as opposed to COBOL and modern-day BASIC languages), although its compactness causes some confusion if you do not know the language. FORTRAN is not regarded as a *self-documenting* language, a sometimes-overused term applied to languages that offer some readability for non-programmers. Nevertheless, FORTRAN appears to have its foothold in the scientific community, and it will for some time. In fairness, FORTRAN has lost ground over the years to PL/I, Pascal, and C, but its superior math capabilities keep FORTRAN far from obsolete.

151

> **Reward:** FORTRAN has been standardized by the ANSI committee. ANSI is the American National Standards Institute, an organization that attempts to sift through all the versions of programming languages and offers a standard set of commands for each one it adopts. Language vendors do not have to follow the ANSI standard, but if the companies do not, they risk losing customers who believe in the advantages that standards provide. Most companies prefer to program in an ANSI standard language; by doing so, they help ensure that new programmers will be versed in the same version as those that came before them.

The Business of COBOL

Grace Hopper, the Naval Admiral who is credited with discovering the first computer bug (refer back to Chapter 3 for a refresher if you need it), is also known as the author of COBOL. In 1960, Admiral Hopper and her team of programmers decided they needed a language for the business side of computing (even the Navy has to meet a payroll and pay its bills). FORTRAN was taking care of the scientific side of things, but the FORTRAN language was never designed to handle business transactions. Programmers were also discovering that FORTRAN's cryptic nature slowed down programming maintenance chores as well.

Admiral Hopper's team developed COBOL, an acronym for *COmmom Business Oriented Language.* The COBOL design team's primary goal was to develop a self-documenting language that could process a large amount of business data such as inventory and personnel records. A sample of their achievement is shown in Listing 6.2. This is a program that performs the very same processing as its FORTRAN counterpart in Listing 6.1, yet the COBOL listing is almost twice as long. Take a few minutes to peruse the listing and become familiar with the nature of COBOL.

Note: All COBOL programs are separated into four divisions. The identification division describes the program. The environment division describes the computer system running the program. The data division describes the format of all data in the program. The procedure division contains the code that processes the data. See if you can find these four divisions in Listing 6.2.

Listing 6.2. A sample COBOL program.

```
IDENTIFICATION DIVISION.
PROGRAM-ID.     'PAYROLL'

ENVIRONMENT DIVISION.
INPUT-OUTPUT SECTION.
FILE-CONTROL.
    SELECT GET-DATA, ASSIGN TO KEYIN.
    SELECT OUT-DATA, ASSIGN TO DISPLAY.

DATA DIVISION.
FILE SECTION.
FD  GET-DATA
    LABEL RECORDS ARE OMITTED.
01  GET-REC.
    02 AMOUNT        PICTURE 9(5)V2.

FD  OUT-DATA
    LABEL RECORDS ARE OMITTED.
01  OUT-REC.
    02 FILLER        PICTURE X(80).

WORKING-STORAGE SECTION.
01  ARITHMETIC-DATA.
        02 TOT-OVR      PICTURE 9(5)V2 VALUE ZERO.
        02 HOURS        PICTURE 9(3)V1 VALUE ZERO.
        02 RATE         PICTURE 9(5)V2 VALUE ZERO.
        02 TAX-RATE     PICTURE 9(5)V2 VALUE ZERO.
        02 GROSS-PAY    PICTURE 9(5)V2 VALUE ZERO.
        02 NET-PAY      PICTURE 9(5)V2 VALUE ZERO.
```

continues

153

Listing 6.2. continued

```
01   OUT-LINE-1.
     02 FILLER        PICTURE X(28)
        VALUE 'What were the hours worked? '.
     02 FILLER        PICTURE X(52) VALUE SPACES.
01   OUT-LINE-2.
     02 FILLER        PICTURE X(25)
        VALUE 'What is the hourly rate? '.
     02 FILLER        PICTURE X(55) VALUE SPACES.
01   OUT-LINE-3.
     02 FILLER        PICTURE X(22)
        VALUE 'What is the tax rate? '.
     02 FILLER        PICTURE X(58) VALUE SPACES.
01   OUT-LINE-4.
     02 FILLER        PICTURE X(17)
        VALUE 'The gross pay is '
     02 OUT-GROSS     PICTURE $ZZ,ZZZ.99.
     02 FILLER        PICTURE X(53) VALUE SPACES.
01   OUT-LINE-5.
     02 FILLER        PICTURE X(15)
        VALUE 'The net pay is '
     02 OUT-NET       PICTURE $ZZ,ZZZ.99.
     02 FILLER        PICTURE X(55) VALUE SPACES.

PROCEDURE DIVISION.
BEGIN.
   OPEN INPUT GET-DATA.
   OPEN OUTPUT OUT-DATA.

   MOVE OUT-LINE-1 TO OUT-REC.
   WRITE OUT-REC.
   READ GET-DATA.
   MOVE AMOUNT TO HOURS.

   MOVE OUT-LINE-2 TO OUT-REC.
   WRITE OUT-REC.
   READ GET-DATA.
   MOVE AMOUNT TO RATE.

   MOVE OUT-LINE-3 TO OUT-REC.
   WRITE OUT-REC.
   READ GET-DATA.
   MOVE AMOUNT TO TAX-RATE.

   IF HOURS > 40.0
      THEN COMPUTE TOT-OVR = (40.0 - HOURS) * RATE * 2
           COMPUTE GROSS-PAY = 40.0 * RATE + TOT-OVR
```

```
ELSE
    COMPUTE GROSS-PAY = HOURS * RATE.
COMPUTE NET-PAY = GROSS-PAY * (1.0 - TAX-RATE).

MOVE GROSS-PAY TO OUT-GROSS.
MOVE OUT-LINE-4 TO OUT-REC.
WRITE OUT-REC.

MOVE NET-PAY TO OUT-NET.
MOVE OUT-LINE-5 TO OUT-REC.
WRITE OUT-REC.

CLOSE GET-DATA, OUT-DATA.
STOP RUN.
```

Admiral Hopper's crew wanted COBOL to be self-documenting so that non-programmers could understand it. Can you figure out what Listing 6.2 is doing just by reading the code? Don't feel bad if you can't; if you get lost in the program's silver-dollar words, don't be dismayed. Instead of being self-documenting, COBOL ended up being very *wordy*. There is so much that gets in the way of the working code that most people would probably agree (even those COBOL fans, of whom there are many thousands) that COBOL does not achieve a self-documenting effect. Nevertheless, it shines as the world's premiere business language of choice, and has for almost 40 years.

There are more lines of COBOL in use today than any other programming language. Most large (and some smaller) businesses use only COBOL in their data processing shops, a trend that the C programming language pundits are fighting, and one that PL/I (described next) fought and failed a few years ago. It will take a long time before COBOL is done away with in today's business.

Clue: Part of COBOL's wordiness problem might be solved if a COBOL compiler vendor allowed some shortcuts. For example, the very first line in Listing 6.2's program, IDENTIFICATION DIVISION. is required, period and all, in every COBOL program in the world. If the line is required in every program, then why is it required at all? Why not do away with it? At least allow for an abbreviated form. Fans of the language argue that adding shortcuts would violate the ANSI standard COBOL, and they are

155

correct if ANSI did not adopt the abbreviated version; ANSI probably would have done so before now if there were ever a possibility of shortcuts being added. Also, despite the fact that COBOL is wordy, lots of people know it; changing the language would do nothing but make it more difficult to relearn for those currently using it.

If you want to have a career in programming, you should plan to make COBOL the second or third language you learn. Having a knowledge of COBOL in your mind's toolkit goes a long way in today's data processing world. To learn COBOL as quickly as possible, you should remember that there are several PC versions available. When you do learn COBOL, learning with the quick response time of a PC might be easier than learning via a mainframe for your first time. (COBOL's home environment is in the mainframe world, and that is where COBOL is used most.)

Reward: ANSI standard COBOL compilers were never plentiful on the PC platform. The microcomputer's limited memory and speed, until recent years, could not support production-level COBOL programming. Smaller languages such as Pascal and C filled the smaller microcomputer programming niche quite nicely. Recently, however, PCs have become quite capable of handling full ANSI-COBOL compilers containing not only the COBOL language itself, but also support programs such as built-in editors, debuggers, and profilers.

Other Languages Through the Years

Once FORTRAN and COBOL gained ground, there was no turning back the software industry. Languages began appearing all over the place. Companies would develop their own in-house programming languages that, supposedly, supported their environment better than the *big two* languages, FORTRAN and COBOL.

So many languages began appearing that the programming community started becoming fragmented, wallowing in the sheer number of possibilities, unable to decide which language was the best to use for any given project. At least, that was the scenario that IBM saw when it decided to create "the only programming language anyone would ever need." IBM saw (or tried to create, there is debate today, even amongst IBMers) a need for a programming language that did it all. The new language would be the best scientific language. It would be the best business language. It would solve any programmer's needs.

Therefore, IBM created the PL/I programming language to solve the problem of too many languages. PL/I stands for *Programming Language I*. IBM designed PL/I by taking the best of the COBOL language, the best of FORTRAN, and the best of some other programming languages of the time. The end result, at least in terms of sales, was never achieved; IBM never had the success with PL/I it had hoped for. Instead of being the only programming language anyone would ever need, PL/I became just another programming language amidst many.

The primary problem with PL/I was that it was too good; it was massive. IBM did make use of the best of every programming language of the day, but in doing so, IBM created a huge language that required massive computing resources to run. During the 1960s, not enough businesses had enough computer power to devote 100 percent of the CPU's time to PL/I compiles. Also, PL/I took too long for programmers to learn. The language was so large that programmers rarely mastered it.

Today, there are companies with PL/I programs in use, and some companies still program in PL/I, but the language never caught hold as IBM hoped. Listing 6.3 shows you part of a PL/I program that performs the same routine as the FORTRAN and COBOL listings you saw earlier. In this example, the code looks more like its COBOL counterpart than FORTRAN, but much of PL/I differs from COBOL. The differences become more apparent as you begin programming scientific and other non-business applications.

Listing 6.3. A sample PL/I program.

```
PAYROLL: PROCEDURE OPTIONS (MAIN);
DECLARE OVRTIM     FIXED DECIMAL (2);
DECLARE HOURS      FIXED DECIMAL (5,2);
DECLARE RATE       FIXED DECIMAL (9,2);
DECLARE TAXRATE    FIXED DECIMAL (9,2);
DECLARE GROSS      FIXED DECIMAL (9,2);
DECLARE NETPAY     FIXED DECIMAL (9,2);

BEGIN: GET LIST(HOURS, RATE, TAXRATE);
   IF HOURS < 40 THEN
      OVRTIM = (HOURS - 40) * RATE * 2
      GROSS = 40 * RATE
   ELSE
      OVRTIM = 0
      GROSS = HOURS * RATE;
   NETPAY = GROSS * (1 - TAXRATE);
   PUT LIST (OVRTIM, HOURS, RATE, TAXRATE, GROSS, NETPAY);
END PAYROLL
```

> **Warning:** Although part of the PL/I language offers some interesting programming concepts, aspiring computer programmers should assign a low priority to learning PL/I. Unless you want to program for a company that you know uses PL/I, you'll be more marketable and your time will be better spent if you learn COBOL, FORTRAN, or C (after learning an introductory language such as BASIC).

Perhaps another reason for PL/I's decline is that it was never ported to a microcomputer environment. Originally, the microcomputer did not have the memory or disk space for a language as large as PL/I. Although today's PCs would have no trouble running PL/I, other languages such as C and Pascal have taken hold in the PC arena and a PL/I compiler would have little chance of success.

Another programming language that has been around for many years is RPG. RPG stands for *Report Program Generator* and exists in newer versions named RPG II and RPG III. As its name implies, RPG began as a report-writer only.

It was originally intended to be a language that non-programmers (shades of COBOL's ideals) could use to generate reports from data in disk files.

RPG is unlike most other programming languages. The languages you have seen so far are *procedural languages.* That is, they offer individual instructions that the computer follows in a sequential manner until the job is done. RPG does not have typical commands, and its logic is non-procedural. (Some of the later versions of RPG do offer limited procedural capabilities.) An RPG program is one that is written using codes that follow strict column placements. Non-programmers, and even veteran programmers who are inexperienced in RPG, have a difficult time deciphering RPG programs. To make matters worse, there are several nonstandard versions of RPG in widespread use.

Listing 6.4 shows you a sample RPG program. The placement of the codes must be exact. If you shift any line of the program to the right or left a few spaces, the program does not work. As you might imagine, an RPG program is difficult to follow and extremely difficult to get right the first time you write one.

Listing 6.4. A sample RPG program.

```
F*      PAYROLL PROGRAM
FOUTP    IP  F    80              KEYBOARD
FINP     O   F    80              SCREEN
IREPORT  AA  01                        1    10RATE
I                                      8    30HOURS
I                                     12    40TAXRATE
C        *PY01         IFGT '40'
C        OVTIM         MULT      RATE*2
C        OVTIM         MULT      HOURS
C                      END
C        *GROSS        IFLE '40'
C        GROSS         MULT      RATE * HOURS
C                      END
OOUTP      H  100 1P
```

Programmers use RPG primarily on minicomputers. RPG is probably used on more minicomputers than any other programming language. (There are only a couple of RPG compilers available for microcomputers, and their sales suffer from severe lack of interest.) As you might recall from Chapter 2, the minicomputer is losing sales to mainframes and microcomputers, and many predict that RPG will go down with the demise of the minicomputer.

Clue: RPG programmers use *RPG specification sheets* to write RPG programs. These sheets are similar to graph paper, with cells labeled for the different RPG commands. By writing out the program using specification sheets, the programmer can help ensure accurate column placement for his or her RPG programs.

In the meantime, RPG is still used on many computers; you should be aware of its report-generating capabilities. If you ever work on a minicomputer, you will almost assuredly run across an RPG program.

Two other programming languages, APL and ADA, have also been used a lot over the years. APL (which stands for *A Programming Language*) is a highly mathematical programming language developed by IBM. APL is a language as different from COBOL and FORTRAN as is RPG. An APL program consists of many strange symbols (housetops, curved arrows, triangles, and so forth) and requires special hardware to generate its symbols. Because of the hardware restriction and its slow speed compared to other programming languages (APL is almost always run in an interpreted mode and rarely compiled), it is losing favor even by those who were fans in the past.

Pitfall: Another problem with APL is that it is difficult to maintain due to its cryptic nature. Companies are finding that a more natural procedural language makes for more productive long-term programming teams than APL allows.

ADA, named aftern Lady Augusta Ada Byron (daughter of the poet, Lord Byron, and girlfriend of Charles Babbage, the father of computers), is used almost exclusively by the Department of Defense and other governmental contracts. The government thought it best to standardize on a programming language so that all of its programs would be consistent and governmental programmers would be familiar with the language of all in-house code. Experts view ADA as a mediocre programming language that is difficult to learn (keep in mind, the government put its blessing on ADA as the language of choice, and the government has never been known for being extremely efficient or logical). One wonders why the Department of Defense, which designed and wrote the first COBOL compiler years earlier, chose to use something besides COBOL when almost every company at the time had adopted COBOL and was having tremendous success using it.

Because the government standardized on the ADA programming language early (it was the Department of Defense that designed ADA in 1979), the ANSI committee adopted an ANSI ADA standard shortly after ADA's release. Therefore, as long as you learn to program in ADA using an ANSI ADA compiler, you are assured of knowing the same language as that used in all governmental contracts.

The reason you might want to learn ADA is that you might someday work for a company that writes software for the government. The government does not do all its own programming. Because so few nongovernmental employees know ADA, ADA programmers are often in demand, especially for aviation, defense, and space applications.

This completes the first discussion of programming languages. In the next chapter, you get a look at some of the newer programming languages (those developed within the last 20 years).

Chapter Highlights

Understanding the inner workings of your computer is a prerequisite for becoming a master programmer. Only after learning about what is "under the hood" can your programming skills blossom. Computer programming has come a long way since the early days of wiring panels and switches. High-level languages such as COBOL and FORTRAN offer a much easier approach to making computers do what you want them to do.

✖ Memory is nothing more than on and off switches.

✖ Electricity can be stored in two states, called *binary states*. The binary digits, or bits, are 1 and 0, representing on and off, respectively.

✖ The computer stores all its data internally as a series of bits.

✖ The pattern of bits that correspond to specific characters is determined by the ASCII table.

✖ Early computers were programmed by physically rewiring the system.

✖ A switch panel improved the speed at which people could program computers because the program could be put in memory along with the program's data.

✖ Once keyboards were attached to computers, many advances began. The earliest non-binary programming language was called *assembler language*. The assembler translates assembler coded mnemonics into 1s and 0s.

✖ Both the assembler language and the machine's language (the 1s and 0s) are called low-level languages.

✖ High-level programming languages provide a much easier programming environment because they are one step closer to spoken language and one step further from the machine's native binary code.

✖ FORTRAN was one of the first high-level programming languages and is still used today in scientific and engineering applications.

✖ COBOL was designed to handle the day-to-day data processing of businesses.

✖ PL/I was IBM's attempt to consolidate all the various programming languages, but PL/I did not end up becoming the major programming language for most people.

✖ RPG began as a report-generating language for non-programmers, but recently has evolved into a regular procedural programming language.

✖ RPG is used mostly on minicomputers.

✖ APL is a mathematical programming language. Its use of strange symbols limits its availability and readability.

✖ ADA is a programming language adopted by the government to standardize all their programming jobs. Defense contractors must submit their programs in ADA or the government will not accept the program.

Programming Languages: Modern Day

Perilous Perry was back on his ship, looking out over the bow. He was worried—there was no land in sight! Will Perilous Perry reach the land of modern computing?

1. What is the primary strength of Pascal?

2. Where is Pascal used the most today?

3. Why is C known as a high low-level language?

4. Is C a large programming language?

5. What is a programming language operator?

6. What advantages does C++ offer?

7. Why is BASIC good for beginners?

8. Why are there so many versions of BASIC?

9. How has BASIC evolved over the years?

10. Which Windows programming tool is easy to use?

11. Which programming language is best?

12. Why do some companies prefer one language over another?

Programming languages have come a long way since the original COBOL compiler in the early 1960s. With each new programming language comes the promise of faster learning time and more maintainable code. Some of the newer languages look similar to those presented in the previous chapter. Being newer does not always mean that the programming languages have to differ greatly from the ones people already know. As a matter of fact, the closer a new language is to an existing one, the faster programmers can get up to speed with it and use it. (This may have been the thinking of the designers of C++, which is a close relative of C yet is light-years ahead of C in what it can accomplish.)

There is a trend among programmers toward graphical programming languages. Programmers and non-programmers are able to produce working programs simply by moving graphical objects around on the screen. Although these programming languages are still in their infancy, they mark an important development in programming that promises to continue through the next several years. Their popularity is a direct result of the popularity of *graphical user interfaces* (*GUIs*) such as the Macintosh computer systems, Microsoft Windows, and IBM's OS/2 operating environments. The procedural languages do not lend themselves well to the needs of the graphical environment. Many graphical user interface programmers today tend to mix GUI programming with procedural languages, using the best each has to offer.

This chapter focuses on the programming languages that have been popular for the last few years. Because use of the microcomputer has grown so much during this time, most of these languages are available on microcomputers, and some are used exclusively in microcomputer environments.

Structured Programming with Pascal

In 1968, Niklaus Wirth wrote the first Pascal compiler. Pascal was named after the French mathematician Blaise Pascal. Pascal is a good general-purpose programming language, offering support for scientific work as well as business. Pascal's input/output capabilities are not as advanced as other programming languages used in business, such as COBOL, so it was never a contender for removing COBOL from its business perch. Nevertheless, Pascal is a solid language that does a lot well.

Pascal's biggest advantage is that it supports the structured programming concept so well. The three structured programming constructs—sequence, decision, and looping (see Chapter 5 for a review of the structured programming constructs)—are integrated into the design of Pascal. Pascal's control statements offer several ways to accomplish structured programming constructs within a program.

> **Reward:** It is difficult *not* to write structured programs in Pascal. Spaghetti code is almost non-existent in Pascal programs. Unlike most programming languages, some versions of Pascal do not contain a `GOTO` statement that allows the unconditional branching and jumping other languages provide.

During the 1970s, it was thought that Pascal would become "the only programming language you would ever need." Can you remember where you have heard that before? The previous chapter mentioned that same prediction for PL/I. As with PL/I, Pascal never achieved that lofty goal. Pascal's usage seemed to shrink as quickly as it grew. The 1970s saw a tremendous growth in Pascal and the 1980s saw it decline. Today, Pascal is rarely used in business and engineering. Pascal is used mostly as a teaching tool for programming and on home computers by people who enjoy the language.

There is a lot of debate as to why Pascal lost ground to other programming languages when it had such a strong start. Perhaps the competition from C and C++ languages (the usage of which grew tremendously in the 1980s at the expense of Pascal) was just too strong for Pascal to regain its lead.

Listing 7.1 shows you a sample Pascal program. Do not expect to understand the code in full. You should be able to see where data is initialized and where it is output to the screen, however.

> **Reward:** Unlike FORTRAN and COBOL, Pascal (as are all of the modern-day languages) is *free form*. That means that you can put as many blank lines and spaces in the program (called *whitespace*) as you like to make the program more readable. Pascal programmers often indent lines of code that go together and add blank lines between sections of their programs to help clarify the parts of the programs and make them easier to modify later.

Listing 7.1. A sample Pascal program.

```
{ Typed constant arrays with records
  that hold people's statistics }
PROGRAM People;
USES Crt;
TYPE PersonTypes  = (Employee, Vendor, Customer);
     PersonString = STRING[9];
     PersonRecord = RECORD
                        Name:    PersonString;
                        Balance: WORD;
                     END;
   PersonNameArray = ARRAY[PersonTypes] OF PersonRecord;
CONST People: PersonNameArray =
               ((Name: 'Sally'; Balance: 323.56),
                (Name: 'Ted';   Balance:   0.00),
                (Name: 'John';  Balance: 1212.37));
VAR Person: PersonTypes;

{The primary output routine appears next }
BEGIN
   CLRSCR;
   WRITELN( '*** People in System ***'):
   WRITELN;
   FOR Person := Employee TO Customer DO
     WITH People[Person] DO
        BEGIN
           WRITELN( Name, ' has a balance of $',
                    Balance, '.');
           WRITELN;
        END;  {with}
END.  {People}
```

One of Pascal's biggest promoters in the PC industry is Borland International, which has achieved the reputation of being the premiere supplier of Pascal programming products since its first Pascal language, called *Turbo Pascal 1.0*. Turbo Pascal is now in its seventh version with comprehensive graphics and database libraries available. Some feel that without Borland's support of Pascal for the past ten years, the language would have died away completely. Thanks to Borland, there is still a base of Pascal programmers and support publications available. Even though Pascal did not achieve success as "the only programming language you will ever need" as first thought, it will remain as a programming language option for many years to come.

> **Note:** Colleges and universities almost always require their programming students to take a Pascal course immediately after learning BASIC. Pascal's structured programming support is so strong that educators feel that, although the mainstream computer world may not use Pascal, budding programmers learn a lot about how to program correctly by using Pascal. By learning Pascal, you develop good programming habits that should stay with you as you move into other programming languages. Therefore, Pascal is still strong today at the education level, and probably will be for some time to come.

C

C was developed at Bell Laboratories by two men named Brian Kernighan and Dennis Ritchie, men whose programming language made their names as famous in the computer industry as Charles Lindbergh is in aviation. In 1972, the Bell Laboratories needed to write a new operating system. Until that point, all operating systems were written in assembler language because the high-level programming languages were not efficient enough given the lack of computer power back then. The problem with the low-level programming of assembler language is that the code is difficult to maintain. As the operating systems were updated, programmers dreaded the nightmares that updating assembler code brought.

169

Clue: The operating system that resulted from this endeavor was called *UNIX*, which is still in widespread use today on minicomputers.

Bell did not want their new operating system to be as difficult to maintain as previous ones were, but there was simply no high-level language at the time that could do the job. Therefore, they set out to write a new programming language, one that would be as easy to maintain as high-level programming languages tend to be, and one that was almost as efficient as assembler code.

Kernighan and Ritchie (known in the industry as simply *K&R*) made several attempts, finally coming up with the C programming language. (The story goes that their first two attempts, A and B, failed, but the third time was a charm.)

C is known as a *high low-level language*, meaning that it supports all the programming constructs of any high-level language, including structured programming constructs, but also compiles into extremely tight and efficient code that runs almost as fast as assembler language. The Bell Labs ended up with an operating system that was efficient but still easy to maintain and update.

The Success of C

C's popularity grew rapidly. Companies liked the idea of having more efficient programs. A C program might run up to ten times faster than an equivalent COBOL program. Although it will be many years before C displaces COBOL, the C programming language is now the language that most people want to learn. Scan any computer bookshelf and you'll see scores of titles on the C programming language. Fans of C are saying that C is "the only programming language you will ever need."

Okay, you know the story of that line by now. First, PL/I was going to be the only programming language anyone would ever need and it never achieved that title. Years later, Pascal was going to be the only programming language anyone would ever need, and although it achieved a fair amount of success, its decline happened just as rapidly as its growth.

Given the track record of such a statement as "the only programming language you will ever need," you might roll your eyes with a "Here we go again" attitude and move onto the next language. The amazing thing, however, after years of hearing that a programming language would finally solve all your problems, is that C has almost become "the only programming language anyone will ever need." The computer industry has never seen such a widespread acceptance and movement towards a single programming language. Critics of C quickly become pundits. Schools are facing the largest number of enrollments in their C classes. The sales of C book titles continue to set records. Many companies have moved all their programming departments to straight C data processing shops. The help-wanted ads in the programming newspaper sections all seem to want C programmers. It has gotten to a point where, if you do not know C, you had better learn it fast.

Note: Most of the PC programs you use are now written in C, whereas they used to be written in assembler. Popular spreadsheets and word processors are almost always coded in C these days to gain as much efficiency as possible while still being maintainable. Almost all Windows programs are written in C because the internal Windows routines that your Windows programs must integrate with are written in C and designed to be executed from a C program. As graphical user interfaces continue to grow in usage, so, it appears, will the need for C programmers.

C is not necessarily a good choice for your first computer language. There are some good books and classes that teach you C and don't assume any prior programming knowledge on your part, but if you learn another language as your first exposure to programming before tackling C you will probably be a better C programmer as a result. BASIC, although a very different language from C, makes a good introduction to C. Because the next few chapters of this book teach you the fundamentals of BASIC programming, you might find that C can be your next step after this book. If so, plan to take it easy, though, and don't expect to master C within a week or two.

> **Clue:** Whatever your programming goals are, plan to make C the language you eventually learn. Over the next few years, it appears that the jobs in C (and its successor C++, described later in this chapter) will remain plentiful.

The C Language

Some consider C to be a cryptic programming language. C can be cryptic if it is not written and documented well. C is a free-form language and allows comments so you can describe what is going on inside the program. This helps alleviate some of the cryptic nature of C programs. C programs are not necessarily difficult to follow; a well-written C program is easier to understand than a badly written COBOL program, even though COBOL is supposedly a self-documenting programming language and readable by non-programmers.

C is known as a programming language "written for programmers by programmers." Many programming languages have lots of rules that restrict the programmer. C's philosophy assumes that dull tools are useless, so C lets programmers get away with much more than other programming languages allow. In doing so, programmers must keep a sharp eye out for logic errors. Because the C compiler checks for fewer errors, programmers assume more responsibility to ensure that their code is accurate. C offers a lot of programming power, but with that power comes responsibility.

C is a language that has few words and numerous operators. The C programming language has only 32 commands, all of which are shown in Table 7.1. Languages such as COBOL and BASIC have well over a hundred commands, but C tries to be more succinct.

Table 7.1. The 32 C commands.

auto	double	int	struct
break	else	long	switch
case	enum	register	typedef
char	extern	return	union
const	float	short	unsigned
continue	for	signed	void
default	goto	sizeof	volatile
do	if	static	while

C has more operators than any other programming language with the exception of the scientific APL language described in the previous chapter. An operator is usually a special character that performs some operation on data. Not all operators are mathematical, but the primary math operators are the most obvious way to learn about operators because you are already used to them. In the expression 5 + 6, the plus sign (+) is an operator. Most programming languages use the four operators shown in Table 7.2 as their primary math operators. C is no exception.

Table 7.2. C's primary math operators.

Operator	Example	Description
+	5 + 6	Performs addition
-	10 - 4	Performs subtraction
*	4 * 7	Performs multiplication
/	27 / 9	Performs division

The asterisk is used in programming languages for multiplication because the small letter *x* is often available for other things, most notably for naming data values. There is no division symbol on computer keyboards, so the forward slash is almost universally used to mean division.

As you learn a programming language, you will learn how the command names work and how the operators manipulate the data. Unlike with most languages, learning how C's operators work is of utmost importance. Most of your time learning C will be spent working with C's operators. It is the large number of operators that make people think that C is a cryptic or mathematical language. Actually, C's operators (a complete list is shown in Table 7.3) are not all mathematical. Many of them take the place of commands used by other languages. It is the abundant use of operators in C that make it very efficient and succinct.

Table 7.3. A complete list of C's operators.

++	--	()	[]	->	.
!	~	-	+	(*type*)	*
&	sizeof	/	%	<<	>>
<	<=	>	>=	==	!=
^	¦	&&	¦¦	?:	=
+=	-=	*=	/=	%=	>>=
>>=	&=	^=	¦=	,	

> **Note:** Two of the operators, (*type*) and sizeof, appear to be command names, but the C compiler treats them as if they were operators.

Listing 7.2 shows a sample C program. As you can probably gather, a C program looks a lot like the other programs you have seen in this and the previous chapter. Learning more than one programming language is more of an exercise in spotting how they are similar instead of how they are different. Look through the program and see if you can determine its purpose.

Listing 7.2. A sample C program.

```
/* Letter guessing game */
#include <stdio.h>
#include <time.h>
#include <stdlib.h>
main()
{
   int tries = 0;
   char compAns, userGuess;

   /* Save the computer's letter */
   srand(time(NULL));  /* Randomize the random-number generator */
   compAns = (rand() % 26) + 65;    /* Generate a random letter */

   printf("I am thinking of a letter...");
   do {
     printf("What is your guess? ");
     scanf(" %c", &userGuess);
     tries++;   /* Add 1 to the guess counter */
     if (userGuess > compAns)
        { printf("Your guess was too high\n");
          printf("\nTry again...");
        }
     if (userGuess < compAns)
        { printf("Your guess was too low\n");
          printf("\nTry again...");
        }
   } while (userGuess != compAns);  /* Quit when a
                                       match is found */

   /* User got it right, announce it */
   printf("*** Congratulations!  You got it right! \n");
   printf("It took you only %d tries to guess.", tries);
   return 0;
}
```

This C program is a letter-guessing game. The computer generates a random letter and loops until the user correctly guesses the letter. You don't have to understand any of the C instructions (lines of program instructions are often called *statements*) to get a good idea of how this program works. You can read the text throughout the program and figure out a lot just from the text. The instructions themselves are not all extremely cryptic. `printf` obviously prints something on the screen. The program has ample comments (descriptions that are not C instructions, but are notes to people looking at the program); C comments always appear between `/*` and `*/`. As you can see, C programs are not always as cryptic as touted, but to really master C, learning another language first is most helpful.

C++: A Better C

C is not losing ground as the most popular language of today, but its successor, C++, is gaining extensive support all the time. C++ is a newer version of C. It was designed by a Swedish programmer named Bjarne Stroustrup in the early 1980s. The advantage that C++ has over other new languages is that it is based on C. As a matter of fact, many C++ programs look exactly like C programs, because most of C++ is C. C++ offers a few additional commands and operators but is mostly just another way to program in C.

> **Reward:** The biggest reason for the current success of C++, as well as the reason you should learn it, is that it contains *object-oriented programming* capabilities. Object-oriented programming (called *OOP* for short) is a different way of writing programs that helps programmers write programs more quickly and with fewer errors. OOP also helps speed the program maintenance process later. Chapter 14, "The Future of Programming" explains more about object-oriented programming.
>
> Although there is some debate in the industry, most people agree that you should learn C before moving to C++'s object-oriented programming style. Many predict that C++ will replace C as the programming language of choice in the 1990s.

C++ is a more restrictive language than regular C. C++ does not give the programmer the freedom that C allows, but C++ also does not let as many hidden errors creep into the code because it is more strict than C.

The C++ language adds only a few more commands and operators to regular C. The popularity of C++ is attributed to its object-oriented capabilities and its more restrictive nature. Listing 7.3 shows you the C++ version of the letter-guessing game. As you can see, it looks very similar to C code.

Listing 7.3. A sample C++ program.

```
// Letter guessing game
#include <iostream.h>
#include <time.h>
#include <stdlib.h>
main()
{
   int tries = 0;
   char compAns, userGuess;

   // Save the computer's letter
   srand(time(NULL));   // Randomize the random-number generator
   compAns = (rand() % 26) + 65;    // Generate a random letter

   cout << "I am thinking of a letter...";
   do {
     cout << "What is your guess? ";
     cin >> userGuess;
     tries++;    // Add 1 to the guess counter
     if (userGuess > compAns)
        { cout << "Your guess was too high\n";
          cout << "\nTry again...";
        }
     if (userGuess < compAns)
        { cout << "Your guess was too low\n";
          cout << "\nTry again...";
        }
   } while (userGuess != compAns);  // Quit when a
                                    // match is found

   // User got it right, announce it
   cout << "*** Congratulations!  You got it right! \n";
   cout << "It took you only " << tries << " tries to guess.";
   return 0;
}
```

The BASICs

This discussion on specific languages concludes with an explanation of BASIC to springboard your thoughts into the next chapter, which teaches you a modern-day version of BASIC called QBasic. BASIC was originally developed at Dartmouth College for teaching beginners how to program. The FORTRAN programming language was a little too complex for students to learn quickly enough to use it in their studies. John Kemeny and Thomas Kurtz, who taught at Dartmouth, used FORTRAN as a basis for creating BASIC. BASIC stands for *Beginner's All-purpose Symbolic Instruction Code*, a name that is more foreboding than the language itself.

BASIC is typically run in an interpreted environment, although modern-day versions of BASIC can be compiled. By being interpreted, beginners can concentrate on the programming language and not worry about the details of compiling a program. As with any interpreted language, interpreted BASIC programs run slower than compiled programs, so interpreted BASIC programs are not used much in business.

Over the years, BASIC has been distributed in many different forms. The original BASIC language had very little structure and had a strict set of coding rules. It was thought that the strict rules would take away some of the ambiguity present in other programming languages and speed the beginner's learning of the language. Listing 7.4 shows a version of a program written in the original BASIC language. You can tell from the use of GOTO statements that the language was not very well structured and provided avenues for spaghetti code. Also, each line required a line number. The common practice was to increment the line numbers by tens so you could insert up to nine more lines between existing lines if you had to later.

Listing 7.4. A sample original BASIC program.

```
10   REM Letter-guessing game in BASIC
20   REM Generate a random number from 65 to 90
30   REM (ASCII 65 is A and ASCII 90 is Z)
40   NUM = (INT(RND * 26)) + 65
50   CA$ = CHR$(NUM)
```

```
60   CLS
70   PRINT "*** Letter Guessing Game ***"
80   PRINT
90   PRINT "I am thinking of a letter..."
100  INPUT "What is your guess"; UG$
110  TR = TR + 1
120  IF (UG$ > CA$) THEN GOTO 150
130  IF (UG$ < CA$) THEN GOTO 180
140  GOTO 210
150  PRINT "Your guess was too high"
160  PRINT "Try again..."
170  GOTO 200
180  PRINT "Your guess was too low"
190  PRINT "Try again..."
200  GOTO 100
210  REM Here if guess was correct
220  PRINT "*** Congratulations!  You got it right!"
230  PRINT "It took you only"; TR; "tries to guess."
240  END
```

The output of this program appears below. Try to follow the program to see how the output was produced. This will prepare you for the next chapter, where you learn how to write your own BASIC programs. As you look through the program, try to answer these questions: Where is the program's remark? (A remark is a statement that comments the program. Remarks are ignored by BASIC when you run the program. Remarks are there for you to document the code so someone looking through the program listing has a better idea what the program is supposed to do.) Where is the program's loop? What BASIC command produces output?

```
*** Letter Guessing Game ***

I am thinking of a letter...
What is your guess? A
Your guess was too low
Try again...
What is your guess? Z
Your guess was too high
Try again...
What is your guess? M
Your guess was too low
Try again...
What is your guess? V
```

```
Your guess was too high
Try again...
What is your guess? S
*** Congratulations!  You got it right! It took you only 5 tries to
guess.
```

Although BASIC began as a language for beginners and is still quite useful for introducing programming, today's versions of BASIC rival Pascal and C by providing a rich assortment of structured programming elements. Here are a few of the names of BASIC as it has evolved through the years:

- ✖ BASICA (for *BASIC Advanced*)
- ✖ GWBASIC (for *Gee Whiz BASIC*)
- ✖ Power BASIC
- ✖ Turbo BASIC
- ✖ QuickBASIC (a compiled version)
- ✖ QBasic (which began shipping with MS-DOS starting with Version 5.0 of DOS)
- ✖ Visual Basic (a Windows programming environment)

One of the biggest factors in BASIC's success was Microsoft's adoption of BASIC. Microsoft Corporation, the company that develops operating systems for Apple computers and PCs, has offered many versions of BASIC through the years, improving the language with each version they release. Microsoft was one of the first companies to offer a compiled BASIC (QuickBASIC) for PCs. Microsoft is the company that supplied QBasic (an interactive structured version of BASIC that you will learn starting in the next chapter) in DOS 5.0 and all higher versions. Microsoft also wrote and sells Visual Basic, a graphical programming tool with which you can write customized Windows programs (described in the next section).

One of the biggest changes Microsoft made in the BASIC language was when they introduced QuickBASIC, a compiled version of BASIC. Up until then (around 1984), BASIC was always run in an interpreted environment. The line numbers were required in interpreted versions so the programmer could keep track of the order of the program statements and rearrange statements if the programmer needed them reordered. The line numbers were not required in QuickBASIC because the compiler came with its own full-screen editor. With QuickBASIC, BASIC left the ranks of amateur programming languages and moved into the category of a well-written, structured, compiled programming language that rivaled both Pascal and C.

Clue: Perhaps it was the success of QuickBASIC that helped cause the Pascal demise. QuickBASIC offered structured programming constructs while retaining the ease of learning facilities found in previous versions of BASIC.

Listing 7.5 shows you a QuickBASIC version of the letter-guessing game you saw earlier in the chapter. Notice that there are no line numbers and that the program is free-form and easy to follow, features that the rigid BASICs of old could not have boasted. QuickBASIC is almost C-like or Pascal-like in its appearance.

Listing 7.5. A sample QuickBASIC program.

```
' Newer BASIC allows the more succinct ' for a remark instead of REM
' A letter-guessing game

num = (INT(RND * 26)) + 65    ' Generate a random number from 65 to 90
                              ' (ASCII 65 is A and ASCII 90 is Z)
compAns$ = CHR$(num)      ' Converts the number to a letter
tries = 0

CLS   ' Clear the screen
PRINT "*** Letter guessing game ***"
PRINT
PRINT "I am thinking of a letter..."

DO
   INPUT "What is your guess"; userGuess$
   tries = tries + 1
   IF (userGuess$ > compAns$) THEN
      PRINT "Your guess was too high"
      PRINT "Try again..."
```

continues

Listing 7.5. continued

```
    ELSE
        IF (userGuess$ < compAns$) THEN
            PRINT "Your guess was too low"
            PRINT "Try again..."
        END IF
    END IF
LOOP WHILE (userGuess$ <> compAns$)    ' Quit when a match is found

' User got it right, announce it
PRINT "*** Congratulations!  You got it right!"
PRINT "It took you only"; tries; "tries to guess."
END
```

Microsoft won industry favor with its QuickBASIC compiler. Finally, there was a compiler for BASIC—not just a compiler, but an integrated full-screen editor as well. Most BASIC versions before QuickBASIC included their own line-editor or limited full-screen editor. Many people feel that Microsoft's integrated full-screen editor played as important a role in QuickBASIC's success as the improved language itself.

Microsoft helped ensure its leadership in the BASIC arena when it introduced QBasic, an interpreted version of BASIC that now comes supplied with every version of MS DOS. If you have MS DOS 5.0 or later, you have QBasic. Its sheer numbers of machines around the world (almost every PC uses a version of MS DOS) means that QBasic is available to almost anyone with a PC. QBasic is the language of choice for most beginning programmers in the world, and this book is no exception. It is QBasic that you will learn starting in the next chapter.

Figure 7.1 shows a screen from the QBasic programming editor. It supports the use of a mouse, pull-down menus, and an online help feature. By moving the cursor (via the keyboard arrow keys or mouse) over a QBasic command and then pressing F1 to request help, QBasic supplies help for that command. Figure 7.2 shows help being given for the PRINT command. QBasic's help is known as *context-sensitive help*; that is, QBasic gives you help on whatever you are doing at the time by looking at your cursor's location and supplying help on that location's topic.

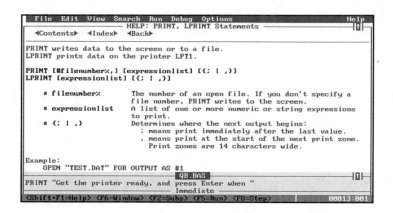

```
 File  Edit  View  Search  Run  Debug  Options                        Help
┌──────────────────────────── QB.BAS ────────────────────────────────────┐
│LINE INPUT "What is your name? "; nm$                                     │
│LINE INPUT "What is your address? "; ad$                                  │
│LINE INPUT "What is your city? "; ct$                                     │
│LINE INPUT "What is your state? "; st$                                    │
│LINE INPUT "What is your zip code? "; zp$                                 │
│                                                                          │
│PRINT "Get the printer ready, and press Enter when "                      │
│INPUT "you want me to begin printing..."; en$                            │
│                                                                          │
│LPRINT nm$      ' Print first label                                       │
│LPRINT ad$                                                                │
│LPRINT ct$; ", "; st$; SPC(5); zp$                                        │
│LPRINT                                                                    │
│LPRINT    ' Skip two spaces to the next label                             │
│                                                                          │
│LPRINT nm$      ' Print second label                                      │
│LPRINT ad$                                                                │
│LPRINT ct$; ", "; st$; SPC(5); zp$                                        │
│──────────────────────────── Immediate ─────────────────────────────────│
└──────────────────────────────────────────────────────────────────────────┘
<Shift+F1=Help> <F6=Window> <F2=Subs> <F5=Run> <F8=Step>         00011:001
```

Figure 7.1. *Viewing a program in QBasic.*

```
 File  Edit  View  Search  Run  Debug  Options                        Help
┌──────────────── HELP: PRINT, LPRINT Statements ─────────────────────────┐
│  ◄Contents► ◄Index► ◄Back►                                               │
│PRINT writes data to the screen or to a file.                            │
│LPRINT prints data on the printer LPT1.                                  │
│                                                                          │
│PRINT [#filenumber%,] [expressionlist] [{; ¦ ,}]                         │
│LPRINT [expressionlist] [{; ¦ ,}]                                        │
│                                                                          │
│  ■ filenumber%       The number of an open file. If you don't specify a  │
│                      file number, PRINT writes to the screen.           │
│  ■ expressionlist    A list of one or more numeric or string expressions │
│                      to print.                                          │
│  ■ {; ¦ ,}           Determines where the next output begins:           │
│                        ; means print immediately after the last value.  │
│                        , means print at the start of the next print zone.│
│                        Print zones are 14 characters wide.              │
│                                                                          │
│Example:                                                                  │
│    OPEN "TEST.DAT" FOR OUTPUT AS #1                                      │
│──────────────────────────── QB.BAS ─────────────────────────────────────│
│PRINT "Get the printer ready, and press Enter when "                      │
│──────────────────────────── Immediate ─────────────────────────────────│
└──────────────────────────────────────────────────────────────────────────┘
<Shift+F1=Help> <F6=Window> <F2=Subs> <F5=Run> <F8=Step>         00013:001
```

Figure 7.2. *Getting help with the* PRINT *command.*

One of BASIC's strongest assets is its support for *string data*. String data consists of characters, words, and sentences, as opposed to numeric data. BASIC has many built-in routines that can left-justify strings, right-justify strings, and pick out one or more characters from strings. These string capabilities are not nearly as easy in C, Pascal, COBOL, or FORTRAN as they are in BASIC.

183

Pitfall: Although Microsoft's versions of BASIC, especially QuickBASIC and QBasic, are the de facto industry standards, the ANSI committee has not worked on a BASIC standard for a long time. Their previous ANSI BASIC is outdated and does not support several of the language features that have been available for several years.

If you write BASIC programs for your company, keep in mind that you will probably be using a version that the ANSI committee has not approved, and that the program is not guaranteed to work on other computer versions of BASIC.

Despite this warning, as long as you stick to one of the mainstream BASICs, especially QuickBASIC or QBasic, you will probably have compilers and interpreters around for many years that will run your programs.

Graphical Programming with Visual Basic

Perhaps the most impressive programming language of all is Visual Basic. Visual Basic is really less of a programming language and more of a collection of graphical controls with which you build BASIC programs. Visual Basic is a Windows programming environment that you can use to write Windows programs. When you first start Visual Basic, you see the screen shown in Figure 7.3. As you can see from the screen, the term *visual* is an extremely accurate description.

Do not let the randomness of the Visual Basic screen frighten you. As you learn more about Visual Basic, you'll better understand how the different parts of the screen fit together and you'll learn ways to make the screen look more like the way you prefer. Visual Basic lets you rearrange and hide certain parts of the screen so that you can customize the look and feel of the screen and make it appear exactly as is best for you.

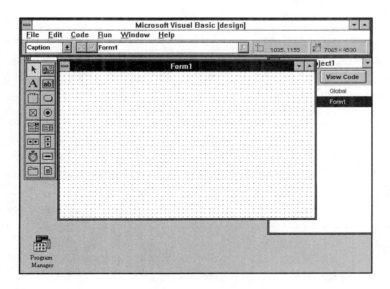

Figure 7.3. *The opening screen of Visual Basic.*

Windows programs are inherently difficult to write for both beginners and advanced programmers who are not used to its environment. Windows programs are *event driven*. Unlike procedural programs that perform a sequence of actions based on the user's expected input, a Windows program must be able to expect almost anything at any given time. For example, the user might press a key, move the mouse, press a mouse button, or select from a menu. If Windows programs were as procedural in nature as other programs are, the programs could respond to a mouse movement only when the program was ready, not when the user was ready. By being event driven, the program responds to events in any order that they happen.

A Windows program might be stopped at any time, or temporarily put on hold while the user executes another Windows program. Because Windows programs run inside windows on the screen, the programs must be able to respond to resizing commands that the user might issue. A user might want to see a Visual Basic program run in a window at the top of the screen and see an animated graphing sequence at the bottom of the screen. Writing a Windows program from scratch, especially for beginning programmers, was a nightmare until Visual Basic came along. Visual Basic takes care of all the petty details of the Windows application, enabling the user to resize the program's window, select from a menu, click with the mouse, or press a key. Visual Basic ensures that the proper event occurs when it is called for. The programmer only has to tell Visual Basic what he or she wants done when certain events occur.

Visual Basic is not a true compiler, so a Visual Basic program runs slower than a compiled program. Figure 7.4 shows how a regular programming language program in memory compares to a Visual Basic program. Notice how much farther away the Visual Basic program is from the hardware. With the Visual Basic *runtime interpreter* (a kind of mix between a compiler and interpreter, but slower than a compiler), Windows, and DOS between the hardware and the Visual Basic program, there is a lot of software interaction that slows down the running program.

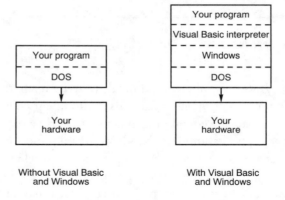

Figure 7.4. *A Visual Basic program requires a lot of overhead to run.*

In addition to all the software that is in memory, the bookkeeping that Windows continually performs also slows down a Visual Basic program. Windows must monitor several activities that a normal non-Windows MS-DOS program doesn't have to worry about. Nevertheless, Visual Basic is the first Windows programming tool that enables a novice to create simple Windows programs without knowing C. Before Visual Basic, most Windows programs were written in C using Microsoft's Software Developer's Kit (*SDK*). The only prerequisite to learning Visual Basic is knowing how Windows applications work in general. If you are familiar with one or two applications in Windows, such as the Word for Windows word processor, you know all you need to know to begin writing programs in Visual Basic.

Warning: Visual Basic is a far cry from BASIC, and is quite unlike QuickBASIC as well. Although the language underneath the graphical interface of Visual Basic programs is simliar to QuickBASIC, the visual elements and event-driven handlers in Visual Basic will be new even to veteran BASIC and QuickBASIC programmers.

Visual Basic is not the answer to all your Windows programming needs. Because the Visual Basic system does so much of the work for the programmer, the programmer has less to worry about. However, the programmer also has less control over the final program than she or he would have if writing the program using a high-level programming language such as C.

Pitfall: Do not fall into the trap of thinking that programming environments such as Visual Basic are object oriented. Visual Basic is graphically oriented, but it is not an object-oriented language. Chapter 14 helps explain what determines whether or not a programming language is object-oriented.

The following example walks you through the creation of a fully functional Visual Basic program. Although you have yet to write your first program, this example shows you that Visual Basic is written for non-programmers as well as programmers. (Even for the easy Visual Basic environment, you have to learn quite a bit about programming on its command level before you can write truly powerful and customizable programs with it.) You may not have access to a Visual Basic system, and you may not have ever used Windows. Even so, this example gives you a glimpse of the new visual programming tools that will be released in the coming years.

To write a fully functional Visual Basic Windows program, all you have to do is start Visual Basic. If you then move the mouse to the box in the center of the screen and double-click the mouse, you see a window open up such as the one shown in Figure 7.5.

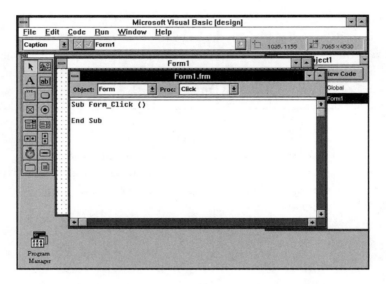

Figure 7.5. *After clicking on the middle window in Visual Basic.*

This program requires only one programming statement. If you type PRINT "I am programming!" and press the function key labeled F5 (F5 is the shortcut keystroke for running a Visual Basic program), you'll see the program run. (You can also select **R**un **S**tart from the pull-down menu at the top of the screen to run the program.) The program produces a blank window on the screen. Every time the mouse button is pressed, the message I am programming! appears on the screen. The result of this Visual Basic program after clicking the mouse several times to produce the message in the window is shown in Figure 7.6.

The reason the program is so amazing is that it took a mouse click, one programming statement, and the F5 keypress, and that was it. Visual Basic took care of the rest. Visual Basic displayed a window on the screen, but not just any window: a *resizable* window. With the mouse, you can expand the window, shrink it, move it, and reduce it to a Windows icon with one mouse click (you have to be familiar with Windows to understand everything being described here). The normal Windows control menu is available by clicking on the box in the upper left corner of the program's window. Finally, the program responds to the mouse event by displaying the message every time the mouse button is pressed.

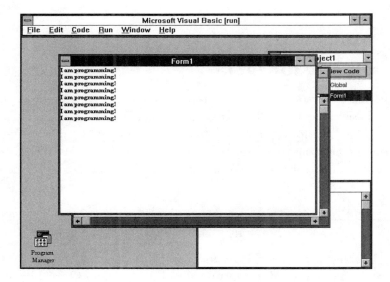

Figure 7.6. *The resulting Visual Basic program.*

You have to admit, writing *that* program took very little effort. The end result is that the program does not do a whole lot on the surface, but it is a beginning. The same program would have taken a couple of pages of code if you wrote it using C, the usual programming language of Windows.

189

Reward: Visual Basic is not really a programming language like the other languages that this book describes and that programming courses teach. However, Visual Basic is a new tool that offers programming ease never seen before and gives you a glimpse at the programming tools of the future. It will be a long time before a programming environment such as Visual Basic replaces C, C++, COBOL, and FORTRAN, because Visual Basic by its very nature limits what the programmer can do. Nevertheless, using Visual Basic is a treat and you should reward yourself by trying Visual Basic the next chance you get.

Visual Basic for DOS

After the success of Visual Basic, Microsoft introduced a non-Windows version of Visual Basic called *Visual Basic for DOS*. As you can see from the screen in Figure 7.7, Visual Basic for DOS is a text-based version of the Visual Basic graphical programming environment. Programs you write for Visual Basic for DOS are compatible with Visual Basic for Windows. Therefore, you can write one set of programs that works in both environments.

Reward: One of the nice features of Visual Basic for DOS is that it also runs programs written in QBasic and GWBASIC. Although these programs cannot take advantage of many of the features of Visual Basic for DOS, at least your investment in software is not made obsolete by the new programming environment.

Which Language Is Best?

There are so many programming languages in the world that you might wonder which is best. The answer to that is difficult, if not impossible to determine. Which music is the best? Which period of art is the best? Which car is the best? The answer is a resounding "It depends." The best programming language depends on the job that you need to perform.

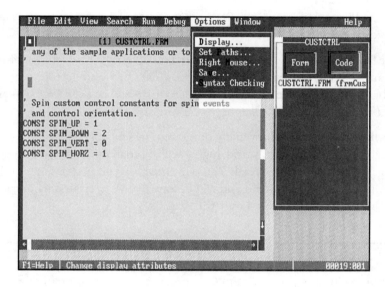

Figure 7.7. A screen from Visual Basic for DOS.

If you really want to know which language is the best to learn first, this book has already answered that question. BASIC (or preferably one of its derivatives such as QBasic or QuickBASIC) is the best all-purpose language for beginning programmers. The next chapter begins to develop your QBasic programming skills. As you hone your QBasic skills, you might find that QBasic is the only programming language you ever need to learn because it does everything you would ever need a programming language to do. If that is the case, then there is nothing wrong with staying with QBasic.

Most people, however, will need more power than QBasic can supply. Once they master an introductory language such as QBasic, many people move onto Pascal or C. The current jobs available require that you know C, C++, or COBOL. If you feel that you would like to work in large organizations programming mainframes, you should learn COBOL as soon as you feel you are ready (once you get comfortable with QBasic). However, most people have access to microcomputers, and the microcomputer is nice to learn programming with because it offers quick feedback and you can learn to program at home. As you learned earlier in this chapter, C and C++ are the languages most in demand these days, and in the PC environment, no other programming languages are more important to learn than C and C++.

The languages you know often determine the language in which you program. If you are working on a rush project (as most data processing projects are), you won't have time to master a new language, so if BASIC or FORTRAN is all you know at the time, that is the language you will probably use.

It is hard to determine how many programming languages a "good" programmer should know. Some highly paid, highly skilled programmers know only a single language, but most know several. You will find that you prefer some programming languages over others and you will become truly expert in only one or two, although you may learn several over the years.

Note: Whatever happens in your computer education, plan to keep learning as long as you program. Computers are always an exciting field to work in because there is always something new around the corner.

Less than 15 years ago, integrated programming environments such as Turbo C would have amazed the programming community; today those programming environments are commonplace. Visual BASIC would have been nothing less than magic before it was introduced in 1991; now beginners use such programming tools to create powerful Windows applications.

The language a company uses to write a particular application is determined by many factors. The company might have only one or two compilers. If so, their applications will be written using one of those compilers. Mainframe compilers can cost several thousand dollars, so it is difficult for companies to move around from language to language looking for the best one. Often, the language currently owned is made to work.

The type of application also helps determine the best language to use. A scientific application would require FORTRAN if the choice were between FORTRAN and COBOL. COBOL would be the mainframe language of choice for processing a large amount of business transactions.

Note: Companies generally prefer programming languages that are common over those that are more obscure. For instance, there is an object-oriented programming language called *Actor* that is a very good language, but only a handful of programmers know it. C++ would be a much wiser selection if someone else might have to take care of program maintenance in the future.

The best thing to remember about high-level programming languages is that they are general-purpose enough to use in writing almost any application. COBOL might be a lousy choice for scientific applications, but you can make it work if COBOL is all you have to use.

Whatever you end up using, programming is a rewarding career and is fun as well. Get ready to join the ranks of programmers. Turn the page to begin Chapter 8 and get started writing programs in QBasic.

Chapter Highlights

As programming languages mature, they become easier to use. Most of today's programming languages include integrated environments and offer support for structured programming. Today's graphical user interfaces such as Microsoft Windows require more complex programming tools, but easy-to-use languages such as Visual Basic are easing even beginning programmers into the graphical world of programming.

✖ Modern-day programming languages offer tremendous improvements over previous languages. They are more structured and offer integrated programming environments.

✖ Pascal is a good general-purpose programming language that boomed during the 1970s and declined in use in the 1980s. Pascal is still used today for teaching structured programming concepts and is a good second language for programming students.

✖ C, developed by Bell Labs, is a highly efficient, high low-level programming language. C is fast becoming the most-used programming language in existence. C is a small language with a rich collection of operators, but it takes some time to master.

✖ C++ is a newer and improved version of C. C++'s biggest improvement over its predecessor is its ability to provide support for object-oriented programming (OOP).

✖ Many feel that C++ will become the major programming language of the 1990s.

✖ BASIC and its family of languages, such as QBasic and QuickBASIC, offer the best programming language for beginners.

✖ Windows programming is made easier by a special version of BASIC called Visual Basic. Visual Basic takes care of the tedium of Windows programming by letting you concentrate on your application instead of the details of Windows.

✖ There is a DOS-based version of Visual Basic called Visual Basic for DOS. You can use Visual Basic for DOS to create DOS-based applications that require a mouse and pull-down menus.

✖ The programming language you use depends on lots of factors. Most languages are best suited to certain kinds of programs. The language you select can depend on how scientific- or business-oriented your application is. Also, you must give consideration to how many other programmers know the language you select in case someone else has to maintain your programs later.

Your First Language: QBasic

Perilous Perry's journey brought him to the island. With hammer in hand, Perilous Perry contemplated what to build first. Will our hero choose wisely? Will Perilous Perry be able to brave the storms of his programming paradise?

1. How do I enter and run a QBasic program?

2. What if there is an error in my QBasic program?

3. What is a variable?

4. How do I name variables?

5. What is the difference between a string variable and a numeric variable?

6. How do I print the results of calculations on-screen?

7. How do I print the results of calculations on the printer?

8. How does QBasic perform math?

9. What are the QBasic math operators?

10. How can I clear the screen before a program runs?

This chapter is your first exposure to the specifics of a programming language. It begins by taking you through a QBasic programming session. You then learn how to store QBasic data and see the results of calculations. After you finish this chapter, you will be able to write your own QBasic programs.

Although you cannot become a programming expert in a single chapter, this chapter lays the groundwork for your future as a programmer. All the programming concepts you learn here carry over to any other language you learn in the future.

Getting Started

In Chapter 5, "The Programming Process," which described program editors, you saw how to start the QBasic full-screen editor. Remember that you must use the editor to write your programs. The QBasic editor is more than an editor; it is also a QBasic interpreter. From within the QBasic editor, you can write a program, run it, change it, view its output, and save your program to a disk for long-term storage.

Although programming languages are all different, as you learn QBasic and others, you will see that almost all programming languages have a lot in common with other languages. They all have ways to print output and to get values from the keyboard and a disk. They all have commands that loop by repeating one or more statements. They all can make decisions. Some perform these actions more elegantly and naturally than other programs do. What is important, though, is that every time you learn a new programming language, the next one becomes even easier to learn. QBasic is a great place to start your programming career. Even if you do not end up programming in QBasic for a living, you will find the programming skills that you develop with QBasic very useful.

Familiarize yourself with the QBasic environment by going through a sample QBasic session. You are given a program to type in and run. Just to keep things interesting, the program contains an error that you must fix before the program will run correctly.

Keep the following points in mind as you work with the QBasic editor:

✖ Use the arrow keys to move the cursor around the screen.

✖ The Insert key turns insert mode on and off (when you first begin QBasic, insert mode is on). When insert mode is on, existing characters are pushed to the right as you type the new characters. When insert mode is off (called *overtype* mode), the characters you type replace those they walk on.

✖ The Delete key deletes the character under the cursor. Whenever you delete characters, the ones to the right move over and fill in the gap left by the deleted characters.

✖ You can use the PageUp and PageDown keys to scroll the screen. Use them when your program is too long to fit within a single screen. This scrolling action works like a camera panning a scene.

Follow these steps to enter and run your first QBasic program.

1. Start QBasic. At the DOS prompt, type QBASIC (in either uppercase or lowercase). You will see the QBasic startup screen.

2. Press the Escape key to clear the Help option from the editing window. (Later, you might want to view some of the Help screens available from this opening screen.)

3. Type the following program into QBasic. (The blank lines are optional, as are the indented lines. The extra whitespace makes the program more readable.)

```
REM My first QBasic program
BEEP
REM Ask the user for his or her first name
CLS
INPUT "What is your first name"; nm$
PRINT

REM Sound the siren!
FOR up = 1000 TO 1500 STEP 25
    SND up, 3
NEXT up
```

```
REM Print the name down the screen
col = 1
FOR row = 1 TO 24
    LOCATE row, col
    PRINT nm$
    col = col + 2
NEXT row
END
```

4. Make sure that the program you type looks exactly like the one in Step 3. Double-check it to ensure that it is correct. QBasic cannot read your mind, and accuracy counts in programming. However, you can type the commands in either upper- or lowercase—QBasic converts commands you type in lowercase to uppercase.

5. Run the program. To do so, select Run Start from the pull-down menu by pressing Alt-R (to choose Run) and then pressing Enter (to choose Start). You can also use the Shift-F5 key combination as a shortcut key to run programs; it is faster than using the menu. All of the menu options have their shortcut key equivalents next to them on the menu. (Some menu options, however, do not have shortcut key equivalents.) The Alt key is always the key you press to access the menus.

6. Because the program contains an error, it will not run. QBasic spots the error and displays the message box shown in Figure 8.1. Anytime QBasic displays an error message, you have two options. You can get more help about the error message by choosing Help inside the error message box. If you don't need more help, choose OK to remove the error message box. Either way, QBasic highlights the place in the code where it found the error. As you can see, QBasic does not like the command SND.

7. There is no SND command in QBasic. The command should be SOUND. Change the line so that it looks like this:

   ```
   SOUND up, 3
   ```

8. Run the program again. When you do, the screen clears and QBasic beeps. Then it asks you for your first name. After typing your name, a siren sounds and your name appears down and across the screen as shown

in Figure 8.2. QBasic always displays the `Press any key to continue` message before returning to your program so that you can see the final results of the output screen.

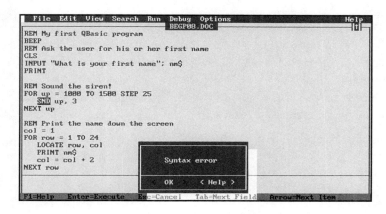

Figure 8.1. *QBasic spots a syntax error in the program.*

```
George
 George
  George
   George
    George
     George
      George
       George
        George
         George
          George
           George
            George
             George
              George
               George
                George
                 George
                  George
Press any key to continue
```

Figure 8.2. *The result of running your first program.*

Reward: When your screen returns to the program editing window, you can go back and view the output screen by selecting View Output Screen from the pull-down menu or by pressing the F4 shortcut key.

9. If you want to save the program so you can run it later, select File Save, type a filename such as FIRST.BAS, and then press Enter. All QBasic programs should have the .BAS filename extension. The first part of the filename follows the standard DOS file naming rule that says the first part of the filename must be from 1 to 8 characters long.

Congratulations! You have just successfully typed, corrected, and run your first QBasic program. Now learn the specifics of the language so that you can write your own programs from scratch.

Delving into QBasic

It is now time to develop an understanding of the QBasic language. Throughout this book, you learn about the importance of writing programs that are easy to maintain. The programs you write should not only work, but they should be easy to read. Very likely, you or someone else may need to update your program later. Having code that is clear makes that task much easier.

Reward: There is another advantage of writing clear, well-documented programs. You will finish your programs faster and they will have fewer errors. Being organized always pays off when programming.

Some of the most important statements you can put in QBasic programs are completely ignored by QBasic. They are remarks documenting what the program is doing. The QBasic program you typed earlier had four remarks. A QBasic remark is any statement that begins with REM.

The QBasic interpreter completely ignores remarks. Remarks appear in programs for the benefit of people who look at the programs. The remarks exist solely to document the program, telling in plain English what the program is about to do. For example, you can see from the four remarks exactly what the program is doing without knowing anything about QBasic except for the REM statement.

Clue: Many programmers like to begin a program with a remark that states the programmer's name and the date on which the program was written. This is especially important if you are one among many programmers in a data processing department. When others have to modify programs, they can track down the original programmer in case they have questions.

QBasic allows a shortcut for remarks. You can use an apostrophe (') in place of REM. Listing 8.1 shows you the same program you saw earlier with the shortcut remark in place of REM. As you can see from Listing 8.1, the shortcut remarks can go to the right of QBasic statements; they do not have to reside on lines by themselves as REM statements do.

Listing 8.1. The QBasic program with shortcut remarks.

```
' My first QBasic program
BEEP
' Ask the user for his or her first name
CLS
INPUT "What is your first name"; nm$
PRINT                              ' Print a blank line

' Sound the siren!
FOR up = 1000 TO 1500 STEP 25   ' Loop to control the siren
    SOUND up, 3                 ' Sound a tone on the speaker
NEXT up                         ' End of the sound loop

' Print the name down the screen
col = 1
```

continued

Listing 8.1. continued

```
FOR row = 1 TO 24            ' Loop several times
   LOCATE row, col           ' Position the cursor
   PRINT nm$                 ' Print the user's name
   col = col + 2
NEXT row                     ' End of the printing loop
END
```

Not all lines require remarks. Use them to clarify what your code is doing. Some programmers insert a remark every three or four lines; for them that is sufficient. The best number of remarks is however many it takes to clarify the program code you write.

Storing Data

As its definition implies, data processing means that your programs process data. That data must somehow be stored in memory while your program proceses it. In QBasic programs, as in most programming languages, you must store data in variables. You can think of a variable as if it were a box inside your computer holding a data value. The value might be a number, character, or string of characters.

Note: Actually, data is stored inside memory locations. Variables keep you from having to remember which memory locations hold your data. Instead of remembering a specific storage location (called an *address*), you only have to remember the name of the variables you create.

Your programs can have as many variables as you need. There is a limit to the number of variables a single program can have, but the limit depends on the type of data you are holding. (Anyway, the number is so large that you will not run out of variables in your program.) Variables have names associated with them. You do not have to remember which internal memory location holds data; you can attach names to variables to make them easier to remember. For instance, `Sales` is much easier to remember than the 4376th memory location. You can use almost any name you want, provided that you follow these naming rules:

✘ Variable names must begin with an alphabetic character.

✘ Variable names can range in length from 1 to 40 uppercase or lowercase characters.

✘ After the first alphabetic character, variable names can contain numbers. There are a few special characters that can also be part of variable names (such as `.`, `&`, and `^`), but some other special characters are not allowed (such as `(`, `*`, and `+`). Therefore, it is safest to stay with letters and numbers.

Pitfall: Avoid strange variable names. Try to name variables so that their names help describe the kind of data being stored. `Balance93` is a much better variable name for your 1993 balance value than `X1y96a`, although QBasic does not care which one you use.

Here are some examples of valid and invalid variable names:

Valid	*Invalid*
Sales93	Sales-93
MyRate	My$Rate
ActsRecBal	93ActsRec
row	REM

Warning: You cannot give a variable the same name as a QBasic command.

Variables can hold numbers or character strings. If you follow the naming rules just listed, the variables can hold numbers.

There is one special character that is useful to use at the end of variable names. If you put a dollar sign ($) at the end of a variable name, the variable can hold one or more alphabetic or special characters. Therefore, the following variables can hold characters, words, and even sentences:

```
nm$
Company$
show$
Employee$
```

Assigning Values

All that discussion about variable names was worth your patience. The majority of QBasic program statements use variable names. QBasic programs often do little more than store values in variables, change variables, calculate with variables, and output variable values.

When you are ready to store a data value, you must name a variable to put it in. You must use an assignment statement to store values in your program variables. The assignment statement includes an equal sign (=) and an optional command LET. Here are two example assignment statements:

```
sales = 956.34

LET rate = .28
```

Reward: The LET keyword is optional and requires more typing if you use it. Therefore, most programmers save typing time and leave off the LET from their assignment statements. I do not know of any good reason to use LET; old versions of BASIC (in the 1960s) required it, so programmers who learned it then might still use it.

Think of the equal sign in an assignment statement as a left-pointing arrow. Whatever is on the right side of the equal sign is sent to the left side to be stored in the variable there. Figure 8.3 shows how the assignment statement works.

A=23

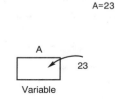

Figure 8.3. *The assignment statement stores values in variables.*

If you want to store character string data in a variable, you must enclose the string inside quotation marks. Here is how you store the word *QBasic* in a variable named `lang$`:

```
lang$ = "QBasic"    ' Enclose strings in quotation marks
```

Once you put values in variables, they stay there for the entire run of the program, or until you put something else in them. A variable can hold only one value at a time. Therefore, the two statements

```
age = 67
age = 27
```

result in age holding 27, because that was the last value stored there. The variable age cannot hold both values.

You can also assign values of one variable to another and perform math on the numeric variables. Here is a short program that stores the result of a calculation in a variable and then uses that result in another calculation:

```
pi = 3.1416
radius = 3
area = pi * radius * radius
halfArea = area / 2
```

> **Reward:** QBasic zeros all variables for you. This means that anytime you name a variable, QBasic assumes that the value of the variable is 0 (zero) until another value is assigned to it. Therefore, if you want a variable to begin with a zero, you do not have to assign a zero to it.

Once you store values in variables, you must have a way to display them on the screen and printer. The next few sections describe how to output your data values.

Looking at Values

The PRINT statement outputs data to the screen. PRINT is used in almost every QBasic program because displaying data on the screen is so important. Your users must be able to see results and read messages from the programs they run. Figure 8.4 shows you an illustration of what PRINT does.

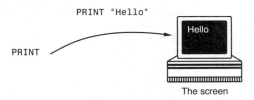

Figure 8.4. *PRINT sends output to the screen.*

There are several ways to use PRINT. The easiest way to print words on your screen is to enclose them in quotation marks after the PRINT statement. The following two statements print names on the screen:

```
PRINT "Sally Brown"
PRINT "John Wilson"
```

These statements produce the following output:

```
Sally Brown
John Wilson
```

The quotation marks never appear around printed strings; the marks simply enclose the character strings to be printed. Whatever appears inside quotation marks prints exactly as it appears inside the quotation marks. The PRINT statement

```
PRINT "5 + 7"
```

does *not* print 12 (the result of 5 plus 7). Because quotation marks enclose the expression, the expression prints exactly as it appears inside the quotation marks. This PRINT statement produces this output:

```
5 + 7
```

If, however, you print an expression without the quotation marks, QBasic prints the result of the calculated expression. For example,

```
PRINT 5 + 7
```

does print a 12. Variables printed without quotation marks print as well. Here is an expanded version of some code you saw in the previous section. Now it has output statements so you can see the results of the calculations.

```
' Program that calculates and prints the area
' of a circle and half circle
pi = 3.1416          ' Mathematical PI
radius = 3           ' Radius of the circle
area = pi * radius * radius    ' Compute circle area
halfArea = area / 2            ' Compute half the circle area
PRINT "The area of a circle with a radius of 3 is"
PRINT area
PRINT "The area of one-half that circle is"
PRINT halfArea
END
```

Clue: The END statement at the end of QBasic programs is optional. Most programmers put the END statement there so that others looking at the program know when they have reached the end instead of wondering if there might be another page to the program.

Here is the output of this program:

```
The area of a circle with a radius of 3 is
28.2744
The area of one-half that circle is
14.1372
```

Notice that each PRINT statement causes a new line to be printed. Follow the program and see how its output is produced.

Using the Semicolon

If you want to print several different values on the same line, you can do so by separating them with a semicolon. For example, the following series of PRINT statements

```
PRINT 15
PRINT 20
PRINT 25
```

produces these three lines of output:

```
15
20
25
```

If you separate the three numbers with semicolons, however, they appear on a single line. Therefore, the statement

```
PRINT 15; 20; 25
```

prints all three values on a single line, like this:

```
15 20 25
```

Using the semicolon, you can improve the previous program by making the values appear directly after the desciptions of the calculations instead of on the next line. Here is the improved program:

```
' Program that calculates and prints the area
' of a circle and half circle
pi = 3.1416          ' Mathematical PI
radius = 3           ' Radius of the circle
area = pi * radius * radius     ' Compute circle area
```

```
halfArea = area / 2                ' Compute half the circle area
PRINT "The area of a circle with a radius of 3 is"; area
PRINT "The area of one-half that circle is"; halfArea
END
```

Here is the output from this program:

```
The area of a circle with a radius of 3 is 28.2744
The area of one-half that circle is 14.1372
```

The semicolon can also go at the end of a PRINT, as in

```
PRINT "Sally ";
```

so that a subsequent PRINT will continue the output on the same line as the previous one. Often, you might want to print the results of several calculations on a single line. By printing each one with a trailing semicolon at the end, you can print them as you calculate them throughout the program and still ensure that they all print next to each other.

Printing with Commas

The comma acts similarly to the semicolon in that it lets you print values together on the same line with a single PRINT statement. Unlike the semicolon, which causes the values to print directly after one another, the comma causes the next value to print in the next *print zone*.

There is one print zone for every 14 columns of your computer screen. Figure 8.5 shows how your screen is divided into five print zones. Each comma in a PRINT causes the next value to print in whichever print zone comes next.

> **Note:** QBasic always prints a space after every number printed and always prints positive numbers with an extra space before them. The leading space takes the place of a supressed plus sign. Negative numbers always print with a minus sign and no extra space. Strings are never printed with leading or trailing spaces.

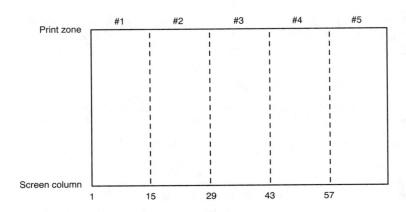

Figure 8.5. *The print zones appear every 14 columns of your screen.*

The following PRINT demonstrates the use of the comma:

```
PRINT 15, 20, 25
```

This PRINT prints the 15 (after a leading space), then the 20 in column 15, and then the 25 in column 29, like this:

```
 15            20            25
```

The comma is useful for printing a table of values. The comma ensures that the columns of the table line up under each print zone. In the following program, the names print starting in the same four columns, even though the names are of different lengths.

```
' Illustrates the use of commas
PRINT "Sam", "Jesse", "Charles", "Susan"
PRINT "Christine", "Ron", "Jayne", "Martha"
PRINT "Johnny", "Thomas", "Francis", "Kerry"
PRINT "Kim", "Barbara", "Lea", "William"
END
```

Here is the output from this program:

```
Sam           Jesse         Charles       Susan
Christine     Ron           Jayne         Martha
Johnny        Thomas        Francis       Kerry
Kim           Barbara       Lea           William
```

As you work with more data and print several values at a time, you will appreciate the help that the print zones offer when you want your data to line up in columns.

Printing on the Printer

You can send output to the printer as well as to the screen. The LPRINT statement is to the printer what the PRINT statement is to the screen. The LPRINT statement sends data to the printer in the same way that PRINT works. If you LPRINT strings inside quotation marks, they print on the printer exactly as they appear in the quotation marks. If you print variables and expressions without quotation marks, QBasic prints the values of those variables and expressions.

Clue: Computer printers are sometimes called *line printers*, hence the name of the LPRINT command.

Using the semicolons and commas inside the LPRINT causes the printed values to appear either next to each other or in the next print zone, respectively. The following program prints the names in columns on the printer:

```
' Illustrates the use of commas
LPRINT "Sam", "Jesse", "Jackson", "Susan"
LPRINT "Christine", "Ron", "Jayne", "Martha"
LPRINT "Johnny", "Thomas", "Francis", "Kerry"
LPRINT "Kim", "Barbara", "Lea", "William"
END
```

Often, your programs will print both to the screen and the printer.

Clearing the Screen

Before your program displays anything on the screen, you probably want a blank screen. If your program does not first clear the screen before printing to it, all previous output will be on the screen, including the command you typed to start QBasic from DOS.

It is very easy to clear the screen in QBasic. The CLS statement is all you need. When QBasic reaches a CLS statement in your program, it clears the contents of the output screen. It is always a good idea to clear the screen at the beginning of any program.

The following short program erases the screen and prints a message at the top of the cleared screen:

```
CLS
PRINT "QBasic is fun!"
```

> **Warning:** Be sure your programs erase the screen if you write programs that display critical data. For example, if you write programs for a payroll department, you might want to make sure that your programs always clear the screen before their END statement. The cleared screen ensures that sensitive payroll figures aren't left on the screen for unauthorized eyes to see.

Math with QBasic

QBasic performs mathematical calculations in the same way as most programming languages. It uses the same primary math operators for addition, subtraction, multiplication, and division that you saw in the previous chapter, as well as some additional ones unique to QBasic. Table 8.1 lists the QBasic math operators with which you should familiarize yourself.

Table 8.1. The QBasic math operators.

Operator	Description
( )	Groups expressions together
^	Exponentiation
*, /, \, MOD	Multiplication, division, integer division, and modulus
+, -	Addition and subtraction

The order of the operators in Table 8.1 is important. If more than one of these operators appears in an expression, QBasic does not always calculate the values in a left-to-right order. In other words, the expression

```
v = 5 + 2 * 3
```

stores the value *11* in v, not *21* as you might first guess. QBasic does not perform calculations in a left-to-right order, but rather in the order given in Table 8.1. Because multiplication appears before addition in the table, QBasic computes the 2 * 3 first, resulting in 6; it then computes 5 + 6 to get the result of 11.

Clue: The order in which operators are evaluated is often called *operator precedence*. Every programming language, except APL, computes expressions based on a precedence table. Different programming languages might use different operators from the ones shown in Table 8.1, although almost all of them use parentheses and the primary math operators (*, /, +, and -) in the same way as QBasic does.

Parentheses have the highest operator precedence. Any expression enclosed in parentheses is calculated before any other part of the expression. The statement

```
v = (5 + 2) * 3
```

does assign the value of 21 to v because the parentheses force the addition of 5 and 2 before its sum of 7 is multiplied by 3.

The exponentiation operator raises a number to a particular power. In the following statement, 100 is placed in the variable named x because 10^2 means raise 10 to the second power (10 times 10).

```
x = 10 ^ 2
```

You can also raise a number to a fractional power with the ^ operator. For example, the statement

```
x = 81 ^ 0.5
```

raises 81 to the one-half power, in effect taking the square root of 81. (If this math is getting deep, have no fear; some people program in QBasic for years and never need to raise a number to a fractional power. If you need to, though, you can, thanks to QBasic.)

Division is handled three different ways in QBasic. The forward slash (/) produces normal division. The statement

```
d = 3 / 2
```

puts *1.5* into d. The back slash (\) performs *integer division.* An integer is a whole number, and integer division always produces the whole number result of the division (the decimal portion is discarded). Therefore, the statement

```
d = 3 \ 2
```

puts *1* into d, and the *.5* is ignored.

One of the strangest QBasic operators is not a symbol—it looks more like a command. It is the MOD operator. The MOD operator returns the integer remainder from a division. For example, the statement

```
m = 20 MOD 3
```

puts a *2* in m, because 20 divided by 3 is 6 with a remainder of 2. There are some specialized math operations that require modulus (integer remainder) arithmetic, and QBasic supplies the MOD operator to meet that need.

To sum up (pardon the pun) math operators, here is a program that prints the result of calculations that use all the QBasic operators described in this chapter. The output of the program is shown in Figure 8.6 after the program listing.

```
' Program to demonstrate the QBasic math operators
num1 = 12
num2 = 5
CLS
PRINT "num1 is "; num1
PRINT "num2 is "; num2
' Print the result of several calculations using 12 and 5
value = num1 + num2
PRINT "num1 + num2 equals"; value
value = num1 - num2
PRINT "num1 - num2 equals"; value
value = num1 * num2
PRINT "num1 * num2 equals"; value
value = num1 / num2
PRINT "num1 / num2 equals"; value
value = num1 \ num2
PRINT "num1 \ num2 equals"; value
value = num1 MOD num2
PRINT "num1 MOD num2 equals"; value
value = num1 ^ num2
PRINT "num1 ^ num2 equals"; value
value = num1 + num2 * 4
PRINT "num1 + num2 * 4 equals"; value
value = (num1 + num2) * 4
PRINT "(num1 + num2) * 4 equals"; value
END
```

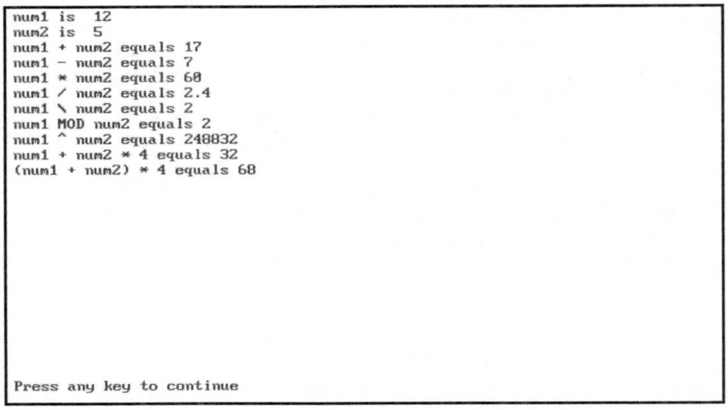

```
num1 is  12
num2 is  5
num1 + num2 equals 17
num1 - num2 equals 7
num1 * num2 equals 60
num1 / num2 equals 2.4
num1 \ num2 equals 2
num1 MOD num2 equals 2
num1 ^ num2 equals 248832
num1 + num2 * 4 equals 32
(num1 + num2) * 4 equals 68




Press any key to continue
```

Figure 8.6. *Viewing the output of the calculations.*

217

You do not have to be a math expert to use QBasic; it does all the math for you. You only have to understand how QBasic performs the math so that you can properly set up the equations you need to calculate.

Chapter Highlights

QBasic is one of the best implementations of BASIC that beginning programmers can use. As you learned in this chapter, writing programs in the QBasic programming language is not only easy, but it can be fun as well. The programs in this chapter show you how to store data in variables and output results to both the screen and the printer.

✖ In this chapter, you learned how to type QBasic programs and run them.

✖ You can switch between the program editing screen and the program output screen by pressing the F4 key.

✖ One of the most important QBasic statements is not a command at all, but a remark to people. The REM statement (which has a shortcut of ') contains English descriptions of the code. The remarks enable others to look at the program later and tell what is going on without having to search through the code.

✖ Variables hold the data that your programs process.

✖ All variables have names. If you put a dollar sign ($) at the end of variable names, the variables can hold string data. Without the dollar sign at the end of variable names, variables can hold only numeric data.

✖ The PRINT statement outputs values to your screen. You can display strings, calculated results, and values of variables with PRINT.

✖ You can control how the PRINT statement works by placing semicolons and commas in the output. Semicolons cause the next printed value to appear directly after the one just previously printed. The comma causes printed values to appear in the next print zone.

✖ The LPRINT statement produces printed results on your printer in the same manner that PRINT prints to the screen.

✖ You can clear your screen with the CLS command. You can put CLS anywhere in your programs; when QBasic reaches a CLS, it erases everything on your screen.

✖ Although you do not have to be a mathmetician to write powerful QBasic programs, you do have to understand how QBasic performs arithmetic.

✖ QBasic uses an operator precedence table to evaluate certain operators before others in an expression. The highest operator of them all is the pair of parentheses. Anything inside parentheses is calculated first.

✖ QBasic has three different ways to compute division: regular division, integer division, and modulus (or remainder) division.

Data Processing with QBasic

Perilous Perry kneeled outside his hut and rubbed two sticks together to start a fire. He would have to make the right decisions to get a really good fire going. Will Perilous Perry figure out how to get fired up?

1. How do I ask the user for data?

2. What is a prompt?

3. How do I display a prompt with INPUT?

4. Can I print money amounts to two decimal places?

5. How does QBasic make decisions?

6. What does the ELSE statement do?

7. What are the relational operators?

8. How can I repeat a section of code a certain number of times?

9. What is the difference between a DO-WHILE and a DO-UNTIL loop?

10. How do I flowchart a DO-WHILE or DO-UNTIL statement?

This chapter extends your knowledge of QBasic by showing you how to input, compare, and loop with QBasic. In the previous chapter, you learned how to output values with PRINT. This chapter shows you how to do the opposite: get values from the user at the keyboard. The data processing model includes input as well as output, and programs should have a means to ask the user questions. The user's responses then guide the flow of the program.

This chapter teaches you how to write programs that make decisions and repeat sections of code while processing data throughout a loop. With the concepts you learn in this chapter, you can write powerful programs to do what you need done. You will find yourself thinking of new ideas and new ways to use your computer, so hang on, put on your thinking caps, and start your DP engines.

Getting Keyboard Data with *INPUT*

The INPUT statement is the opposite of PRINT. As Figure 9.1 shows you, INPUT gets values from the keyboard. Those values typed by the user go into variables. In the previous chapter, you learned how to assign values to variables. You used the assignment statement because you knew the actual values. However, you do not often know all the data values when you write your program.

Think of a medical reception program that tracks patients as they enter the doctor's office. The programmer has no idea who will walk in next, and so cannot assign patient names to variables. The patient names can be stored in variables only when the program is run.

When a program reaches an INPUT statement, it displays a question mark and pauses until the user types a value and presses the Enter key. Here is an INPUT statement:

```
INPUT age     ' Wait for user to type a value
```

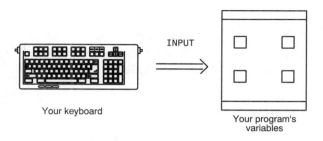

Your keyboard

Your program's variables

Figure 9.1. INPUT *gets values from the keyboard at program runtime.*

When it reaches this statement, the computer displays a question mark on the screen. The question mark is a signal to the user that something is being asked and a response is desired. How does the user know what the question is? It is the programmer's responsibility to include before every INPUT statement a PRINT statement that asks the user for whatever type of value is needed. The PRINT statement *prompts* the user for the input. A prompt message is a question that you ask before a user's input is expected. The prompt message puts a complete question before the INPUT question mark. Consider these three lines from a program:

```
PRINT "What is your age";
INPUT age
PRINT "Thank you!"
```

When the computer reaches the first PRINT, it prints the message as usual. The semicolon at the end of the PRINT keeps the cursor on the same line so that whatever is printed next appears after the question. Do you remember what the INPUT does? It prints a question mark. Because of the semicolon, the question mark appears after the question, and the user sees this:

```
What is your age?
```

The words appear because of the PRINT, and the question mark appears because of the INPUT. The program does not continue to the next PRINT statement until the user answers the question by typing a value and pressing Enter.

Pitfall: Resist the temptation to put a question mark inside your program's prompt questions. If you do, the INPUT will repeat the question mark, and your messages will look like this is on the screen:

```
What is your age??
```

Follow the program in Listing 9.1 and study the output that appears below it. You can see how a variable with no value is filled by an INPUT statement.

Listing 9.1. Demonstrating INPUT.

```
' Demonstrates the INPUT statement
'
PRINT "Before the INPUT, the variable named x is"; x
PRINT
PRINT "What value do you want x to have now";
INPUT x
' x now has the value entered by the user
PRINT
PRINT "After the INPUT, x is"; x
END
```

QBasic zeroes all variables for you when a program begins. This means that the value of x is zero until you give it a value via INPUT. Here is a sample output from the program. The user entered 27 for the value of x.

```
Before the INPUT, the variable named x is 0

What value do you want x to have now? 27

After the INPUT, x is 27
```

Clue: QBasic waits at the INPUT statement as long as it takes for the user to type a value in response to the INPUT statement. The INPUT is finished only when the user presses the Enter key.

Inputting Strings and Multiple Variables

Any type of variable, numeric or string, can be entered with INPUT. For example, these lines wait for the user to enter a string value:

```
PRINT "What is your first name";
INPUT first$
```

If the user types the name in response to the question, the name is put into the first$ variable.

> **Warning:** If the user only presses Enter, without entering a value in response to INPUT, QBasic puts a value called *null* into the variable. A null value is a zero for numeric variables, or an empty string for string variables. An empty string—a string variable with nothing in it—is literally zero characters long.

A single INPUT statement can gather more than one value if your application requires it. You can list more than one variable, separating them with commas, after the INPUT statement. The following INPUT statement waits for the user to type three values:

```
PRINT "What are your first name, age, and salary";
INPUT first$, age, salary
```

Here is a sample run of these statements:

```
What are your first name, age, and salary? Fred, 41, 1904.95
```

Notice that the user has to know that commas are required between the values entered. If no commas are typed, the user receives an error message saying Redo from start—a none-too-descriptive advisory. The error message informs the user that the values were not entered in the expected format. One of the drawbacks to gathering multiple values in a single INPUT is that the user does not always know how to enter the values. It is safer and more expedient to ask for each value individually. For example:

```
PRINT "What is your first name";
INPUT first$
PRINT "How old are you";
```

```
INPUT age
PRINT "What is your salary";
INPUT salary
```

This set of three INPUT statements is far less likely to generate errors when the program is run. The user only has to enter the three values one at a time; there is no worry about putting commas between them. Notice how the following program output leads the user through the questions one at a time:

```
What is your first name? Fred
How old are you? 41
What is your salary? 1904.95
```

Clue: One design factor that you should consider when writing a program is the style of user input. You must remember that people will use your program who might know very little about computers. The user of a program should not need to know how your program works. If you write a program strictly for your own use, you can take more liberties with INPUT statements because you know what your own programs expect. However, the user of a program written by someone else must be instructed clearly. Write your programs so that a user must enter values one at a time when prompted, not two or more values following a single INPUT. Multi-valued INPUT statements are prone to cause errors.

Combining *PRINT* and *INPUT*

You have seen the importance of printing an INPUT prompt message with a PRINT before your INPUT statements. Your programs should not display an INPUT's question mark without printing a message beforehand telling the user what kind of input you expect. The designers of QBasic realized the importance of displaying a prompt along with every INPUT in your program. They added a feature to the INPUT statement itself to include the prompt message along with the input. Instead of having pairs of PRINT-INPUT statements throughout your program, you can have single INPUT statements that both prompt the user and receive input.

A simple example shows how the prompt message works. The following statements should be old hat to you by now. The PRINT asks the user a question, and the INPUT gets the user's answer.

```
PRINT "What is the month number (i.e., 1, 5, or 11)";
INPUT monNum
```

The PRINT displays a prompt that tells the user what input is expected.

Here is an equivalent statement. It does the same thing as the previous PRINT-INPUT, but in a single line of code:

```
INPUT "What is the month number (i.e., 1, 5, or 11)"; monNum
```

This is what the user sees when QBasic reaches this line in the program:

```
What is the month number (i.e., 1, 5, or 11)?
```

The user can then answer the question, in effect supplying the variable monNum with a month number, and the program then continues with the rest of its execution.

Clue: Some questions cannot be asked in a single INPUT prompt. Therefore, there might be times when you have to put extra PRINT statements before an INPUT to fully describe the input you expect. Here is an example that does just that:

```
PRINT "You must now enter the last four digits of your "
INPUT "extended zipcode.  What are those four digits"; eZip
```

Listing 9.2 shows a program that a small store might use to compute totals at the cash register. The INPUT statements in this program are required; only at runtime will the customer purchase values be known. As you can see, getting input at runtime is vital for "real world" data processing.

Listing 9.2. A cash register program for a small store.

```
' Demonstrates INPUT by asking the user for several values
' at a store's cash register and prints a total of the sales
CLS      ' Clear the screen
PRINT , "** Mom and Pop's Store **"
```

continues

Listing 9.2. continued

```
PRINT
INPUT "How many bottles of pop were sold"; pop
popTotal = pop * .75
INPUT "How many bags of chips were sold"; chips
chipTotal = chips * 1.25
INPUT "How many gallons of gas were sold"; gas
gasTotal = gas * 1.19

' Calculate total sale and add 7% sales tax
fullSale = popTotal + chipTotal + gasTotal    ' Total sale
sTax = .07 * fullSale
netSale = fullSale + sTax

' The following INPUT gets a null value just to pause the program
INPUT "Press Enter when you are ready for the invoice..."; ans
' Print an invoice on the screen
PRINT
PRINT
PRINT , "** Invoice Mom and Pop's Store **"
PRINT
PRINT "************************************************"
PRINT pop; "bottles of pop:", popTotal
PRINT chips; "bags of chips:", chipTotal
PRINT gas; "gallons of gas:", gasTotal
PRINT "------------------------------------------------"
PRINT "Total sale:", fullSale
PRINT "Sales tax:", sTax
PRINT "Final total:", netSale
PRINT
PRINT "Thank the customer!"
END
```

Figure 9.2 shows you the result of running this program. As you can see, the program would be helpful for a small store.

There is one problem with the program; it does not print to exactly two decimal places, which a program calculating dollars and cents should do. You can use an additional option on the PRINT (or LPRINT) statement, called USING. The USING option describes how you want your data printed. There is so much to the USING option that it would take an entire chapter to explain it thoroughly. At this point in your programming career, you probably just need USING to print two decimal places for dollars and cents. Currency printing is probably what most QBasic programmers use USING for.

```
              ** Mom and Pop's Store **
How many bottles of pop were sold? 4
How many bags of chips were sold? 3
How many gallons of gas were sold? 19
Press Enter when you are ready for the invoice...?

              ** Invoice Mom and Pop's Store **

*****************************************************
 4 bottles of pop:         3
 3 bags of chips:          3.75
 19 gallons of gas:        22.61
_____
Total sale:     29.36
Sales tax:      2.0552
Final total:    31.4152

Thank the customer!



Press any key to continue
```

Figure 9.2. *Running the cash register program.*

Here is a PRINT statement that ensures the variable total prints to two decimal places:

```
PRINT USING "#####.##"; total
```

The #####.## might look strange to you. It is a picture clause describing how the next variable should look. If there were three pound signs after the decimal point, three decimal places would result, even if they all happened to be zeros. If total does not have five digits before the decimal point, leading spaces appear in the number.

Note: When you use PRINT USING, QBasic follows the pattern in your USING string and ignores the way it would normally print values. Therefore, there is no automatic space before positive numbers if you print them with a USING string.

Listing 9.3 has several PRINT USING statements that show you how to have the output results printed in various formats.

Listing 9.3. Demonstrates various PRINT USING options.

```
' Printing with PRINT USING
PRINT 2223.329
PRINT USING "####.##"; 2223.329
PRINT USING "####.#"; 2223.329
PRINT USING "####.#    ###.#    ##.###"; 2223.329; 12; 12
PRINT USING "#####,.##"; 2223.329
END
```

The output from the program is as follows:

```
 2223.329
2223.33
2223.3
2223.3    12.0    12.000
  2,223.33
```

The last PRINT USING shows you that putting a comma immediately before the decimal point in a USING string instructs QBasic to insert a comma at every third digit in the number. Printing numbers with commas helps the user read the value more easily.

Listing 9.4 shows the same cash register program you saw earlier. Because of the PRINT USING statements, the program prints all of its output to two decimal places, ensuring that the output is properly rounded to dollars and cents before being printed.

Listing 9.4. Improving the look of dollar values.

```
' Demonstrates INPUT by asking the user for several values
' at a store's cash register and prints a total of the sales
CLS       ' Clear the screen
PRINT , "** Mom and Pop's Store **"
PRINT
INPUT "How many bottles of pop were sold"; pop
popTotal = pop * .75
```

```
INPUT "How many bags of chips were sold"; chips
chipTotal = chips * 1.25
INPUT "How many gallons of gas were sold"; gas
gasTotal = gas * 1.19

' Calculate total sale and add 7% sales tax
fullSale = popTotal + chipTotal + gasTotal    ' Total sale
sTax = .07 * fullSale
netSale = fullSale + sTax

' The following INPUT gets a null value just to pause the program
INPUT "Press Enter when you are ready for the invoice..."; ans
' Print an invoice on the screen
PRINT
PRINT
PRINT , "** Invoice Mom and Pop's Store **"
PRINT
PRINT "*************************************************"
PRINT USING "## bottles of pop: ###.##"; pop; popTotal
PRINT USING "## bags of chips:  ###.##"; chips; chipTotal
PRINT USING "## gallons of gas: ###.##"; gas; gasTotal
PRINT "-------------------------------------------------"
PRINT USING "Total sale:   ####,.##"; fullSale
PRINT USING "Sales tax:     ###,.##"; sTax
PRINT USING "Final total: ####,.##"; netSale
PRINT
PRINT "Thank the customer!"
END
```

```
              ** Mom and Pop's Store **

How many bottles of pop were sold? 4
How many bags of chips were sold? 3
How many gallons of gas were sold? 19
Press Enter when you are ready for the invoice...?


          ** Invoice Mom and Pop's Store **

*************************************************
 4 bottles of pop:   3.00
 3 bags of chips:    3.75
19 gallons of gas:  22.61
-------------------------------------------------
Total sale:    29.36
Sales tax:      2.06
Final total:   31.42

Thank the customer!



Press any key to continue
```

Figure 9.3. *The output looks much better with* PRINT USING.

Comparing Data with *IF*

The structured programming decision construct is very easy to implement in QBasic. The decision construct is represented in flowcharts by a decision symbol that always has two exits. Likewise, a QBasic decision statement always has two possibilities. To decide which path to take in a QBasic program, you must use the IF statement. Most programming languages have an IF statement that works exactly like QBasic's.

Listing 9.5 shows you an example of a program that contains an IF statement. Even though you have never seen QBasic's IF before, you will probably have little trouble figuring out what this program does.

Listing 9.5. Using an IF statement.

```
' Deciding how much of a bonus to pay a salesperson
INPUT "What is the salesperson's name"; sName$
INPUT "What were the total sales made last month"; sales

IF (sales < 5000) THEN
    bonus = 0
    daysOff = 0
ELSE
    bonus = 25
    daysOff = 2
END IF

PRINT
PRINT sName$; " earned a bonus of"; bonus;
PRINT "and gets"; daysOff; "days off."
END
```

Look at the following two sample runs of the program. Pay attention to the fact that the program produces a different bonus depending on the salesperson's total sales. Here is the first sample run:

```
What is the salesperson's name? Jim
What were the total sales made last month? 3234.43

Jim earned a bonus of 0 and gets 0 days off.
```

The salesperson did not get a bonus because the sales were not high enough. Consider the difference here:

```
What is the salesperson's name? Jane
What were the total sales made last month? 5642.34

Jane earned a bonus of 25 and gets 2 days off.
```

The program offers complete control over one of two options via the IF statement. Figure 9.4 shows you the flowchart of this program. The decision symbol is represented by the IF statement in the program.

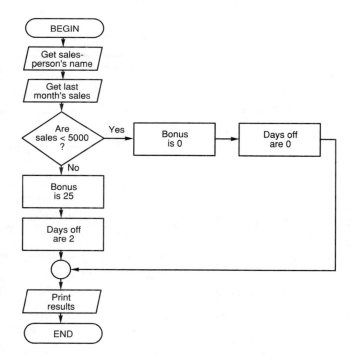

Figure 9.4. *The flowchart of the salesperson program.*

The IF works just like it reads. *If* the statement to the right of the IF is true, the block of statements following IF executes. Notice that the word THEN is required. *If* the statement to the right of IF is not true, the block of statements following ELSE executes instead. The ELSE clause is optional; without it, you are testing to see whether you will execute a single block of statements. For example, here is an IF statement that prints a message only if the statement to the right of IF is true. If it is not, and there is no ELSE, the program continues on the line after END IF:

```
IF (age < 18) THEN
    PRINT "You are not old enough"
END IF
```

The END IF always marks the end of the IF set of statements. Whatever the result of the IF is, the statements following END IF always execute after the IF finishes.

Note: The parentheses around the statement to the right of the IF are not required, but they clarify what exactly is being tested. This statement to the right of IF, typically enclosed within parentheses, is called a *relational test*.

The Relational Test Options

The IF statement reads just as it does in plain English: *if something is true, do one thing; otherwise do something else.* You do not always add an *else* after a spoken *if,* and you do not have to have one in QBasic either. Consider these statements:

If I make enough money, I'll retire early.

If you're out late, call me, or else you'll get in trouble.

If you're in town, we'll eat dinner together.

Note: The similarity of IF to spoken language makes it easy to represent the IF in pseudocode.

As a programming language, QBasic is fairly strict about how you make the IF test. The relational test, the statement to the right of the IF, always includes one of the symbols from Table 9.1.

Table 9.1. The IF statement relational operators.

Operator	Description	Example
<	Less than	IF (sales < maxSales) THEN
>	Greater than	IF (amount > 100.00) THEN
=	Equal to	IF (age = 21) THEN
>=	Greater than or equal to	IF (grade >= 90) THEN
<=	Less than or equal to	IF (price <= 1.00) THEN
<>	Not equal to	IF (year <> 1993) THEN

You learned about the math operators in Chapter 8. QBasic supplies these relational operators so you can test certain conditions with an IF statement. There are always two possibilities with the relational operators. Something is either less than something else, or it is not. Something is either greater than something else, or it is not. Something is either equal to something else, or it is not.

Clue: The two possibilities that the relational operators allow provide the means for duplicating the two-legged decision symbol in a flowchart. A decision symbol has two possible outcomes, and so does the IF. IF is either true or false.

The statements following the THEN and ELSE can be any QBasic statements. When the ELSE contains an IF in its block, you must combine the ELSE and IF into a single statement: ELSEIF. This language rule of QBasic is easier to understand than it first looks. Listing 9.6 contains a set of IF statements that prints first, second, third, or fourth depending on the number entered by the user.

Listing 9.6. An IF within the ELSE must become ELSEIF.

```
' Prints a description based on user's number
INPUT "How many years have you been in school"; years
IF (years = 1) THEN
   PRINT "This is your first year"
ELSEIF (years = 2) THEN
   PRINT "This is your second year"
ELSEIF (years = 3) THEN
   PRINT "This is your third year"
ELSEIF (years = 4) THEN
   PRINT "This is your fourth year"
ELSE PRINT "You did not enter 1, 2, 3, or 4"
END IF
END
```

As this program shows, you can test whether the user enters acceptable data by using the IF. This is known as *input validation*. You can validate some input values to make sure the user entered what you expected. For instance, you can check an age to make sure it is greater than 0. There is not always a way to determine whether the user's input value is exactly correct, but you can check to see if it is reasonable.

The *SELECT CASE* Statement

There is a special type of decision statement in QBasic called the SELECT CASE statement. The SELECT CASE statement is useful for testing several conditions. Although each condition has only two possibilities, as with IF conditions, the SELECT CASE can replace a series of IF statements within another IF statement, as in the program in Listing 9.6.

SELECT CASE is extremely easy to understand. Listing 9.7 shows a rewritten version of the program you saw in Listing 9.6 in the previous section.

Listing 9.7. Using SELECT CASE to select from several tests.

```
' Prints a description based on user's number
INPUT "How many years have you been in school"; years

SELECT CASE years
    CASE 1
        PRINT "This is your first year"
    CASE 2
        PRINT "This is your second year"
    CASE 3
        PRINT "This is your third year"
    CASE 4
        PRINT "This is your fourth year"
    CASE ELSE
        PRINT "You did not enter 1, 2, 3, or 4"
END SELECT
END
```

In this program, there are five possible cases. The user could enter 1, 2, 3, 4, or something else. The case that matches the user's input executes and the other cases do not. SELECT CASE is often useful for replacing the slightly more complicated IF within IF statements.

Clue: Use IF statements when you must select from one or two relational conditions. If there are several more relational conditions to test for, a SELECT CASE is generally easier to understand. The easier your code is to understand, the faster you will finish your program, and the easier your code is to maintain later on.

Looping Statements

Looping statements are another important feature of any programming language. QBasic supplies several statements that control loops. Your computer will never get bored. It will loop over and over, quickly repeating statements as long as you need it to.

Loops have many uses. You might need a loop to ask the user for several people's data, to calculate a combined total, or to print several lines of data. QBasic's three primary looping statements are

✖ FOR-NEXT loops

✖ DO-UNTIL loops

✖ DO-WHILE loops

The following sections describe each of these looping statements.

The *FOR-NEXT* Loop

The FOR-NEXT loop is actually a loop of statements enclosed between the FOR and the NEXT statement. Before you look at the FOR-NEXT statement, an analogy to things in everyday life might be helpful. As with the IF, the FOR loops are natural ways of expressing an idea. Consider the following description:

> *For each of today's invoices:*
> *check the accuracy of the invoice,*
> *add the total amount to the daily sales total.*
> *Look at the next invoice.*

You can sense from this description of invoice totaling that a repetitive process happens. If there are five invoices, the process repeats for each of those five invoices.

The computer's FOR loop works just like the *for each* concept in the invoice description (that's why it's called FOR). To ease you into FOR loops, Listing 9.8 shows a simple loop that explains the FOR and NEXT statements.

Listing 9.8. Using FOR and NEXT to control a counting loop.

```
' First FOR-NEXT Program
' This program prints the number 1 through 10
CLS
```

```
FOR i = 1 TO 10
   PRINT i
NEXT i
END
```

Here is the output from Listing 9.8's program:

```
1
2
3
4
5
6
7
8
9
10
```

The FOR and NEXT statements work in pairs; they enclose one or more state-ments. The statements inside the FOR-NEXT loop repeat until the loop finishes. The loop is controlled by the FOR statement's variable. In Listing 9.8's program, the control variable is i (you can use any variable name). The FOR statement is saying the following: *For each i (with i having a value of 1 the first time, 2 the second time, and so on until it gets to 10), perform the statement between FOR and NEXT.*

Note: As you can gather from Listing 9.8, the FOR-NEXT loop automati-cally *increments* (adds one each time to) the control variable. The body of the FOR loop (the statement or statements between the FOR and NEXT) loops once for every increment of the variable until the variable reaches its final value specified in the FOR statement.

Listing 9.9 shows a program that does exactly the same thing as Listing 9.8, but without using a FOR loop. You can see that the FOR loop makes repetitive state-ments much easier to code. (Consider how much easier it would be to use a FOR-NEXT statement to print the numbers from 1 to 100, instead of writing two hun-dred lines of code to print those numbers if you used the method in Listing 9.9.)

Listing 9.9. Printing without a FOR-NEXT loop.

```
' Prints from 1 to 10 without a FOR-NEXT statement
CLS
i = 1
PRINT i
i = 2
PRINT i
i = 3
PRINT i
i = 4
PRINT i
i = 5
PRINT i
i = 6
PRINT i
i = 7
PRINT i
i = 8
PRINT i
i = 9
PRINT i
i = 10
PRINT i
END
```

You do not have to print the value of the loop variable as done in Listing 9.8. Often, a FOR loop controls a set of statements, determining the number of times those statements repeat, without using the control variable for anything else. Listing 9.10, controlled by a FOR loop, prints a message 15 times.

Listing 9.10. Printing a message several times.

```
' Message-printing program
CLS
FOR i = 1 TO 15
    PRINT "Happy Birthday!"
NEXT i
END
```

Another example will make this clearer. Look at the program in Listing 9.11. A teacher might use it to print a grade sheet. The program asks the teacher how many test scores are to be entered. It uses that answer to loop through a series of statements asking for the next child's name and grade. As the teacher enters the data, the values are printed to the printer. At the end of the program, there is a complete listing of names and grades. (In Chapter 12, you learn how to program an *accumulator* to add all the grades together and to print a class average.)

Listing 9.11. A teacher's grade-printing program.

```
' Grade-printing program
CLS

PRINT , "** Grade-listing Program **"
PRINT
INPUT "How many tests are there today"; numTests
PRINT

LPRINT "** Grades for the Test **"
LPRINT
LPRINT "Name", , "Grade"
FOR i = 1 TO numTests
  INPUT "What is the next student's name"; sName$
  PRINT "What is "; sName$; "'s grade";
  INPUT grade
  LPRINT sName$, , grade
NEXT i
END
```

Figure 9.5 shows what the program looks like on-screen. If the teacher has five students, the FOR loop will loop five times. If the teacher says there are ten students, the program loops ten times. Because the teacher's input value controls the FOR loop, the program is of general purpose and able to handle any number of students.

```
                    ** Grade-listing Program **

How many tests are there today? 5

What is the next student's name? Joe Santiago
What is Joe Santiago's grade? 87
What is the next student's name? Julie Moore
What is Julie Moore's grade? 98
What is the next student's name? Eddie Kerry
What is Eddie Kerry's grade? 56
What is the next student's name? Linda Smith
What is Linda Smith's grade? 78
What is the next student's name? Carol Jones
What is Carol Jones's grade? 88




Press any key to continue
```

Figure 9.5. *Running the grade-printing program.*

Here is a listing of the program's output, given the names and scores entered in the session shown by Figure 9.5:

```
** Grades for the Test **

Name                      Grade
Joe Santiago               87
Julie Moore                98
Eddie Kerry                56
Linda Smith                78
Carol Jones                88
```

Controlling the *FOR* Loop

There are additional ways you can control a FOR loop. You can make the control variable increment by a value other than 1 each time through the loop. You can also make the count variable count down instead of up. By adding the STEP option to the FOR statement, you make the control variable step (change) by a different value, by either a positive or negative amount.

Listing 9.12 shows you a program that counts down from 10 to 1 and then prints Blast off! at the end of the loop. To carry out the countdown, a negative STEP value had to be used. The FOR statement says that a loop is requested, with i looping from 10 to 1. Each time through the loop, −1 is added to i, causing the descending count.

Listing 9.12. Counting down from 10 to 1.

```
' A countdown program
CLS

FOR i = 10 TO 1 STEP -1
    PRINT i
NEXT i

PRINT "Blast Off!"
END
```

Here is the output from the program:

```
10
9
8
7
6
5
4
3
2
1
Blast Off!
```

You can specify any value for a STEP amount. Listing 9.13 shows you a program that prints the even numbers below 15 and then the odd numbers below 15. Two loops control the counting. The first one begins counting at 2, and the second one begins counting at 1. Each loop adds a STEP value of 2 to the initial FOR value to produce the sets of even and odd numbers.

Listing 9.13. Printing the first few even and odd numbers.

```
' Print the first few even and odd numbers
CLS

PRINT "Even numbers from 2 to 14:"
FOR number = 2 TO 15 STEP 2
  PRINT number
NEXT number
```

continues

243

Listing 9.13. continued

```
PRINT "Odd numbers from 1 to 15:"
FOR number = 1 TO 15 STEP 2
  PRINT number
NEXT number
END
```

Figure 9.6 shows the output from this program.

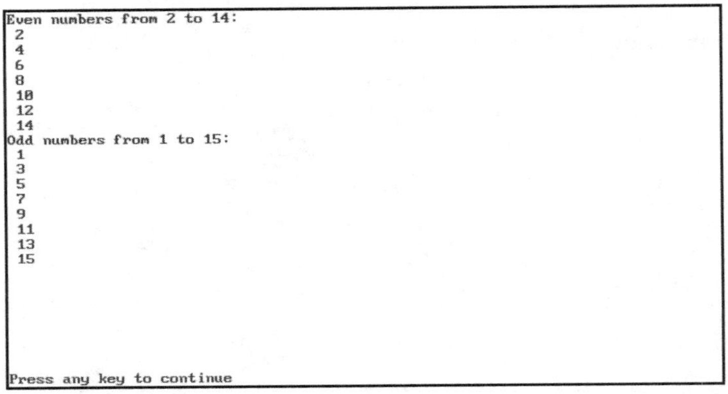

Figure 9.6. *Printing some even and odd numbers.*

You can also cause a FOR loop to exit early with the EXIT FOR statement. There might be times when you expect to loop for a fixed number of times, as specified by the FOR control variable. Then, because of special input from the user, you have to exit the FOR loop early. The EXIT FOR statement exits a FOR loop whenever QBasic encounters it in your program. Listing 9.14 shows how EXIT FOR works. In the next chapter, you learn how to use EXIT FOR when you want to prompt the user for disk data.

Listing 9.14. Demonstrating the EXIT FOR statement.

```
' Using EXIT FOR to quit a FOR loop earlier
' than its natural conclusion.
CLS
FOR i = 1 TO 100      ' Would normally loop 100 times
   PRINT i               ' Prints the numbers from 1 to at most 100
   INPUT "Continue (Y/N)"; ans$   ' See if user wants to continue
   IF (ans$ = "N") THEN
      EXIT FOR                       ' Quit early if user wants
   END IF
NEXT i
PRINT "That's all folks!"
END
```

Here is a sample run of this program. Notice that the FOR loop would have run 100 times, printing the numbers from 1 to 100, if the user had not stopped the process early by entering N in response to the prompt.

```
1
Continue (Y/N)? Y
2
Continue (Y/N)? Y
3
Continue (Y/N)? Y
4
Continue (Y/N)? Y
5
Continue (Y/N)? Y
6
Continue (Y/N)? N
That's all folks!
```

Note: Any entry other than an uppercase N causes the program to continue.

The FOR loop offers much loop control, but it is designed to count through the control loop's value. Not all of your loops can be determined by a counting variable. Sometimes you need loops that loop while a certain condition is true or until a certain condition is met.

The *DO-WHILE* Loop

The DO-WHILE loop supplies a way to control loops through a relational test. The loop's relational test uses the same relational operators used with IF statements (refer back to Table 9.1 for a complete listing of relational operators).

Suppose the teacher with the grade-printing program doesn't know exactly how many students took the test, and doesn't want to take the time to count them. Because the total number of tests must be specified to control the FOR loop properly, another method is required. Listing 9.15 shows you the same program, but controlled by a DO-WHILE loop. Notice that the DO-WHILE continues looping *while* a certain condition is true. The condition is the teacher's answer in response to having more tests to enter.

Listing 9.15. Controlling the grade printing with a DO-WHILE loop.

```
' Grade-printing program using DO-WHILE
CLS

PRINT , "** Grade-listing Program **"
PRINT

LPRINT "** Grades for the Test **"
LPRINT
LPRINT "Name", , "Grade"
DO
  INPUT "What is the next student's name"; sName$
  PRINT "What is "; sName$; "'s grade";
  INPUT grade
  LPRINT sName$, , grade
  INPUT "Are there more grades (Y/N)"; ans$
LOOP WHILE (ans$ = "Y")
END
```

This program keeps looping until the teacher indicates that there are no more grades to enter. Notice that the body of the loop is enclosed between the DO and LOOP WHILE statements, and that the WHILE is followed by a relational test, the result of which (true or false) determines whether the loop repeats again or quits.

The *DO-UNTIL* Loop

The DO-UNTIL loop is similar to the DO-WHILE loop you saw in the preceding section. DO-WHILE loops as long as the relational condition is true; DO-UNTIL loops as long as the relational condition is false.

The choice of DO-WHILE versus DO-UNTIL depends on your application. You can use both interchangeably in most programs; just be sure to reverse the conditional test being performed. Here is a DO-WHILE loop:

```
DO
   PRINT "A"
   INPUT "Again"; ans$
LOOP WHILE (ans$ = "Y")
```

Here is the same code using a DO-UNTIL loop:

```
DO
   PRINT "A"
   INPUT "Again"; ans$
LOOP UNTIL (ans$ = "N")
```

The tests being performed in the two sets of loops are the opposite of each other. The first program loops *while* a certain condition is true; the second loops *until* a certain condition is true. Figure 9.7 shows a flowchart of each set of loops. The decision symbol's question is different for each one, but the logic used is the same.

Listing 9.16 shows you how to use the DO-UNTIL loop to control a number-guessing game. The computer keeps asking the user for a number until the user's number matches the computer's.

Listing 9.16. A number-guessing game.

```
' Number-guessing game
CLS

compNum = 47     ' The computer's number

PRINT "I am thinking of a number..."
PRINT "Try to guess it."
PRINT
```

continues

Listing 9.16. continued

```
DO
    INPUT "What is your guess (between 1 and 100)"; guess
LOOP UNTIL (guess = compNum)

PRINT "You got it!"
END
```

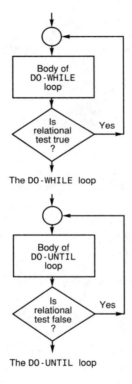

Figure 9.7. Flowcharting the two DO loops.

Figure 9.8 shows a sample run of this program. DO-UNTIL is the perfect control statement, because the program must keep looping, asking for another number, until the user enters the correct number.

```
I am thinking of a number...
Try to guess it.

What is your guess (between 1 and 100)? 80
What is your guess (between 1 and 100)? 60
What is your guess (between 1 and 100)? 50
What is your guess (between 1 and 100)? 30
What is your guess (between 1 and 100)? 40
What is your guess (between 1 and 100)? 44
What is your guess (between 1 and 100)? 47
You got it!




Press any key to continue
```

Figure 9.8. *Guessing the computer's number.*

Chapter Highlights

Congratulations! You can now enter data into a QBasic program and format the resulting output. You have also mastered the true power of any programming language—looping. The programs you saw in this chapter are getting to be powerful, yet you have seen that programming is easy.

✖ The INPUT statement gets values from the keyboard.

✖ You should always prompt the user before getting input so the user knows what kind of data is needed.

✖ You can ask the user for numeric or string values with INPUT.

✖ The USING option of the PRINT statement enables you to format your output. With a USING string, you can ensure that all dollar amounts print with two decimal places.

✖ QBasic uses statements that mirror real life statements that you say every day.

✖ The IF statement is QBasic's decision control statement.

✖ IF uses a relational test to determine whether a condition is true or false.

✖ IF has an ELSE statement that executes when the IF statement is false.

✖ A set of relational operators enable you to test for any relational condition. A relational condition, like the decision symbol in a flowchart, always has two possibilities.

✖ The FOR loop enables you to repeat one or more statements for a specified number of times.

✖ A FOR loop always has a control variable that counts up or down, controlling the loop.

✖ The STEP option of the FOR loop determines how the loop control occurs.

✖ You can exit a FOR loop early with EXIT FOR.

✖ The DO-WHILE loop continues looping *as long as* a certain relational test is true.

✖ The DO-UNTIL loop continues looping *until* a certain relational test is true.

✖ DO-WHILE and DO-UNTIL are useful for looping when you do not know beforehand how many times the loop should repeat. (Use FOR when you do know exactly how many times you want the loop to repeat.)

Managing Data and Disk Files

10

Perilous Perry revelled in the treasure his adventuring had brought him. But will Perilous Perry be able to manage his treasure and figure out how to store it for the long term?

1. What is an array?

2. How do I reserve memory for arrays?

3. How do I erase arrays?

4. What is a subscript?

5. What advantage do disk files have over program variables?

6. What are the three modes of file access?

7. What is the difference between a record and a field?

8. How is a file handle used?

9. How do I open a disk file?

10. How do I close a disk file?

11. How do I write to a disk file?

12. How do I read from a disk file?

Y ou are well on your way to becoming a QBasic programmer! If you were enrolled in a programming course, the material you just finished in Chapter 9 would take you through the first half of the course. Although this has been a whirlwind tutorial, you can see (hopefully) that fighting the perils of programming is not as precarious as exploring a lion-infested jungle, no matter what your first expectations might have been.

When you finish this chapter, you will have had a tremendous, albeit quick, exposure to QBasic and programming. The good news is that all programming languages contain the same types of statements you are learning about here. Just as all spoken languages includes verbs and nouns, all programming languages include variables, loops, and decision statements. The syntax of a statement in another language might be slightly different than in QBasic, but the types of available commands are identical.

Reward: The similarity among programming languages is the primary reason that programmers often know more than one. It is very easy to learn a second or third language once you master your first one.

This chapter teaches you about some advanced ways to store your data. In the previous chapters, you learned about how to work with variables. Variables are adequate for simple data, but for more advanced applications, you need to understand an advanced use of variables called *arrays*. An array is nothing more than a list of variables that you can treat as a single group. You will also see some commands that store data to your disk file. Unless you can store your data long-term, your programs cannot keep track of data over time. By storing your variables and arrays to disk, you can process them whenever it is convenient.

Clue: Disk files enable you to store many things: name and address information, so you can print mailing lists whenever you want them; employee records, so you can process payroll every month; and business data, so you can print reports when requested. You would not want to re-enter all that data every time you run a program. With disk files, you enter your data once and then save it to disk. Your data will be immediately available when future programs want to use it.

Chapter 12 describes some advanced programming techniques common to all programming languages and uses them in code examples. Once you understand those advanced techniques, seeing them used in a programming language with which you are already familiar will help you apply them in any programming language you use later on, be it QBasic, C, or something else.

Introduction to Arrays

Often, you must keep track of several items that are the same kind of data. For example, a teacher might need to keep track of 30 test scores, a company might need to track 150 products, or you might need to keep track of the money you've invested monthly into your retirement account. Although you could do so, it would be time-consuming to store similar data in the kind of variables you have seen. To keep track of them, you would have to give each one a different name.

For example, consider a teacher's test scores. If there are 30 pupils, the teacher might call the scores score1, score2, score3, and so on. The teacher must know what student's name goes with each score, so there would also have to be 30 separate string variables, probably called something like Sname1$, Sname2$, Sname3$, and so on. Such variable names make for tedious processing and program-writing. Listing 10.1 shows you a partial listing of what is involved in such a program.

Listing 10.1. A partial program that requests student names and grades without using arrays.

```
' Program that begs to have arrays instead of regular variables
CLS
INPUT "What is the next student's name"; Sname1$
INPUT "What is the test score for that student"; score1
```

continues

255

Listing 10.1. continued

```
PRINT                         ' Prints a blank line
INPUT "What is the next student's name"; Sname2$
INPUT "What is the test score for that student"; score2
PRINT                         ' Prints a blank line
INPUT "What is the next student's name"; Sname3$
INPUT "What is the test score for that student"; score3
PRINT                         ' Prints a blank line
INPUT "What is the next student's name"; Sname4$
INPUT "What is the test score for that student"; score4
PRINT                         ' Prints a blank line
INPUT "What is the next student's name"; Sname5$
INPUT "What is the test score for that student"; score5
PRINT                         ' Prints a blank line
' This process continues for 25 more students
```

Anytime you find yourself writing two or more sets of statements and the only differences are the variable names, you are probably not taking advantage of a better programming style. The program in Listing 10.1 begs you to use array variables. Given what you know about programming so far, you won't be able to do anything different if you need to keep all 30 variables in memory for later use (perhaps to calculate an overall class average or some such statistic).

Pitfall: Another drawback to using a different variable name for all 30 variables is that you cannot take advantage of the powerful loop statements you learned in the previous chapter. The goal of programming is to make your life simpler, not harder. Whenever you can put repetitive code such as that in Listing 10.1 into a loop, you save wear and tear on your fingers by writing only a single pair of INPUT statements wrapped inside a FOR or DO-WHILE loop.

An array is a list of similar variables. Each of the like variables is called an *array element*. Instead of each individual array element having a different name, the entire array has one name. Each element in the list is distinguished by a subscript.

The top of Figure 10.1 shows you what five of the first 30 test score variables look like in memory. Each variable has a different name. The bottom of Figure

10.1 shows you how the same set of variables stored in an array would appear. There are still five variables, and each one is separate and distinct. Unlike the differently named variables, each of the array variables has the same name. They are distinguished not by their names, but by a *subscript*, which is the number inside the parentheses after the array name. Every element in every array has a subscript. This way you know which element in the list to refer to when you want to distinguish one value from another.

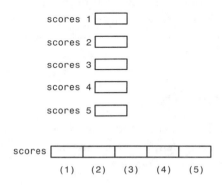

Figure 10.1. Separate variables stored as an array.

Now that the teacher stores the variables in 30 array elements called scores, the teacher can use a loop to step through them. The ability to loop through array elements, either initializing or printing them, makes arrays extremely powerful and easy to program. Consider the section of code in Listing 10.2. Notice how the program asks for the student's name and score only once; that request is then repeated inside a loop.

Listing 10.2. Improving the grade program with arrays.

```
' Loop through the questions with array subscripts
CLS
FOR i = 1 TO 30
    INPUT "What is the next student's name"; Sname$(i)
    INPUT "What is the test score for that student"; scores(i)
    PRINT                      ' Prints a blank line
NEXT i
' Rest of program follows
```

The first time through the FOR loop, i is 1. The teacher enters the value for Sname$(i) (which is really Sname$(1)) and scores(i) (which is really scores(1)), and then the loop increments i to 2. This continues until the teacher enters all 30 names and scores. The subscript runs through the data and makes the code much cleaner.

Reward: QBasic zeros out all the elements of numeric arrays and puts null strings in all the elements of string arrays before you use them.

Reserving Array Space

Often, you must tell QBasic beforehand how much array space you will need. QBasic permits only 10 array elements before requiring you to request more with a DIM statement. DIM stands for *dimension*; it is the statement that reserves array space for your program.

You have to include the appropriate DIM statement at the top of a program that uses array elements to make it work properly. Here is the statement that dimensions 30 student names and scores:

```
DIM Sname$(30), scores(30)    ' Reserve space for 30 elements each
```

Note: Actually, QBasic, unlike many of the older versions of BASIC, lets you use subscript 0. Therefore, when you dimension to 30, you are really reserving *31* elements: scores(0), scores(1), and so on through scores(30). Many QBasic programmers ignore the zero element.

You can tell QBasic that you don't want to reserve the zero element when you dimension arrays with the OPTION BASE command. If you use this command before a DIM statement

OPTION BASE 1

QBasic starts the array elements at 1, not 0. The first array subscript you can use is scores(1) if that is the array you dimension next. Using the OPTION BASE 1 command saves you a little memory because QBasic does not reserve the zero element. The amount you save, however, is negligible.

Listing 10.3 shows a complete program for storing student names and scores. It dimensions array memory, asks for all the names and scores, and prints all the values to the printer. Without arrays, there isn't an easy way to duplicate this program, short of having 30 pairs of differently named student variables and inputting them with 30 different sets of statements.

Listing 10.3. The grade program that stores data and prints it later.

```
' Student name and grade listing program
DIM Sname$(30), scores(30)

CLS
FOR i = 1 TO 30
   INPUT "What is the next student's name"; Sname$(i)
   INPUT "What is the test score for that student"; scores(i)
   PRINT                           ' Prints a blank line
NEXT i
' Now that all the data is entered, print it
LPRINT , "** Grade Listing **"
LPRINT "Name", "Score"            ' Column Heading
FOR i = 1 TO 30
   LPRINT Sname$(i), scores(i)
NEXT i
END
```

Reward: To make the program in Listing 10.3 usable for any situation, write the program to dimension all 30 elements (assuming that is the total number of students in the class), and then ask the teacher how many students took the test. The FOR loop can then loop for however many students actually took the test. If the entire class took the test, all 30 array elements are filled. If fewer took the test, the FOR loop only loops for as many students as there are test scores.

Parallel Arrays

The student name and grade listing demonstrates a popular use of arrays. The Sname$() and scores() arrays are known as *parallel arrays*. That is, the arrays each have the same number of elements, and each element in one corresponds to an element in the other.

With parallel arrays, you can store arrays with any type of data. Although a single array can hold only one type of data, you can have several parallel arrays that correspond to each other on a one-to-one basis. Using parallel arrays, you can keep track of an entire set of names, addresses, phone numbers, and salaries in a payroll program.

Erasing Arrays

There is a quick way to erase the contents of any numeric or string array. The ERASE statement enables you to erase the contents of any array. This puts the array back to its initial state. If you want to reuse an array in the last part of a program for a different set of data, you first need to erase the array to prepare it for new values.

To erase two arrays named amount() and Cust$(), you would write this:

```
ERASE amount, Cust$
```

The program in Listing 10.4 fills an array with the numbers from 1 to 10 and prints the array. It then erases the array and prints the new contents.

Note: Older versions of BASIC required that you loop through an entire array, assigning zero to each element, before you could be assured that the array was properly erased. QBasic's ERASE statement increases your programming productivity by doing the work for you.

Listing 10.4. A program that erases an array.

```
' Erases an array
DIM nums(10)

FOR i = 1 TO 10
   nums(i) = i       ' Put 1 through 10 into each element
NEXT i

CLS
PRINT "The array before erasing it:"
FOR i = 1 TO 10
   PRINT nums(i) ,
NEXT i

ERASE nums
PRINT "The array after erasing it:"
FOR i = 1 TO 10
   PRINT nums(i) ,
NEXT i
END
```

Clue: The numbers print across the page because of the trailing commas at the end of each PRINT.

You can see from the following output that the ERASE statement erases the array in a single statement.

```
The array before erasing it:
 1            2            3            4            5
 6            7            8            9            10
The array after erasing it:
 0            0            0            0            0
 0            0            0            0            0
```

Introduction to Disk Files

Arrays are great for storing program data, but arrays are stored in your computer's memory, which is erased when you turn off the computer. For long-term storage, you must store data in a disk file.

Your computer acts like an electronic filing cabinet, storing files that your programs create. Disk files are *non-volatile*; that is, they remain on the disk when you turn off the computer. Each file on the disk has a unique filename, just as files in your filing cabinet have a unique label. The filename is how you designate which file to read or write from your programs.

Computer filenames have two parts, just as a person has two names (a first and last name). Figure 10.2 describes the parts of a filename. The first part can be from one to eight characters long. The second part is optional. It is called the *extension*. If you supply one, you must separate it from the first part of the name with a period.

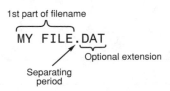

Figure 10.2. The parts of a filename.

Keep all special characters, except for letters and numbers, out of a filename. Although some special characters are allowed in the name, many are not allowed. It is safest to keep special characters out of the filename. Here are some valid filenames:

```
SALES.DAT     EMPLOYEE     PAYROLL.93     MYGRADE.TXT
```

Any kind of data can reside in a file. Generally, it is repetitive data that has similar patterns, such as all your employees' names and addresses, customer lists, invoice balances, and so on.

Records and Fields

A disk file is divided into *records*. A record is loosely defined as a line in the file. Although records can physically span more than one line in a file, a record is a collection of related file data usually written on one line. To clarify the concept of a record, look at Table 10.1. It shows a customer file. There are five records in the table; other records continue from those, but they are not shown in the table.

Table 10.1. A customer data file.

Customer Number	Customer Name	Customer Balance	Customer Account Code
30432	Smith, Julie	213.42	EB432
93845	Johnson, Tom	9434.34	BG895
30201	Kerry, Kim	3432.67	YT009
10392	Jensen, Judy	411.59	EW437
90323	Post, Paul	2883.45	TW326

Each record in a file is broken down further into *fields*. A field is a column of data. Table 10.1 contains a file that has four fields. If there were 20,000 records in the file, it would still contain four columns of data; therefore, it would contain four fields.

If the file shown in Table 10.1 contained far more data than those four fields, you might see how a single record can span more than one line in the file, yet still be considered a single record of data.

> **Reward:** Think of a file's records as a collection of cards. Each card is a separate record of information in the card file. On each card, you have several fields of data.

Types of Access

There are only three things you can do with a data file:

- ✖ Create one by writing to it
- ✖ Read from one
- ✖ Add to the end of one

That is all you do with a filing cabinet file as well. You either create a new file by filling out a file folder label and putting things into the folder, add to an existing file by putting new items into it, or read a file's contents.

With a filing cabinet file, you must open the proper file folder before you can read from a file. In QBasic, you must open files with the OPEN statement. The OPEN statement tells QBasic how you want to access a file.

> **Clue:** When you use the OPEN statement, QBasic does a lot behind the scenes. It searches the disk for the proper file that you want to read or append to one already opened. If you are creating a file, QBasic makes sure the filename is acceptable, and it ensures that the disk is properly prepared to hold the data. OPEN makes sure the disk is not write-protected.

If you choose to write-protect a floppy disk, you will not be able to write or append to any file on that disk.

OPEN has another useful purpose: It attaches a *file handle* to the disk file that you are opening. A file handle is a number you assign to a file in the OPEN statement. Once OPEN attaches a file handle to the file, the rest of your program refers to the file by its handle and not by the full filename.

The easiest way to learn about the OPEN statement is to look at a few examples. Suppose you want to open and read a file called SALES.DAT that resides on disk drive D:. The read mode of OPEN is called *input*. Here is the OPEN statement that you might use:

```
OPEN "D:SALES.DAT" FOR INPUT AS #1
```

The #1 is the file handle. If QBasic finds the file on drive D:, it will attach the #1 file handle to the file. Subsequent disk I/O (input/output) statements will use the #1 instead of the filename. You can type the drive name and the name of the file using any combination of upper- or lowercase characters, as with any DOS filename.

Reward: If the filename resides on the *default disk drive* (the drive that was active when you first started QBasic, usually C:), you do not have to specify the drive name before the filename.

If you want to have several files open in the same program, you must assign each one a different file handle. A different file handle for each file lets QBasic know which disk file you are reading from or writing to in subsequent file I/O commands.

Warning: If you attempt to open a file for input, but the file does not exist, QBasic issues a `File not found` error message. You can only read from a file when it already exists.

The following OPEN statement opens a file for *output* mode. Output mode means that you want to write to the file. Output mode assumes the file does not exist, or if the file does exist, output mode assumes that you want to overwrite it. You must be careful about opening files in output mode, because if you inadvertently open a file that exists, QBasic destroys its contents to make room for the new data. The output mode always assumes that you want to create a brand new file.

```
OPEN "Payroll.93" FOR OUTPUT AS #3
```

Subsequent file-writing commands file handle #3 to send data to the file named *Payroll.93* on the default disk drive.

There might be a time when you want to add to the end of a data file. You might be adding new customers, new engineering statistics, or new inventory records. Adding to the end of a file is known as *append mode*. Here is an OPEN statement that sets up a file as file handle #2 and ensures that subsequent writes to file handle #2 add to the end of the file and do not destroy any of the original contents:

```
OPEN "STATS.NUM" FOR APPEND AS #2
```

Clue: If you open a file for append mode, and the file does not already exist, QBasic creates the file for you.

Closing Open Files

Before getting into the actual file I/O commands, you should look at the CLOSE command. You should always close every file you open in a QBasic program. (If you don't close a filing cabinet, you could hurt yourself running into it, or lose important data that falls out.) Although DOS closes a file for you once your QBasic program ends and returns to DOS, you are being sloppy if you do not specifically close every open file. Even more important, your power could go out while a file is still open. Even if you are no longer reading from the file or writing to it, there is a chance that you could lose data and possibly lose the entire file.

The CLOSE command is simple. To close the file associated with file handle #1, you can do one of the following:

```
CLOSE 1
```

or

```
CLOSE #1
```

As you can see, the pound sign is optional. You can close more than one file in a single CLOSE statement, like this:

```
CLOSE 1, 2, 3
```

Creating Output Files

Once you open an output file, the WRITE # command writes data to it. As Figure 10.3 shows, WRITE # is to a data file what PRINT is to the screen; write sends data to the file. The file handle must appear after WRITE # (the pound sign precedes the file handle).

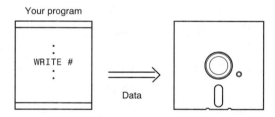

Your program

```
    :
 WRITE #
    :
```

Data

Figure 10.3. The WRITE # command writes data to a file.

The WRITE # writes *comma-separated* data to a disk file. Unlike PRINT, which prints data exactly like you type it, WRITE # does more for you than simply send data to a file. WRITE # separates each field in the data file with commas. To aid you in reading the data later (with the INPUT # command discussed in the next section), WRITE # also encloses all string data in quotation marks, instead of appending all the strings together in one long record.

To see the effects of WRITE, look at the program in Listing 10.5. The first few statements assign values to variables, and the last line writes that data to disk. The program is short; only one record is written to the disk file. In reality, more records would be written in an actual application. Nevertheless, the program shows you how WRITE # formats the line of data. Study the program, and then take a look at the data as it actually gets written to the file.

Listing 10.5. Using WRITE # to write a record to a file.

```
' First disk writing program
CLS

' Initialize some variables that will be written to the disk
Cname$ = "Jim Smith"
Age = 40
Addr$ = "146 E. Oak"
City$ = "Miami"
St$ = "FL"
Zip$ = "34029"

OPEN "first.dat" FOR OUTPUT AS #1    ' Open file for output
WRITE #1, Cname$, Age, Addr$, City$, St$, Zip$
CLOSE #1

END
```

Here is what the newly created file, *first.dat*, looks like after this program created it:

```
"Jim Smith",40,"146 E. Oak","Miami","FL","34029"
```

Notice that QBasic put commas between each of the values and quotation marks around all the strings. The next section shows you how to read such a file.

> **Reward:** Using the techniques you learned in Chapter 5, you can use Edit or Edlin to view the contents of the data files your QBasic programs create.

Listing 10.6 is a more common example of how data files are created. In this program, the user controls how many records are written to the file. The program uses both arrays and the disk to keep track of the data entered. The program first collects all the data—up to 100 values—in parallel arrays. The last part of the program stores those arrays to the disk file *first.dat*.

Listing 10.6. Writing the file based on more user input.

```
' Disk writing program based on user input
DIM Cname$(100), Age(100), Addr$(100), City$(100), St$(100), Zip$(100)

CLS

PRINT , "** Data gathering program for a disk file **"

' Loop getting data that will be written to the disk
FOR i = 1 TO 100
  PRINT
  INPUT "What is the customer name"; Cname$(i)
  INPUT "What is the customer's age"; Age(i)
  INPUT "What is the customer's address"; Addr$(i)
  INPUT "What is the customer's city"; City$(i)
  INPUT "What is the customer's state"; St$(i)
  INPUT "What is the customer's zipcode"; Zip$(i)
  INPUT "Are there more values to get (Y/N)"; ans$
  IF (ans$ <> "Y") THEN
      EXIT FOR
  END IF
NEXT i

OPEN "first.dat" FOR OUTPUT AS #1    ' Open file for output
' At this point, variable i holds the total number
' of records actually entered
FOR j = 1 TO i
   WRITE #1, Cname$(j), Age(j), Addr$(j), City$(j), St$(j), Zip$(j)
NEXT j
CLOSE #1

END
```

Here are the contents of *first.dat* after the program is run and a few records are entered:

```
"Tom Wesley",32,"102 E. Lane","Miami","FL","34023"
"Joe Yard",32,"9345 West 8th","Reno","NV","54905"
"Rush Righter",38,"210 E. 5th Ave.","New York","NY","10012"
"Tina Johnson",21,"1013 Sycamore","Coweta","OK","74429"
```

Pitfall: You might wonder why the ZIP code is stored in a string variable, even though it contains only numeric digits. Avoid using numeric variables for any data with which you are not going to do any math. A general rule of thumb is to use numeric nonstring variables only for number values with which you will calculate, and to store all other kinds of data in string variables. The digits in some numeric variables can lose accuracy because of rounding when you store their initial values. Keep ZIP codes, telephone numbers, Social Security numbers, and the like in string variables and you will never have any trouble with them.

Reward: Whenever you have to get user data that might have commas in it, such as an address, use LINE INPUT instead of INPUT. In Listing 10.6, the addresses entered for the sample output file had no commas, but if they did, you would have to use LINE INPUT. LINE INPUT is exactly like INPUT, except that you can get only one input string value with it. That string value may include any character. A comma, however, is not allowed in the INPUT statement because it would be the separating character if you were inputting more than one variable with a single INPUT.

If you want the user to enter a last name separated from the first name with a comma, LINE INPUT would be required in the name prompt as well. LINE INPUT will not generate an automatic question mark for you, so you must put a question mark at the end of the prompt if you use it.

Reading the Disk File

Reading disk files is easy. As long as you create files with WRITE #, a corresponding INPUT # reads the data into separate variables. INPUT # is a mirror-image command from WRITE #. For instance, if you wrote values to the disk with the WRITE # command

```
WRITE #1, Cname$, Age, Addr$, City$, St$, Zip$
```

you could read those values back into variables, such as from within another program, with this INPUT #:

```
INPUT #1, Cname$, Age, Addr$, City$, St$, Zip$
```

> **Warning:** You need to know the format of the data file you are reading. Every INPUT # must match, in type, the data being read. You cannot use a numeric variable as the first variable listed after the INPUT # statement if the first field in the file contains string data.

There is one additional problem with reading data files that you would not encounter when you create them. The program reading a data file may not know exactly how many records are in the file. There is a built-in routine inside QBasic (called a function) that tells you when you have reached the end of an input file. When this routine tells you that the end of a file is reached, your program has to stop reading the data.

The end-of-file routine is called EOF(); you have to put the file handle inside the parentheses. EOF() equals –1 if you just read the last record from the file. EOF() equals 0 if there are still records left to be read. Generally, you will find the DO-UNTIL to be a useful control loop for reading a file until you reach the end. Here is the general format that your programs should follow when reading files:

```
INPUT #1, variables go here
DO
    ' Process the input data here
    INPUT #1, variables go here
LOOP UNTIL ( EOF(1) = -1)
' Rest of program follows
```

The initial INPUT # reads the first data record from the file. This routine assumes there is always at least one record in the file (if there were not, OPEN would have failed because the file would probably not exist). The subsequent INPUT # statements immediately before the end-of-file check ensure that the file is read until the end of the file is reached. Then the loop terminates and the rest of the program continues.

Listing 10.7 reads the data file created in Listing 10.6. The program continues reading the file's records, printing them to the screen, until the end of the file is reached. Figure 10.4 shows you the output of this program, given the file's contents shown earlier.

Listing 10.7. Reading a data file from the disk.

```
' Disk-reading program
' The program will read the data file into these arrays
DIM Cname$(100), Age(100), Addr$(100), City$(100), St$(100), Zip$(100)

CLS

PRINT , "** Data printing program from a disk file **"
PRINT

OPEN "first.dat" FOR INPUT AS #1
i = 1

' Loop getting data from the disk
  INPUT #1, Cname$(i), Age(i), Addr$(i), City$(i), St$(i), Zip$(i)
DO
  i = i + 1      ' Add 1 to subscript
  INPUT #1, Cname$(i), Age(i), Addr$(i), City$(i), St$(i), Zip$(i)
LOOP UNTIL (EOF(1) = -1)
CLOSE #1         ' Close file since all data has been read

' At this point, variable i holds the total number of records
FOR j = 1 TO i
   PRINT
   PRINT "Name: "; Cname$(j), "Age:"; Age(j)
   PRINT "Address: "; Addr$(j)
   PRINT "City: "; City$(j)
   PRINT "State: "; St$(j), "Zipcode: "; Zip$(j)
NEXT j

END
```

```
              ** Data printing program from a disk file **

   Name: Tom Wesley         Age: 32
   Address: 102 E. Lane
   City: Miami
   State: FL      Zipcode: 34023

   Name: Joe Yard           Age: 32
   Address: 9345 West 8th
   City: Reno
   State: NV      Zipcode: 54905

   Name: Rush Righter       Age: 38
   Address: 210 E. 5th Ave.
   City: New York
   State: NY      Zipcode: 10012

   Name: Tina Johnson       Age: 21
   Address: 1013 Sycamore
   City: Coweta
   State: OK      Zipcode: 74429


   Press any key to continue
```

Figure 10.4. The data from the file created earlier.

Appending to a Data File

Adding data to the end of an existing file is easy. The WRITE # command writes the data just as it would if you were creating the file. The only difference between creating a new file and appending to the end of one is the OPEN command.

Clue: Remember that opening a disk file in APPEND mode does not destroy the file's contents. APPEND only adds to the end of an existing file. If you open a nonexisting file in APPEND mode, QBasic creates the file without issuing an error. In effect, you are appending to the end of an empty file.

Listing 10.8 shows you a program that opens the data file created earlier and then asks the user for more values.

Listing 10.8. Appending to the end of a file created earlier.

```
' Disk appending program
CLS

PRINT , "** Appending new data to the end of a file **"

OPEN "first.dat" FOR APPEND AS #1    ' Open file for append mode

' Loop getting data that will be appended to the disk
DO
  PRINT
  INPUT "What is the next customer name"; Cname$
  INPUT "What is the next customer's age"; Age
  INPUT "What is the next customer's address"; Addr$
  INPUT "What is the next customer's city"; City$
  INPUT "What is the next customer's state"; St$
  INPUT "What is the next customer's zipcode"; Zip$
  WRITE #1, Cname$, Age, Addr$, City$, St$, Zip$

  INPUT "Are there more values to append (Y/N)"; ans$
LOOP UNTIL (ans$ = "N")

CLOSE #1
END
```

At this point, you can run the file-reading program in Listing 10.7 to print the file as it is now written, with the new records appended to it.

Two or More Files Open

The example programs you have seen in this chapter have been simple, yet powerful. You have seen how to store data in disk files for long-term storage. It is easy to create, read, and append to disk files using QBasic.

All of the examples you have seen have had only one file open at a given time. Therefore, they used only file handle #1 for the file access. The program in Listing 10.9 opens two files at the same time. The first file (the *first.dat* file created in the last few program listings) is the input file, and a new file (the output file called *backup.dat*) is created. This program reads an entire record from *first.dat* and writes that same record to *backup.dat* until all the records have been written. The program makes an exact duplicate of the first file. This might be a useful program for backing up important data files for safekeeping.

Listing 10.9. Creating a backup file.

```
' Opens two files at once
CLS
PRINT "Backing up the data file..."

OPEN "first.dat" FOR INPUT AS #1
OPEN "backup.dat" FOR OUTPUT AS #2

DO
    INPUT #1, Cname$, Age, Addr$, City$, St$, Zip$
    WRITE #2, Cname$, Age, Addr$, City$, St$, Zip$
LOOP UNTIL (EOF(1) = -1)

CLOSE #1
CLOSE #2
PRINT
PRINT "The file is now backed up."
END
```

Advanced Data Files

There are some advanced ways to access files in QBasic that this chapter does not discuss. This chapter describes *sequential file processing*, a fancy term for reading, writing, and appending to files. Another form of access, called *random-file access*, is helpful when you want to both read and write to the same file inside the same program. Using random-file access, you can change specific file data, such as a customer's balance, without having to recreate the entire file.

There is not enough room in this book to discuss a subject so complex as random-file access. When you study QBasic in more detail, with an entire book or class devoted to QBasic, you will learn all about random-file access and see its advantages.

Despite its advantages, random-file access is not an answer to everything. Many very advanced programming applications use the sequential file access techniques you learned in this chapter.

Chapter Highlights

Beginning programmers often think arrays are difficult, but as you have seen, arrays are just another way to hold data for your QBasic programs to process. Once you load arrays with data, you can safely tuck the data away to a disk file for later processing.

✖ Arrays offer advanced variable storage capabilities. Instead of having different names for many variables of the same kind, you can have a list of values with the same name. The list of values is called an array.

✖ You differentiate between the array elements with a numeric subscript. The subscript lets you search through an array by means of a loop.

✖ Before using a large array, you must reserve storage for it with the DIM statement.

✖ The OPTION BASE statement lets you begin an array with either 0 or 1 as a subscript. The default, if you do not supply an OPTION BASE statement, is to begin all array subscripts at 0.

✖ Parallel arrays are arrays with different kinds of data that correspond to each other. Parallel arrays always have the same number of elements. (Two arrays, one holding the inventory's part numbers, and the other holding the quantity of each part number, are an example of parallel arrays.)

✖ The ERASE statement erases an entire array.

✖ Disk files enable you to save data for long-term storage. Variables are volatile; they lose their values when your program ends or when you turn off your computer.

✖ There are three modes of access for disk files: output, input, and append.

✖ You must open all disk files with the OPEN statement before you access them.

✖ Close all files with the CLOSE statement when you are through with them.

✖ If you open a file in output mode, QBasic creates the file. If the file already exists, QBasic overwrites the old one.

✖ If you open a file in input mode, QBasic lets your program read the file. If the file does not exist, QBasic issues an error message.

✖ If you open a file in append mode, QBasic lets your program add data to the end of the file. If the file does not exist, QBasic creates one for you.

✖ You can have more than one file open simultaneously, as long as you open them with different file handles.

Having Fun with QBasic

11

Perilous Perry lowered himself down the face of the rocky cliff. What awaits our hero at the bottom of the waterfall? Will Perilous Perry ever have any time for relaxation during his adventures?

1. How do I beep my computer's speaker?

2. How does the SOUND command work?

3. What does *hertz* mean?

4. Can I play music on my PC?

5. How can I prepare my screen for graphics?

6. What command turns on a graphics dot?

7. What command turns off a graphics dot?

8. How do I draw lines on the screen?

9. How do I draw boxes on the screen?

10. How do I draw circles on the screen?

11. Must I have a graphics adapter to generate graphs?

12. Can I change the location of the next PRINT statement's screen output?

Now is the time to sit back and have some fun with QBasic. Sure, programming is fun in itself, and you know how easy and enjoyable it is writing programs with QBasic. However, there is more you can do with QBasic than write data-processing programs for business and engineering. You can also use QBasic to generate sounds and graphics.

The material you master in this chapter will give you the framework for adding pizzazz to your programs. You will get an idea of how game programmers do their job. You will learn some fundamental concepts that you need to write programs that capture the user's attention.

To use the graphics commands in this chapter, you must have a color monitor and a VGA (which stands for *Video Graphics Array*) graphics adapter card inside your computer. You don't need the graphics adapter to program sounds, but you need it for pictures.

If you do not have a graphics adapter, you cannot program the graphics. You must wait until you get one. If you do have a graphics adapter, but it is not a VGA, you can still write graphics programs; however, they will be more limited than this chapter's. Today's standard is VGA, and most computers purchased (or upgraded) in the last few years have a VGA card inside. If you are unsure, try a few of the graphics programs in this chapter, and you will know right away whether your graphics card is compatible.

> **Note:** There is not enough space in this chapter to cover all the graphics cards available. If you want more information on programming various graphics adapters, you can get more detailed help on QBasic's graphics possibilities in Appendix A.

Beeping the Speaker

Your PC has a built-in speaker. Although the fidelity of the speaker leaves much to be desired, it can be helpful when you need to get the user's attention.

Perhaps the easiest way to get a sound out of your computer is with the BEEP command. Whenever QBasic encounters a BEEP in your program, QBasic sends a signal to the speaker causing it to beep for about one-half second. Listing 11.1 shows a program that beeps the speaker.

Listing 11.1. Getting a beep from the speaker.

```
' Program that beeps the speaker
CLS

BEEP

PRINT "That was the speaker."
PRINT
INPUT "Want to hear it again"; ans$
BEEP
END
```

The *SOUND* Command

The SOUND command gives you much more control over your computer's speaker than the BEEP command does. With SOUND, you can control both what note is sent to the speaker and how long it plays. It is helpful to have some familiarity with a musical keyboard or musical theory before using SOUND. Here is a sample SOUND command:

```
SOUND 880, 36.4      ' Sound a tone on the PC speaker
```

The SOUND command can generate a tone from 37 hertz to 32,767 hertz. *Hertz* (Hz) is the number of cycles per second at which a note vibrates. The first of the two values after SOUND is the value of hertz you are sounding. The higher the hertz is, the higher the note sounds. To give you an idea of the range of hertz, the A below middle C on a piano is 440 Hz, a frequency commonly used for tuning musical instruments. If you halve the value of 440 Hz, getting 220 Hz, you get the next lowest A on the piano. Halving 220 Hz to 110 Hz produces another A an octave lower.

In the opposite direction, doubling 440 Hz to 880 hertz gives you the A above middle C. Table 11.1 shows you where the A notes fall in the range of possible SOUND hertz. To make other notes in between, use hertz values between the hertz values of two A notes.

Table 11.1. The possible SOUND frequency values for different hertz values.

Hertz	Note Sounded
55	Fourth A below middle C
110	Third A below middle C
220	Second A below middle C
440	First A below middle C
880	First A above middle C
1760	Second A above middle C
3520	Third A above middle C
7040	Fourth A above middle C

The second value in the SOUND command is the duration of the note you want to play. Like the hertz value, the duration value can be confusing at first. The duration is the number of CPU clock ticks during which the sound persists. There are a total of 18.2 CPU clock ticks per second. (Your CPU includes a clock to keep everything timed properly inside the computer.) If you want to sound a tone for one second, use *18.2* as the second value of SOUND. To sound a tone for 2 seconds, use *36.4* for the duration value, and so forth.

The program in Listing 11.2 uses the SOUND command to generate every tone possible on the PC for a fraction of time. (Because a duration of 2 is only about one-tenth of a second, each note sounds for only a short time).

> **Warning:** The program takes a while to circulate through all possible notes, even though each note is sounded for just a fraction of a second. With a hertz range from 37 to 32767, there are a lot of notes to cycle through.

Listing 11.2. Producing every note possible on a PC.

```
' Program that produces all notes with SOUND
CLS

PRINT "Get your ears ready..."

FOR Note = 37 TO 32767
    SOUND Note, 2
NEXT Note

PRINT "Things are sounding uppity around here!"
END
```

You can cycle through the sounds faster by adding a step value to the FOR loop. The program in Listing 11.3 takes the sounds up and down again with a couple of FOR loops.

Listing 11.3. Producing a rising and falling siren.

```
' Program that steps up and down through notes
CLS

PRINT "Here's a siren..."
```

continues

Listing 11.3. continued

```
FOR Note = 450 TO 750 STEP 5    ' The siren goes up
   SOUND Note, 2
NEXT Note

FOR Note = 750 TO 450 STEP -5   ' The siren goes down
   SOUND Note, 2
NEXT Note

END
```

By changing a few values and adding SOUND commands, you can create some interesting effects. The program in Listing 11.4 almost sounds as though your computer has two speakers inside, each doing its own thing.

Listing 11.4. Generating strange sounds with SOUND.

```
' Program that produces really weird sounds
CLS

PRINT "Hold your ears..."

FOR Note = 450 TO 750 STEP 5    ' The siren goes up
   SOUND Note, 1
   SOUND 800 - Note, 1
NEXT Note

FOR Note = 750 TO 450 STEP -5   ' The siren goes down
   SOUND Note, 1
   SOUND 750 + Note, 1
NEXT Note

END
```

The *PLAY* Command

QBasic contains an additional command, called PLAY, that offers a more advanced method for generating sounds and music from your PC. You can only generate the music a single note at a time. Therefore, you cannot generate multi-part harmony with PLAY, but you can generate a line from virtually any piece of music.

The PLAY command requires that you master a mini-language within QBasic, the PLAY language. PLAY is a command that requires a string after it. Here is a sample of a PLAY command:

```
PLAY "L4 C2 E G < B. > L16 C D L2 C"
```

The data inside the string after PLAY look cryptic. The PLAY string, called a *command string*, contains a QBasic musical representation. The L4 (for *Length of 4*) tells the computer how long to play the notes that follow—until another L command changes it. A 4 designates a quarter note, 3 a half note, 2 a dotted half note, and 1 a whole note. The letters following each L command are notes on the musical scale. Whenever a number follows a note, that number overrides the L value currently in effect, but just for that particular note.

When you want to raise or lower an octave, you must include a greater than (>) symbol to raise the following notes an octave, or a less than (<) symbol to lower those notes an octave. A period after a note "dots" it, extending the note for another one-half of its original duration.

There are many more commands possible inside the PLAY command string. If you are familiar with music, you probably understood the last few paragraphs and want more information. Otherwise, it might be best to type the PLAY command shown earlier and sit back and enjoy it. If you want more information on PLAY, check Appendix A for some helpful references.

Note: It is possible to add a sound card to your computer so you can generate multiple-note and instrument sounds. Programming those sound cards, however, takes a lot more work than BEEP, SOUND, and PLAY.

285

Introduction to Graphics

Your graphics screen is made up of many columns and rows. A measurement known as *resolution* determines how detailed your screen's graphics can be. The higher the resolution, the better your graphics will look. The lower the resolution, the worse your graphics will look. In its highest graphics resolution mode, a standard VGA screen can display 640 columns and 480 rows of dots, as Figure 11.1 illustrates. Where every column and row intersect there is a graphics dot on the screen. The dot is called a *picture element*, or *pixel* for short. Because 640 times 480 equals 307,200, there are a total of 307,200 pixels on a VGA screen that you can turn on and off.

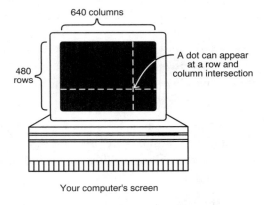

Figure 11.1. The resolution on a typical VGA computer screen.

Note: The column and row numbers begin at 0. Therefore, the 640 columns are numbered from 0 to 639, and the rows are numbered from 0 to 479.

Reward: Although this chapter only shows you how to turn on white pixels over a black background, many colors are possible. QBasic supports a wide range of colors, and the number you can use is determined by your monitor and graphics adapter. After you master black and white graphics, you might want to try your hand at adding color as well.

The *SCREEN* Command

Before you can turn on a graphics pixel, you must tell QBasic to leave its normal text display mode and generate a graphics screen image. The SCREEN command does this for you. There are several possible SCREEN values. The one used throughout this chapter is 12, the highest VGA black and white resolution value. The following SCREEN command sets up your VGA screen in a high-resolution black and white graphics mode:

```
SCREEN 12      ' Places the screen in high-res graphics mode
```

The number after SCREEN can be any number from 0 to 13. Each number represents a different type of display adapter and monitor.

Reward: The SCREEN command automatically clears the screen. You do not need to issue a CLS command before producing graphics.

Warning: If your program sets the video screen to one of the graphics modes, and you are writing a program for general use, be sure to reset the screen to text mode when you are done. You can do so with this command:

```
SCREEN 0        ' Resets the screen back to text mode
```

287

When your program finishes, the text mode is reset to its normal state. If you fail to reset the screen to text, QBasic does it for you. However, there are advanced ways to execute a QBasic program straight from DOS or from within another program, and resetting the adapter back to text mode is a good habit to develop.

Turning Pixels On and Off

The PSET command turns pixels on, and PRESET turns them off. After each of these commands, you must give an *x-coordinate* and a *y-coordinate,* which are nothing more than the column and row numbers that intersect the pixel you want turned on. For example, if you want to turn on the pixel at the intersection of column 100 and row 150 (and provided that, earlier in the program, you have set the screen to a graphics mode), you would do this:

```
PSET (100, 150)    ' Turns on a pixel
```

If you wanted to turn off the pixel at the intersection of column 50 and row 45, you would do this:

```
PRESET (50, 45)    ' Turns off a pixel
```

Clue: There is a handy option you can add to PSET and PRESET that turns pixels on and off at a *relative location* from where you last turned one on or off. The STEP option, placed before the x- and y-coordinates of a PSET or PRESET command, indicates that you want the computer to turn on or off a pixel a given number of pixels away from the previous one. In other words, the command

```
PSET STEP (50, 75)
```

does *not* turn on the pixel at column 50 and row 75. Instead, it turns on the pixel 50 columns and 75 rows away from where the last PSET turned on a pixel.

They say that a picture is worth a thousand words, and the program in Listing 11.5 produces a graphics output you can study to learn how PSET and PRESET work. The program turns on pixels at various locations on the screen; it then uses two FOR loops to draw some lines. (The FOR loops enable you to trace across several columns or rows easily.)

Listing 11.5. Turning on some graphics pixels.

```
' Produces dots on the screen and some lines
CLS
SCREEN 12

PSET (10, 10)
PSET (20, 20)
PSET (30, 30)
PSET (40, 40)
PSET (50, 50)
PSET (100, 200)
PSET (101, 202)
PSET (105, 210)
PSET (200, 33)
PSET (220, 30)
PSET (400, 400)
PSET (300, 25)
PSET (301, 27)
PSET (303, 30)

FOR row = 275 TO 375
   PSET (400, row)
NEXT row

FOR col = 100 TO 500
   PSET (col, 50)
NEXT col
END
```

Figure 11.2 shows you the output from this pixel-setting program. The VGA's resolution is so high that some of the dots are very small. The lines drawn via the FOR loops are easy to spot.

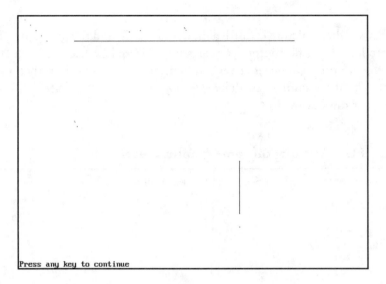

Press any key to continue

Figure 11.2. Setting pixels on the screen.

The program in Listing 11.6 is an extension of the one in Listing 11.5. It first turns on all the pixels that Listing 11.5 did, and then it turns them off with PRESET. Watch carefully; the pixels are erased fairly quickly.

Listing 11.6. Turning on and off some graphics pixels.

```
' Produces dots on the screen and some lines
' then erases them
CLS
SCREEN 12

PSET (10, 10)
PSET (20, 20)
PSET (30, 30)
```

```
PSET (40, 40)
PSET (50, 50)
PSET (100, 200)
PSET (101, 202)
PSET (105, 210)
PSET (200, 33)
PSET (220, 30)
PSET (400, 400)
PSET (300, 25)
PSET (301, 27)
PSET (303, 30)

FOR row = 275 TO 375
   PSET (400, row)
NEXT row

FOR col = 100 TO 500
   PSET (col, 50)
NEXT col

PRESET (10, 10)
PRESET (20, 20)
PRESET (30, 30)
PRESET (40, 40)
PRESET (50, 50)
PRESET (100, 200)
PRESET (101, 202)
PRESET (105, 210)
PRESET (200, 33)
PRESET (220, 30)
PRESET (400, 400)
PRESET (300, 25)
PRESET (301, 27)
PRESET (303, 30)

FOR row = 275 TO 375
   PRESET (400, row)
NEXT row

FOR col = 100 TO 500
   PRESET (col, 50)
NEXT col
END
```

The program in Listing 11.7 uses FOR loops to turn on pixels, showing you how to *nest* loops. Nesting loops is the process of putting one loop inside another loop. The number of times that the inner loop executes is multiplied by the outer loop's controlling variable.

The program in Listing 11.7 is not very long, yet it fills up almost the entire screen by turning on many pixels.

Listing 11.7. Turning on lots of pixels with nested FOR loops.

```
' Paints the screen with pixels
CLS
SCREEN 12

FOR col = 0 TO 639 STEP 3
   FOR row = 0 TO 479 STEP 2
     PSET (col, row)
   NEXT row
NEXT col
END
```

Figure 11.3 shows you the output of the program from Listing 11.7 after the screen is completely painted by the PSET commands.

Clue: Removing both STEP values from the two FOR loops in Listing 11.7 would paint the entire screen solid white instead of creating a plaid effect. If you run a program without the STEP values, have patience; painting an entire VGA screen takes a few seconds.

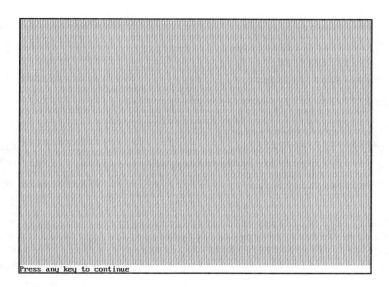

Figure 11.3. Painting the screen with pixels.

Drawing Lines and Boxes

The PSET is too slow for drawing lines and boxes. QBasic supplies the LINE statement to help make your line drawing easier and faster. Instead of collecting a group of PSET statements to draw a line or box, the LINE statement does all the work at once. Depending on the format you use, LINE draws either a line or a box. The simplest format of LINE draws a line from one x,y coordinate to another.

Reward: LINE is faster and easier to use than drawing a straight line of pixels with PSET.

A line is determined by its two end points. To draw a line, you only have to know the x- and y-coordinates of both end points. QBasic does the rest. For example, if you want to draw a line from the pixel at column 100 and row 100 to the pixel at column 200 and row 200, you would specify this LINE command:

```
LINE (100, 100) - (200, 200)
```

As with PSET and PRESET, the LINE command's STEP option draws the line relative to the starting location—the last pixel drawn or turned off. You do not have to include the starting coordinate pair because STEP knows where to begin. Therefore, by using STEP, some of the coordinates might be negative, such as the following:

```
LINE STEP (-12, 0) - (10, 1)
```

Translated, this statement means: Draw a line, one of whose end points is 12 pixels to the left of (and zero rows up or down from) the last pixel turned on, and whose other endpoint is 10 pixels to the right of and down one row from the other endpoint. If you have not already drawn anything, STEP draws pixels from your screen's center point.

> **Note:** You can draw lines up, down, left, or right. QBasic does not care what direction the line travels as long as you specify two end points with the pairs of screen coordinates.

Listing 11.8 shows a program that draws several lines on the screen. Run the program and see how much faster you can draw lines with LINE than by setting individual pixels.

Listing 11.8. Drawing lines with LINE.

```
' Drawing lines on the screen
CLS
SCREEN 12

LINE (100, 100)-(200, 200)
LINE (400, 20)-(620, 400)
```

```
LINE (20, 450)-(5, 30)
LINE (300, 200)-(200, 400)
LINE (100, 20)-(600, 450)
END
```

Figure 11.4 shows you what these lines look like on-screen.

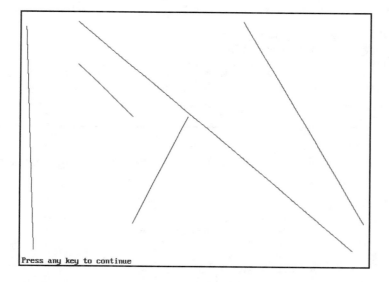

Figure 11.4. After drawing some lines on the screen.

You can add an option to use LINE to draw a box or a rectangle—they are the same thing in QBasic. The LINE statement's B option draws boxes. As with a line, a box is determined by two points, its upper-left and lower-right corners. Here is a LINE command that draws a box on-screen:

```
LINE (40, 50) - (200, 200), , B     ' Draws a box
```

The upper-left corner of the box is at column 40 and row 50, and its lower-right corner is at column 200 and row 200. The B indicates that you want a box and not a line. The two commas before the B are placeholders for an optional color attribute. You must use the two commas if you want to draw a box.

The program in Listing 11.9 draws several boxes on-screen, with some overlapping the others.

Listing 11.9. Drawing boxes on the screen.

```
' Drawing several boxes
CLS
SCREEN 12

LINE (100, 100)-(200, 200), , B
LINE (400, 20)-(620, 400), , B
LINE (20, 450)-(5, 30), , B
LINE (300, 200)-(195, 405), , B
LINE (110, 25)-(600, 450), , B

END
```

Figure 11.5 shows you the result of running the box-drawing program shown in Listing 11.9.

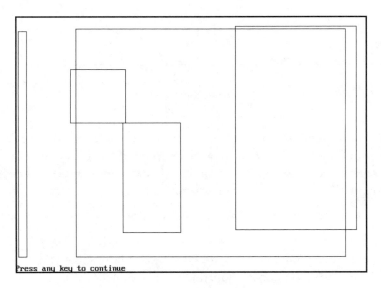

Figure 11.5. After drawing some boxes on the screen.

Drawing Circles

You can draw circles and ellipses on the screen with the CIRCLE command. You will probably have to practice a bit to get circles that are exactly round. Because there are fewer rows than columns, QBasic often draws elongated circles that you must correct. This section shows you the basics of circle-drawing so you can have some fun with them.

To draw a circle, you must specify the radius, in numbers of pixels. The radius of a circle is the distance from its center point to the edge. The following CIRCLE command draws a circle with a center point at column 300 and row 150, and a radius of 125 pixels:

```
CIRCLE (300, 150), 125
```

The program in Listing 11.10 draws several circles on the screen. It uses a FOR loop to move the drawing to the right a few pixels for each circle.

Listing 11.10. Drawing several running circles.

```
' Draws circles across the center of the screen

SCREEN 12

FOR col = 100 TO 520 STEP 50
   CIRCLE (col, 225), 100
NEXT col
END
```

Figure 11.6 shows you the result of running the circle-drawing program.

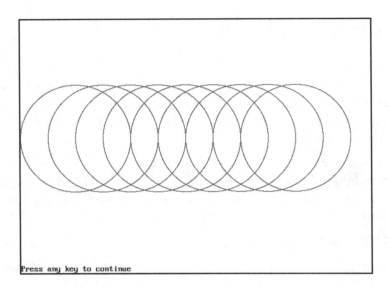

Figure 11.6. After drawing some circles across the screen.

Textual Graphs

Not all graphics require a graphics card, although those with the best resolution do. With a little imagination, you can chart some graphs without leaving the text mode. The program in Listing 11.11 gives you an idea of what is possible. It draws a graph based on the values of children's ages. Instead of using pixels, it prints asterisks on the screen to show which age is the highest (the one farthest to the right).

Listing 11.11. Producing a text graph without graphics.

```
' Draws a textual graph based on children's ages

OPTION BASE 1
DIM ages(8)

ages(1) = 8        ' Fill the 8 array elements with various ages
ages(2) = 9
ages(3) = 5
ages(4) = 6
ages(5) = 10
ages(6) = 6
ages(7) = 6
ages(8) = 9

CLS
PRINT "Here is a graph of the children's ages:"
PRINT

FOR child = 1 TO 8
   PRINT "Child #"; child;
   FOR stars = 1 TO ages(child)
      PRINT "*";        ' The semicolon keeps the cursor on this line
   NEXT stars
   PRINT                ' Moves cursor down for the next child
NEXT child

END
```

The program uses the trailing semicolon after the PRINT statement effectively. The semicolon keeps the cursor on the line being printed until as many asterisks print as the age of the child in years. A blank PRINT then moves the cursor down to the next line ready for the next child's age. Figure 11.7 shows the result of running the program.

```
Here is a graph of the children's ages:

Child # 1 *********
Child # 2 **********
Child # 3 *****
Child # 4 ******
Child # 5 ***********
Child # 6 ******
Child # 7 ******
Child # 8 **********




Press any key to continue
```

Figure 11.7. Displaying a text-based graph.

As you can see from Figure 11.7, you do not always need a graphics adapter to produce visual program output.

Changing the *PRINT* Location

QBasic has a way to print text on various parts of the computer screen. The PRINT statement will print your text at the cursor's current position. Using the LOCATE command, you can move the cursor to another place on the screen. By doing so, you can print anything you want anywhere on the screen while in text mode.

The LOCATE command works like the graphics commands in that it requires a column and row position. Unlike the graphics commands, however, LOCATE works on a maximum of 80 columns and 25 rows (the default limits on most PC text screens). The program in Listing 11.12 uses LOCATE to print the word *QBasic* at four different places on the screen.

Note: Without the LOCATE command, all four occurrences of *QBasic* would print one after another.

Listing 11.12. Using LOCATE to print a word at different locations on the screen.

```
' Print QBasic all over the screen

CLS
LOCATE 22, 60
PRINT "QBasic"

LOCATE 2, 5
PRINT "QBasic"

LOCATE 17, 25
PRINT "QBasic"

LOCATE 3, 40
PRINT "QBasic"

END
```

Figure 11.8 shows the various placements of QBasic on the screen.

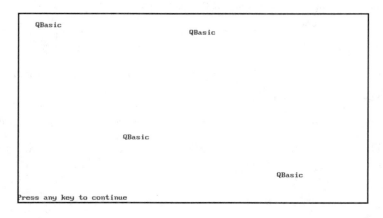

Figure 11.8. Displaying another text-based graph.

Chapter Highlights

As you saw here, QBasic programming is far from boring. By drawing graphics and editing sounds, you can spruce up your programs and really get the user's attention.

✖ The BEEP is one of the easiest ways to get sound on your computer.

✖ The SOUND command is more powerful than BEEP in that it lets you control the duration and the note being sounded.

✖ The duration is measured on a time basis where 18.2 equals one second in real time.

✖ The note played with SOUND is based on hertz (Hz), or the number of cycles per second at which a note vibrates.

✖ The higher the value of hertz is, the higher the note plays. 440 Hz is the A below middle C on a piano's keyboard.

✖ The PLAY command also produces music from within a QBasic program. PLAY does more than SOUND, but requires that you understand musical notation to use it.

✖ It is easy to turn on and off graphics pixels with PSET and PRESET.

✖ The LINE command draws lines and boxes on your graphics screen.

✖ The CIRCLE command draws circles on your graphics screen.

✖ You can produce some text-based graphics without a graphics adapter.

✖ The LOCATE command lets you print messages anywhere on a text screen.

Program Algorithms 12

Perilous Perry stood before the entrance to three caves. He was perplexed. Two of the caves were home to ferocious beasts, but the other one held the treasure. Will Perilous Perry sort out which cave he should enter?

1. What is a counter variable?

2. What is an accumulator variable?

3. How do I swap the values of two variables?

4. What is an ascending sort?

5. What is a descending sort?

6. What is a bubble sort?

7. How do I search for a value in an unsorted list?

8. Can I improve the efficiency of a sequential search?

9. What is meant by the term *binary search*?

10. How can subroutines improve my programming?

This chapter is more theory-oriented than the previous chapters. This chapter presents some programming algorithms that are common across programming languages. An *algorithm* is a common procedure or methodology for performing a certain task. Although this chapter presents the programming examples in QBasic, the concepts you learn here are important no matter which programming language you use.

You will learn how to use your programs to count data values and accumulate totals. The computer is a perfect tool for counting values, such as the number of customers in a day, month, or year, or the number of inventory items in a department's warehouse. Your computer also is capable of lightning-fast accumulations of totals. You can determine the total amount of a weekly payroll or the total amount of your tax liability this year (not that you want to know bad news such as that).

Computers are masterful at sorting and searching for data. When you sort data, you put it in alphabetical or numerical order. There are different methods for doing this, and this chapter presents the most common one. There are also many ways to search a list of data for a specific value. You might give the computer a customer number, have it search a customer list, and then have it return the full name and account balance for that customer. Although computers are fast, it takes time to sift through thousands of data items, especially when searching through disk files (your disk is much slower than memory). Therefore, it behooves you to gain some insight into some efficient means of searching.

The sorting and searching algorithms presented here are varied. They make up a part of every programmer's background and understanding. Rarely will a programmer not need the concepts presented in this chapter. By learning how sorting and searching techniques work, you will have the techniques tucked away in your bag of tricks when the need for them arises. This chapter does not present every concept to you in a program listing. The idea is not to teach you the specific QBasic version, but to give you an idea of how to accomplish the tasks at hand.

Different programming languages have different tools for sorting and searching data. When you master a programming language and are ready to implement one of the algorithms presented in this chapter, you will be able to do so.

Once you master the sorting and searching techniques, this chapter finishes by introducing you to the most important programming tool at your disposal in any programming language: the subroutine.

Counters and Accumulators

When you see a statement such as the following, what do you think?

```
number = number + 1
```

Your first impression might be that the statement is not possible. After all, nothing can be equal to itself plus one. Take a second glance, however, and you will see that in a programming language such as QBasic, the equal sign acts like a left-pointing arrow. The assignment statement, in effect, says "take whatever is on the right side of the equal sign, evaluate it, and put it in the variable to the left of the equal sign." (Most other programming languages also use assignment statements similar to those of QBasic.)

When QBasic reaches the statement just shown, it adds 1 to the variable named number. If number has a 7 to begin with, it now holds an 8. Once it adds the 1 and gets 8, it then stores 8 in number, replacing the 7 that was originally there. The final result is one more than the initial value.

When you see a variable on both sides of an equal sign, and you are adding 1 to the variable, you are *incrementing* that variable. You might wonder how adding 1 to a variable is useful. It turns out to be extremely useful. Many programmers put such an assignment statement inside a loop to count items. Every time the loop repeats, 1 is added to the counter variable, incrementing it. When the loop finishes, the counter variable has the total of the loop.

The program in Listing 12.1 uses such a counter. It is an improved version of a number-guessing game you first saw in Chapter 9. This program gives the user a hint as to whether the guess was too low or too high. The program counts the number of guesses. The Tries variable holds the count.

Listing 12.1. A number-guessing game with a counter variable.

```
' Number-guessing game
CLS

compNum = 47     ' The computer's number

PRINT "I am thinking of a number..."
PRINT "Try to guess it."

Tries = 0

DO
   PRINT
   INPUT "What is your guess (between 1 and 100)"; guess
   IF (guess < compNum) THEN
      PRINT "Your guess was too low, try again."
   ELSEIF (guess > compNum) THEN
      PRINT "Your guess was too high, try again."
   END IF
   Tries = Tries + 1      ' Add one to the counter
LOOP UNTIL (guess = compNum)
PRINT "You got it in only"; Tries; "tries!"
END
```

Clue: In Listing 12.1, the `Tries` variable does not have to be explicitly initialized to zero, because QBasic automatically initializes all variables to zero before you use them. Nevertheless, initializing `Tries` shows your intent of wanting a zero in the variable before using it. Zeroing out variables is a good habit, because not all programming languages zero them for you.

Figure 12.1 shows a sample run of this program. Without the counter, the program cannot tell the user how many guesses are tried.

An accumulator is similar to a counter in that the same variable name appears on both sides of the equal sign. Unlike counter variables, accumulators usually add something other than 1 to the variable. Use accumulators for totaling dollar amounts, people's sales figures, and so forth.

```
I am thinking of a number...
Try to guess it.

What is your guess (between 1 and 100)? 97
Your guess was too high, try again.

What is your guess (between 1 and 100)? 33
Your guess was too low, try again.

What is your guess (between 1 and 100)? 85
Your guess was too high, try again.

What is your guess (between 1 and 100)? 67
Your guess was too high, try again.

What is your guess (between 1 and 100)? 46
Your guess was too low, try again.

What is your guess (between 1 and 100)? 47
You got it in only 6 tries!



Press any key to continue
```

Figure 12.1. *Playing the number-guessing game with a counter.*

In Chapter 10, you saw a teacher's grade-printing program that stored a teacher's input in arrays and then printed a report on the printer that showed each student's name and score. You can use a total to expand on that listing and produce a class average for the bottom of the report.

To compute an average, you must accumulate the test scores, adding one at a time to an *accumulator* (the totaling variable). Because an average is based on the total number entered, you must also count the number of scores entered. Once all the scores are entered, the program must divide the total amount of the scores by the total tests taken. This produces an average. The program in Listing 12.2 shows you how to do this. The counting and accumulating processes shown in this program are used frequently in data processing, no matter what programming language you use.

Listing 12.2. A grade-reporting and averaging program.

```
' Student name and grade listing program
' Print an average at the end of the report
DIM Sname$(30), score(30)    ' Assumes no MORE than 30 students
numStds = 0    ' Initialize counter
Total = 0      ' and accumulator
```

continues

Listing 12.2. continued

```
CLS
DO
   numStds = numStds + 1    ' Increment for number entered
   INPUT "What is the next student's name"; Sname$(numStds)
   INPUT "What is the test score for that student"; score(numStds)
   Total = Total + score(numStds)   ' Must add the latest score
   INPUT "Another student (Y/N)"; ans$
   PRINT                     ' Prints a blank line
LOOP UNTIL (ans$ = "N")

' Now that all the data is entered, print it
LPRINT , "** Grade Listing **"
LPRINT "Name", score              ' Column Heading
FOR i = 1 TO numStds
   LPRINT Sname$(i), score(i)
NEXT i
LPRINT
LPRINT "The average is"; (Total / numStds)
END
```

Here is the output from this program:

```
** Grade Listing **
Name          Score
Tim Jones     98
Jane Wells    45
Heath Majors  100
Chris Reed    78

The average is 80.25
```

Swapping Values

The cornerstone of any sorting algorithm is data swapping. As you sort data, you have to rearrange them, swapping higher values for lower values. As Figure 12.2 shows, swapping values simply means replacing one variable's contents with another's and vice versa.

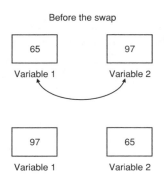

Before the swap

65 | 97

Variable 1   Variable 2

97 | 65

Variable 1   Variable 2

After the swap

Figure 12.2. *Swapping the values of two variables.*

Suppose you assigned two variables named `variable1` and `variable2` with the following statements:

```
variable1 = 65
variable2 = 97
```

The concept of swapping them is simple. How would you do it? If you said the following, you would not be quite correct:

```
variable1 = variable2
variable2 = variable1
```

Can you see why these two assignment statements do not swap the values in the two variables? The first statement assigns `variable2` to `variable1`, which wipes out `variable1`'s original value. The second statement is then redundant, because both variables already hold the same value after the first statement.

Pitfall: QBasic has a `SWAP` command that performs a swap of two variables, but many programming languages do not. If you want to write programs that are easily ported to other languages, you should use the procedure shown here.

311

An accurate approach to swapping variables is to use a third variable, often called a *temporary variable*, because you do not use its value once you swap the original variables. Here is the code to perform the swapping accurately:

```
temp = variable1
variable1 = variable2
variable2 = temp
```

Sorting

The following list of numbers is not sorted:

```
10
54
34
21
23
```

Here is the list sorted in *ascending order* (from lowest to highest):

```
10
21
23
34
54
```

Here is the list sorted in *descending order* (from highest to lowest):

```
54
34
23
21
10
```

You can also sort character string data, such as a list of names. Here is a list of five sorted names (unless otherwise specified, an ascending sort is always used):

```
Adams, Jim
Fowler, Lisa
Kingston, William
Stephenson, Mike
Williams, Pete
```

> **Note:** When sorting a list of string data, your computer uses the ASCII table to compare characters. If a character comes before another in the ASCII table, it is considered to be lower in a sorted list than the other. (Mainframe programs often use the EBCDIC table, an internal table similar to the ASCII table, to perform its sorts.)

There are several ways to sort lists of data. The most popular one for beginning programmers is called the *bubble sort*. The bubble sort is not the most efficient sorting algorithm. As a matter of fact, it is one of the slowest. However, the bubble sort, unlike the other algorithms (such as the heap sort and the quicksort) is easy to understand and to program.

The data that you want to sort is typically stored in an array. Using the array subscripts, you can rearrange the array elements, swapping values, until the array is sorted in the order you want.

In the bubble sort, the elements of an array are compared and swapped two at a time. Your program must perform several passes through the array before the list is sorted. Each pass through the array, the bubble sort places the lowest value in the first element of the array. In effect, the smaller values "bubble" their way up the list, hence the name *bubble sort*.

After the first pass of the bubble sort (controlled by an outer loop in a nested FOR loop, as you will see in the following program), the lowest value of 10 is still at the top of the array (it happened to be there already). In the second pass, the 21 is placed right after the 10, and so on until no more swaps take place. The program in Listing 12.3 shows the bubble sort being used on the five values shown earlier.

Listing 12.3. Sorting a list of values with the bubble sort.

```
' Bubble sorting algorithm
DIM Values(5)

' Fill the array with an unsorted list of numbers
Values(1) = 10
Values(2) = 54
Values(3) = 34
Values(4) = 21
Values(5) = 23

' Sort the array
FOR pass = 1 TO 5          ' Outer loop
   FOR ctr = 1 TO 4        ' Inner loop to form the comparisons each
pass
      IF (Values(ctr) > Values(ctr + 1)) THEN
         t = Values(ctr) ' Swap the pair currently being looked at
         Values(ctr) = Values(ctr + 1)
         Values(ctr + 1) = t
      END IF
   NEXT ctr
NEXT pass

' Print the array to show it is sorted
PRINT "Here is the array after being sorted:"
FOR i = 1 TO 5
   PRINT Values(i)
NEXT i
END
```

Here is the output from the program in Listing 12.3:

```
Here is the array after being sorted:
10
21
23
34
54
```

To give you a better understanding of the bubble sort routine used in this program, Figure 12.3 shows you a flowchart of the bubble sort process. By using the flowchart and by following the program, you should be able to trace through the bubble sort and better understand how it works. At the heart of any sorting algorithm is a swapping routine, and you can see one in the body of the bubble sort's FOR loops.

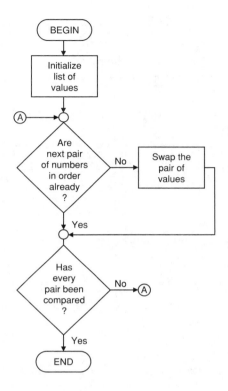

Figure 12.3. *The flowchart of the bubble sort routine.*

Reward: If you want a descending sort, you only have to change one statement in Listing 12.3's program—the first statement inside the FOR loops. Instead of swapping the values if the second item of the pair is lower, swap them if the second item of the pair is higher. The new line looks like this:

```
IF (Values(ctr) < Values(ctr + 1)) THEN
```

If you want to sort names and addresses by ZIP code and store them in several parallel arrays (the names would be in one array, the address lines in another, the cities in another, the state in another, and the ZIP codes in another, each array

315

having the same number of elements), perform the comparison on the ZIP code array. Once you find a pair of ZIP codes that you have to swap, swap them and the corresponding elements in each of the other arrays as well. Figure 12.4 shows you how such parallel arrays might be organized.

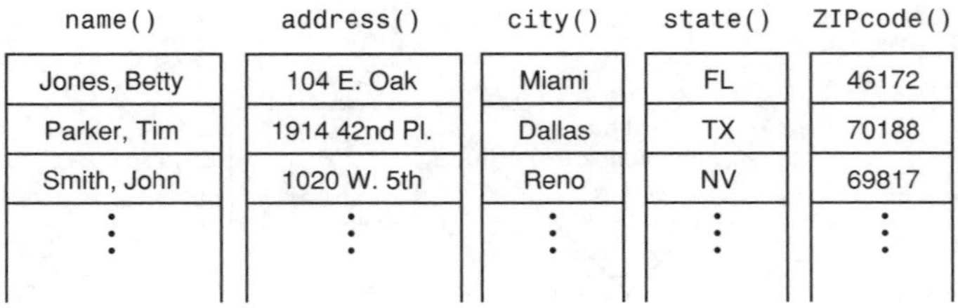

name()	address()	city()	state()	ZIPcode()
Jones, Betty	104 E. Oak	Miami	FL	46172
Parker, Tim	1914 42nd Pl.	Dallas	TX	70188
Smith, John	1020 W. 5th	Reno	NV	69817
⋮	⋮	⋮	⋮	⋮

Figure 12.4. *Parallel arrays for names and addresses.*

Just to show you that a bubble sort works with character string data as easily as with numbers, the program in Listing 12.4 uses the same algorithm as you saw earlier to sort an array of names.

Listing 12.4. Sorting names is as easy as sorting numbers in QBasic.

```
' Bubble sorting algorithm for strings
DIM Names$(5)

' Fill the array with an unsorted list of numbers
Names$(1) = "Breckenridge, Peter"
Names$(2) = "Sands, Tracy"
Names$(3) = "Quincy, Ed"
Names$(4) = "Moore, Diane"
Names$(5) = "Harris, Larry"

' Sort the array
FOR pass = 1 TO 5      ' Outer loop
   FOR ctr = 1 TO 4    ' Inner loop to form the comparisons each pass
      IF (Names$(ctr) > Names$(ctr + 1)) THEN
         t$ = Names$(ctr) ' Swap the pair currently being looked at
         Names$(ctr) = Names$(ctr + 1)
         Names$(ctr + 1) = t$
```

```
      END IF
   NEXT ctr
NEXT pass

' Print the array to show it is sorted
PRINT "Here is the array after being sorted:"
FOR i = 1 TO 5
   PRINT Names$(i)
NEXT i
END
```

The output of Listing 12.4 is as follows:

```
Here is the array after being sorted:
Breckenridge, Peter
Harris, Larry
Moore, Diane
Quincy, Ed
Sands, Tracy
```

Searching Arrays

There are many methods for searching arrays for a specific value. Suppose you have several parallel arrays with inventory data. The first array, `PartNo$()`, holds all your inventory item part numbers. The second array, `Desc$()`, holds the description of each of those parts. The third array, `Price()`, contains the price of each corresponding part. You might keep all the inventory data on the disk and then read that data into the parallel arrays when it is time to work with the data.

One use for an inventory program that uses parallel arrays is a look-up routine. A user could type a part number, and the computer program would search the `PartNo$()` array for a match. When it finds one (for example, at element subscript number 246), you could then print the 246th element in the `Desc$()` and `Price()` arrays, which shows the user the description and price of the part number just entered.

Clue: You often have more disk space than internal memory. Most computers have 30 or more megabytes of disk space and less than 4 megabytes of internal memory. Because your disk drives hold data more often than memory does, you often cannot fit a disk file into memory arrays all at once. (QBasic imposes the additional restriction that no array in your program can take more than 64K of memory.)

Once you begin writing programs with data that needs more memory than your computer has, you will begin using an advanced programming technique (mentioned at the end of Chapter 10, although it is beyond the scope of this book) called *random-access control*. Random-access files enable you to treat your disk file as if it were a huge array. Thus you could rearrange values on the disk as you would in an array. Most programming languages support random-access disk files. You will be ready for them once you become comfortable with the simpler sequential file processing techniques introduced in Chapter 10.

There are several ways to search an array for values. The various searching methods each have their own advantages. One of the easiest to program and understand, the *sequential search*, is also one of the least efficient. The search method you decide on depends on how much data you expect to search through and how skilled you are at understanding and writing advanced searching programs. The next few sections walk you through some introductory searching algorithms that you might use someday in the programs you write.

Warning: Not all of the code examples in the next sections are complete working programs. Often, just the searching algorithm is coded (in QBasic) to give you an idea of how to implement the searching techniques being described.

The Sequential Search

The sequential search technique is easy, but inefficient. With it, you start at the beginning of the array and look at each value, in sequence, until you find a value in the array that matches the value for which you are searching. (You then can use the subscript of the matching element to look in corresponding parallel arrays for related data.)

> **Reward:** The array being searched does not have to be sorted for the sequential search to work. The fact that sequential searches work on unsorted arrays makes them more useful than if they required sorted arrays, because you do not have to take the processing time (or programming time) to sort the array before each search.

Figure 12.5 shows a flowchart of the sequential search routine (as with most flowcharts in this chapter, only the sequential search routine is described, not the now-trivial task of filling the array with data through disk I/O or user input). Study the flowchart and see if you can think of ways to improve the searching technique being used.

The program in Listing 12.5 shows you the sequential search algorithm coded in QBasic. The inventory arrays described earlier are used in the program. The program asks the user for the part number, and then the sequential search routine finds the matching description and price in the other two arrays. After you study the program, you should find that the sequential search is very easy to understand.

Listing 12.5. Using a sequential search in an inventory application.

```
' Sequential search for an item's description and price.
' (This assumes the arrays have been filled elsewhere.)
'
' This code would be part of a larger inventory program.

' ** This program assumes that the variable named TotalNumber
'     contains the total number of items in the inventory,
'     and therefore, in the arrays as well.
```

continues

Listing 12.5. continued

```
CLS
' First, get the part number the user wants to look up
INPUT "What is the number of the part you want to see"; searchPart$

FOR i = 1 TO TotalNumber       ' Look through all inventory items
   IF (PartNo$(i) = searchPart$) THEN
      PRINT "Part Number "; searchPart$; "'s description is"
      PRINT Desc$(i)
      PRINT USING "With a price of ####,.##"; Price(i)
      END     ' Quit the program early once it is found
   END IF
NEXT i        ' Get the next item since it did not match

' If the program flow gets here (and did not END in the loop),
' the searched part number must not be in the inventory arrays.
BEEP    ' Sound an error beep
PRINT
PRINT "** Sorry, but that part number is not in the inventory."
END
```

Improving the Sequential Search

There is one way to improve upon the sequential search. If you are searching an array that is already sorted, you do not always have to search the entire array if the element does not exist (as has to be done with unsorted arrays). If the array you are searching is already sorted, you will know that the search data is not in the array if you find an item that is *higher* (in sorted order) than the one for which you are looking.

For example, consider the following list of part numbers (notice that the list is sorted in ascending order):

```
32345
43495
67545
68878
88983
99000
```

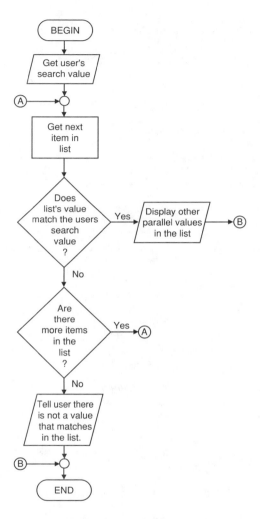

Figure 12.5. *Flowcharting the sequential search technique.*

If you are looking for part number 67994, you do not have to search all six values. As soon as the search takes you to 68878, you know that 67994 is not in the list. Therefore, a simple additional check to the sequential search routine shown earlier implements this change, as Listing 12.6 shows. Remember that this revised sequential search is only advantageous when the item you are looking for is not in the list. If the item you are searching for is in the list, the program in Listing 12.6 is no more efficient than the last. (In reality, Listing 12.6's program is slightly *less* efficient if the search value is found due to the extra checking involved inside the loop. However, the extra time needed for the check is minimal.)

Listing 12.6. Improving the sequential search.

```
' Improved sequential search for an item's description and price.
' (This assumes the arrays have been filled
'   and SORTED in PartNum$ order elsewhere.)
'
' This code would be part of a larger inventory program.

' ** This program assumes that the variable named TotalNumber
'     contains the total number of items in the inventory,
'     and therefore, in the arrays as well.

CLS
' First, get the part number the user wants to look up
INPUT "What is the number of the part you want to see"; searchPart$

FOR i = 1 TO TotalNumber      ' Look through all inventory items
    IF (PartNo$(i) = searchPart$) THEN
       PRINT "Part Number "; searchPart$; "'s description is"
       PRINT Desc$(i)
       PRINT USING "With a price of ####,.##"; Price(i)
       END       ' Quit the program early once it is found
    ELSEIF (PartNo$(i) > searchPart$) THEN      ' Gone too far
       BEEP    ' Sound an error beep
       PRINT
       PRINT "** Sorry, but that part number is not in the inventory."
       END     ' Quit the program
    END IF
NEXT i      ' Get the next item since it did not match or fail

' The searched part was neither found, nor bypassed, if the code
' gets to this point (one of the two END statements above would
' have been triggered otherwise).  Therefore, the last item in
' the array is not larger than the searched value, and the searched
' value was never found.  The "not found" message must be repeated
here.
BEEP    ' Sound an error beep
PRINT
PRINT "** Sorry, but that part number is not in the inventory."
END
```

The biggest drawback to this "improved" sequential search method is that you must sort the array before it works. If you do not sort the array, you must search the entire list. When the list is thousands of elements long, efficiency can be critical. However, the time it takes to sort the list before each search negates the advantage. Figure 12.6 shows you a flowchart of the improved sequential search technique.

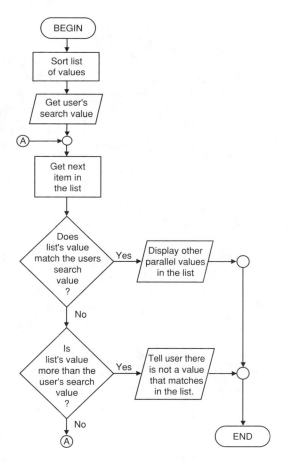

Figure 12.6. *Flowcharting the improved sequential search.*

The improved sequential search is useful for data that you must sort for reasons other than the search itself. For instance, if you are keeping a name and address list in your computer and want to take advantage of bulk mailings, you always want to sort your data in ZIP code order. Because you must sort the data every time you add a new name and address, you might as well use the improved sequential search techniques shown in this section. Sorting just for the sake of searching, however, is not worth the improved search time.

Pitfall: A comparison of Listings 12.6 and 12.5 will show that using improved searching techniques made your programming task more difficult. More work is usually required on your part every time you improve upon an algorithm. If your program will be used a lot, especially for searching large arrays, the runtime efficiencies will more than make up for the extra up-front programming work.

The Binary Search

If your array is already sorted, there is another technique that offers tremendous searching speed advantages over either of the sequential searches shown in the previous sections. This technique is known as the *binary search*. The binary search is more complex to understand and program than the sequential search, but, as with most things in the programming world, it is worth the effort in many cases.

The binary search technique uses a *divide and conquer* approach to searching. One of the primary advantages of the binary search is that with every comparison you make, you can rule out one-half of the remaining array if a match is not found. In other words, if you are searching for a value in a 100-element array, and the first comparison you make fails to match, you only have at most 50 elements left to search (with the sequential search, you would still have a possible 99 elements left to search). On the second search, assuming there is no match, you rule out one-half of the remaining list, meaning that there are only 25 more items to search through.

The multiplicative advantages of a binary search will surprise you. If you have a friend write down a number from 1 to 1,000 and then use the binary search technique to make your guesses (your friend will only have to tell you if you are "too low" or "too high" with each guess), you can often zero-in on the number in 5 to 15 tries. This is an amazing feat when there is a pool of 1,000 numbers to choose from!

The binary search technique is simple. Your first guess (or the computer's first try at matching a search value to one in the list) should be exactly in the middle of the sorted list. If you guess incorrectly, you only need to know if you were too high or low. If you were too high, your next guess should split the *lower* half of the list. If you were too low, you should split the *higher* half of the list. Your new list (one-half the size of the original one) is now the list you split in the middle. Repeat the process until you guess the value.

Suppose your friend thinks of the number 390. Your first guess would be 500 (half of 1,000). When your friend says "too high," you would immediately know that your next guess should be between 1 and 499. Splitting that range takes you to your second guess of 250. "Too low," replies your friend, so you know the number is between 250 and 499. Splitting that gives you 375. "Too low" means the number is between 375 and 499. Your next guess might be 430, then 400, then 390 and you've guessed it. One out of 1,000 numbers, and it only took six guesses.

Listing 12.7 uses the binary search technique to find the correct inventory value. As you can see from the code, a binary search technique does not require a very long program. However, when you first learn the binary search, it takes some getting used to. Therefore, the flowchart in Figure 12.7 will help you understand the binary search technique a little better.

Listing 12.7. Using a binary search.

```
' Binary search for an item's description and price.
' (This assumes the arrays have been filled
'  and SORTED in PartNum$ order elsewhere.)
'
' This code would be part of a larger inventory program.
```

continues

Listing 12.7. continued

```
' ** This program assumes that the variable named TotalNumber
'    contains the total number of items in the inventory,
'    and therefore, in the arrays as well.
CLS
' First, get the part number the user wants to look up
INPUT "What is the number of the part you want to see"; searchPart$

first = 1     ' Must begin the lower-bound of the search at 1
last = TotalNumber    ' The upper-bound of the search

DO
    mid = (first + last) \ 2   ' Note the backslash for integer division
    IF (searchPart$ = PartNo$(mid)) THEN
        PRINT "Part number "; searchPart$; "'s description is"
        PRINT Desc$(mid)
        PRINT USING "With a price of ####,.##"; Price(mid)
        END
    ELSEIF (searchPart$ < PartNo$(mid)) THEN      ' Must half array
        last = mid - 1
    ELSE
        first = mid + 1
    END IF
LOOP WHILE (first <= last)

' The searched part was not found if the code gets here (the END
' statement above would have been triggered otherwise).
BEEP    ' Sound an error beep
PRINT
PRINT "** Sorry, but that part number is not in the inventory."
END
```

Warning: Remember that a binary search always requires that you sort the array before you begin the search. Without sorting the array, the binary search technique will fail.

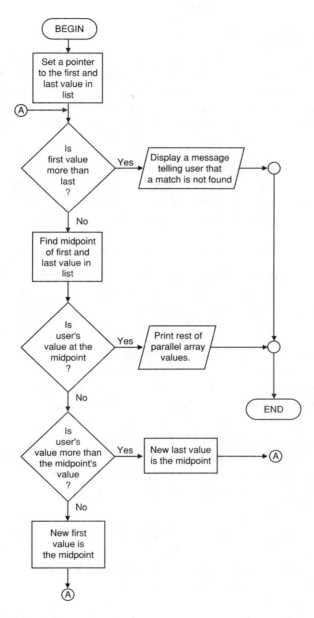

Figure 12.7. *Flowcharting the binary search.*

Subroutines

No text on programming languages would be complete without talking a little about *subroutines*. A subroutine is a set of code inside a program that you execute from another part of a program. A subroutine is like a detour; it is a side trip your program makes for a few statements, and then it gets back on the path it was executing and continues from there.

Subroutines are not difficult to understand. The algorithms presented in this chapter make perfect candidates for subroutines. A subroutine turns your program into a collection of modules that you can integrate together. Instead of one long program, your program becomes lots of little sets (subroutines) of code.

Reward: Subroutines offer tremendous flexibility for writing programs. Once you write several subroutines, you might want to use them in other programs. Over time, the more programming you do, the more your programs become collections of subroutines that you have written before.

Televisions are not repaired today like they were in the old days. In the early days of television, repairing the TV would involve hunting down the offending tube or part, yanking it out of the TV, and replacing that part with another. Today's solid-state television problems are not traced so easily; it would be too costly and time-consuming to hunt down the offending transistor or computer chip and replace it. Therefore, TVs are built in modules—boxes containing different parts of the TV. When the TV has a problem, the module that contains the problem is pulled and a new one is put in its place. The subroutine concept saves a lot of time when repairing TVs.

When you build your collection of subroutines, you won't have to write as much code over the long run. You can pull your module from the disk and place it in your program, producing your final program much more quickly than if you had to "reinvent the wheel" by rewriting the same code over and over.

To call subroutines from QBasic, use the GOSUB statement. Use RETURN to end the subroutine. (There is a collection of more powerful subroutine statements named CALL and SUB, but they are beyond the scope of this book and are more difficult for beginners to master than GOSUB and RETURN.) Other programming languages use similar statements to GOSUB and RETURN.

The Need for Subroutines

Suppose you're writing a program that prints your name and address on the printer several times. Without having subroutines, you would write a program similar to the outline shown in Listing 12.8. The program repeats the same printing code, over and over.

Listing 12.8. A program outline that does not use subroutines.

```
' Long program that prints name and address throughout
' (The rest of the code is not shown.)
'
'    :
'  Program statements go here
'    :
LPRINT "Sally Delaney"
LPRINT "304 West Sycamore"
LPRINT "St. Louis, MO  63443"
'    :
'  More program statements go here
'    :
LPRINT "Sally Delaney"
LPRINT "304 West Sycamore"
LPRINT "St. Louis, MO  63443"
'    :
'  More program statements go here
'    :
LPRINT "Sally Delaney"
LPRINT "304 West Sycamore"
LPRINT "St. Louis, MO  63443"
'    :
'  More program statements go here
'    :
```

continues

Listing 12.8. continued

```
LPRINT "Sally Delaney"
LPRINT "304 West Sycamore"
LPRINT "St. Louis, MO  63443"
'    :
'  More program statements go here
'    :
LPRINT "Sally Delaney"
LPRINT "304 West Sycamore"
LPRINT "St. Louis, MO  63443"
'    :
'  Rest of program finishes up here
'    :
```

Pitfall: Not only is repeating the same code tedious, but by requiring more typing, it lends itself to errors. If you only have to type in the code once, but can still execute that code repeatedly whenever you want (as in a subroutine), your chances of typing errors decrease. Also, if your address ever changes, you only have to change it in one place (inside the subroutine), not everywhere it appears in the program.

If you could put the LPRINT statements in a subroutine, you could save yourself some typing. When you're ready to execute the subroutine, issue a GOSUB (for *go subroutine*) statement that tells QBasic exactly which subroutine to execute. You have to label the subroutine and put that label in the GOSUB statement because you can have more than one subroutine in any program. QBasic has to know which one you want to execute.

Listing 12.9 is an improved version of the previous program outline. Notice that the subroutine's name and address printing code is preceded by a statement that begins PrNmAddr:. This strange-looking message is not a QBasic command, but simply a label that you make up that names the subroutine's location.

> **Note:** The colon is required at the end of all label names in the code.
> When you use a label in a GOSUB, however, you do not type the colon.

Listing 12.9. A program outline that does not use subroutines.

```
' Long program that prints name and address throughout
' (The rest of the code is not shown.)
'
'    :
'  Program statements go here
'    :
GOSUB PrNmAddr           ' Executes the subroutine
'    :
'  More program statements go here
'    :
GOSUB PrNmAddr           ' Executes the subroutine
'    :
'  More program statements go here
'    :
GOSUB PrNmAddr           ' Executes the subroutine
'    :
'  More program statements go here
'    :
GOSUB PrNmAddr           ' Executes the subroutine
'    :
'  More program statements go here
'    :
END             ' Required so subroutine doesn't execute on its
                ' own by the program falling through to it

PrNmAddr:
  LPRINT "Sally Delaney"
  LPRINT "304 West Sycamore"
  LPRINT "St. Louis, MO  63443"
  RETURN
```

Clue: The END is put before the subroutine so the program does not continue through to the subroutine and attempt to execute it one last time before quitting.

At the end of the subroutine is the RETURN statement. RETURN informs QBasic that you want the program's code that called the subroutine to continue from where it left off. GOSUB does not create spaghetti code like a branching statement such as GOTO. GOSUB ensures that execution always returns to the original GOSUB statement that called the subroutine. Execution then proceeds with the original sequence.

You may not see a tremendous advantage in using subroutines when the subroutine is only three lines long, as in this example. However, you can place the searching and sorting algorithms in subroutines and then call them via GOSUB whenever the rest of the program needs to search or sort data. Duplicating 10 or 20 (or more) lines of code every time you want to execute one of the sorting or searching routines takes a lot of programming time away from you. The computer should be your slave; you should not be a slave to it. Subroutines will make your programs more manageable and will ultimately help you write better programs faster.

Reward: By using subroutines instead of duplicating the same lines of code throughout a program, you also save disk space.

Even if you don't have to execute the same routine more than once, grouping a routine into a subroutine makes a lot of sense: it helps organize your program. Listing 12.10 shows a complete program with three subroutines. The subroutines perform the following tasks:

1. Ask the user for a list of numbers.

2. Sort the numbers.

3. Print the numbers.

As you can see, the first part of the program is nothing more than a calling procedure that controls the execution of the subroutine. By breaking your program into modules such as this program does, you can help zero in on code later if you want to change something. If you want to change to a different sorting method, you can quickly find the sorting routine without having to trace through a bunch of unrelated code.

Listing 12.10. A program that uses subroutines for everything.

```
' Program with subroutines
CLS

DIM Values(10)

GOSUB AskForData     ' Get user's list of numbers
GOSUB SortData       ' Sort the numbers
GOSUB PrintData      ' Print the numbers

END

AskForData:          ' Gets 10 values from the user
   PRINT "** Number Sorting Program **"
   FOR i = 1 TO 10
      INPUT "What is a number for the list"; Values(i)
   NEXT i
   RETURN

SortData:            ' Sorts the 10 values
   FOR pass = 1 TO 10
      FOR ctr = 1 TO 9
         IF (Values(ctr) > Values(ctr + 1)) THEN
            t = Values(ctr)
            Values(ctr) = Values(ctr + 1)
            Values(ctr + 1) = t
         END IF
      NEXT ctr
   NEXT pass
   RETURN

PrintData:
   PRINT
   PRINT "After the sort:"
   FOR i = 1 TO 10
```

continues

Listing 12.10. continued

```
      PRINT Values(i); " ";     ' Print list with a space between the
                                ' numbers
    NEXT i
    RETURN
END
```

Clue: By indenting the lines of a subroutine to the right by two or three spaces, you help set apart the subroutine from the rest of the program.

Figure 12.8 shows you the result of this program. Of course, the user has no idea that this program is much better organized than one that does not use subroutines. However, if someone ever has to change this program, that person will be glad that subroutines were used to help group like-code into modules.

```
** Number Sorting Program **
What is a number for the list? 6
What is a number for the list? 3
What is a number for the list? 4
What is a number for the list? 8
What is a number for the list? 7
What is a number for the list? 1
What is a number for the list? 2
What is a number for the list? 9
What is a number for the list? 5
What is a number for the list? 3

After the sort:
  1   2   3   3   4   5   6   7   8   9




Press any key to continue
```

Figure 12.8. *Entering, sorting, and printing with subroutines.*

Chapter Highlights

The techniques you learned in this chapter will be useful throughout your entire programming career. Sorting, searching, and subroutines are needed for useful data processing. The computer, thanks to your programs, can do these mundane tasks while you concentrate on more important things.

✖ Whenever a variable appears on both sides of the equal sign of an assignment statement, it is usually a counter or an accumulator.

✖ A counter variable increments by one each time it is updated.

✖ An accumulator is often called a total variable.

✖ An accumulator variable increments by one or more, in effect keeping a running total of numeric amounts.

✖ By combining a counter and a total variable, you can compute an average of a list of values.

✖ To swap the values of two variables, you need a third variable to hold a temporary value.

✖ Sorting arranges data into an ordered list.

✖ An ascending sort puts values in order from lowest to highest.

✖ A descending sort puts values in order from highest to lowest.

✖ The easiest sorting routine to write is the bubble sort, although it is not the most efficient.

✖ In a bubble sort, the low values rise to the top of the array each time through the sorting loop.

✖ There are many ways to search for values in a list. The most straightforward method is a sequential search.

✖ By sorting the values before performing a sequential search, you can improve the efficiency of the search.

✖ A binary search is one of the fastest methods for finding a value in a list.

✖ By using subroutines, you improve your programming accuracy and maintenance.

How Companies Program

Perilous Perry stood high above Programmer's Ravine, clinging to the rope bridge. Our hero wondered if he was ready for big-time adventuring. Will Perilous Perry "learn the ropes" and make it across?

1. What are company computer departments called?

2. Who pays for a computer department's expenses?

3. Which programming degree is best: a two-year or a four-year degree?

4. Is an additional degree in another field beneficial?

5. Can I get computer experience without a degree or training?

6. Why doesn't a Programmer write programs?

7. What does a Programmer Analyst do?

8. What does a Systems Analyst do?

9. What is a standards manual used for?

10. What is a structured walkthrough?

11. What happens when a program is moved into production?

This chapter attempts to give you an idea of how companies program computers. The focus is on the larger companies with big data processing staffs working on one or more mainframes, minicomputers, and microcomputers. You will also learn about the smaller companies and how they deal with programming staffs and other types of computer personnel.

Companies must coordinate their programming efforts to make the best use of the company's resources. This does not always mean that every program wanted by every person gets written. Actually, the allocation of programming talents is one of the data processing manager's primary tasks.

This chapter describes the different types of available jobs and their titles, and how those people interface with one another. This chapter helps you better understand the wording of the want ads for computer professionals, and you will get an idea of the experience needed to obtain the different jobs in the computer industry.

This chapter is useful to you even if you want to work for a smaller company or start your own. The larger companies have honed the usage of data processing within the corporate umbrella, so seeing how larger companies take care of their programming requests will help you make decisions regarding the computer department you end up in.

Data Processing and Other Departments

A company's data processing department often goes by several names. It is known as *DP*, *Information Services*, *Information Systems*, *IS*, *MIS* (but usually not, strangely enough, by that acronym's meaning: *Management Information Systems*), and *Data Processing*. Whatever the company's people call the computer department, it is commonly in the center of almost every major new project the company takes on. When a company expansion is about to take place, the data processing department must prepare for the additional computing resources needed. When an engineering project begins, data processing supplies the analysis programs for the engineers (although some engineering departments prefer to write their own programs and keep the central DP department in charge of the business side of the company). Whatever new direction a company takes, its data processing staff is usually involved in some way.

As Figure 13.1 shows, the data processing department writes programs for every other department in the company. Unless the company itself is a software-writing company (such as Borland or Microsoft), the company's main focus is not going to be software development. The company has other objectives, but the computer department supplies the computer systems needed to keep the other departments working as effectively as they can.

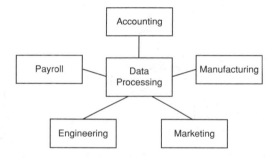

Figure 13.1. The data processing department writes programs for the rest of the company.

Such a corporate setup is natural. In the early years of business computing, the computer department was placed in the accounting department and governed by the accounting staff. The problem with putting the computer department under direct control of accounting is that accounting will tend to write computer systems they need and the engineering, marketing, and upper management's departments might take a back seat. This does not mean that the accounting department would selfishly hoard the computer resources, but the accounting bias would be natural because part of the accounting department's own budget was set aside for the computer and its people.

It was realized in the late 1960s that the data processing department was not directly tied to any one department such as accounting, but instead, computer people worked for the entire company. Therefore, stand-alone computer departments started appearing on the company's organizational charts. Organizations began viewing their computer departments as individual cost centers that required their own budget and autonomy. Figure 13.2 shows how the typical data processing department fits into today's organizational charts. As you can see, the data processing department is located on the same level as accounting, payroll, engineering, and the rest of the departments.

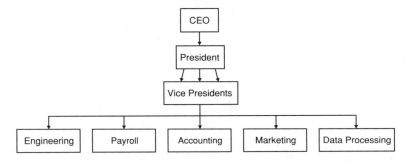

Figure 13.2. *The data processing department is evenly ranked with the other company's departments.*

Despite the fact that the data processing department is now autonomous in most companies, that autonomy still does not ensure proper allocation of computer resources. A data processing department's resources consist of the hardware, peripheral material such as paper and tapes, and people. The people are the most expensive resource in a data processing department. Their office space, desks, supplies, personal computer equipment, benefits, and payroll costs all add up to a tidy sum.

Pitfall: No matter how much money a company makes, it cannot allow unlimited spending for the computer resources just described. There must be some check on the money spent in data processing. Unlike other departments, whose worth is measured in dollars received by outside customers, the company itself is the only customer of its data processing department. (Many of the accounting-related departments often have a similar support role in a company.)

Paying for the Data Processing Department

There are two approaches for budgeting data processing costs. They are *overhead* and *chargeback*. Overhead is the typical way in which other internal support departments are paid. The sales department's cost is paid for by goods sold (the commissions are commensurate with the sales). The engineering department's costs are paid for by breakthroughs made and eventually sold to the public. Unlike engineering and sales, the data processing department fits an internal niche, somewhat like the payroll department, in that it does nothing to generate outside revenue (unless, as mentioned earlier, the company is a computer software company).

Most internal support departments are paid for with overhead funds. That is, each department's budget includes a little extra for overhead expenses (lights, desks, paper, copying, secretarial, and data processing usage). By collecting some of each department's overhead budget, the company can pay for the data processing resources.

This overhead method of paying for data processing costs does not always work well. Overhead is fine for departments such as the general ledger department, but the data processing department's skills are more in demand by other departments. Without checks and balances of some kind, all of the other departments will want programs written with little regard to cost (after all, they've already paid their share of the overhead expense). The computer department can't hire an unlimited supply of programmers just because it gets endless requests for programs.

343

Note: There is not enough incentive with the overhead method to curb unreasonable data processing requests. Under this method, departments from all over the company will constantly hound the computer programmers for more programs.

Companies have been turning away from the overhead approach to another approach called *chargeback*. With chargeback, the data processing center is given no funds from the overhead account (which immediately lowers the overhead expenses for all the other departments). When a department needs a program written, that department requests the program from data processing. The data processing personnel estimate the cost of writing the program and send that estimate back to the original department.

It is then up to the requesting department to accept or reject the charge for the programming. If the department wants the program badly enough, and it has the excess funds in its budget, that department's management can then transfer those funds to the data processing department's budget. DP then begins to work on the program.

One of the biggest advantages of the chargeback method is that a department cannot ask for the world unless they are willing to pay for it. Their own limited resources keep them from requesting more than they really need.

Clue: The money being transferred is really *funny money*. It is made up of internal funds that already belong to the company being passed from department to department. The company is still out the cost of the computing resources, but when it comes directly from the requesting department's budget, that department puts its own check and balance system in place to determine if its data processing requests are reasonable.

The nice thing about chargeback is that the data processing department works like a miniature company within the company, supplying services as long as those services are paid for. The company does not have to worry about skyrocketing data processing costs; after all, if the money is already in a department's budget and that department wants to spend it on data processing, there is nothing wrong with that. The department will not have those funds to spend on other things, and departments have the right to determine how they spend their own budgets.

Reward: At the end of the year, the data processing department often finds that it has made a profit from the other departments. Because the profit is really internal funds, that profit is often distributed *back* to the departments that paid for data processing services at the end of the year. The portion of the refund each department gets is proportional to the amount of data processing dollars that department spent during the year. In this way, the departments know they are spending only as much money as the DP services cost; if they went outside the company for the same services, they would surely pay more because outside DP services would have to make a profit. The profit made by the internal DP department is redistributed back to the company.

Often, the data processing department hires *contract programmers* when the company's requests increase. If the DP department predicts that its workload will increase for a while, such as when another company is bought by the parent company, the data processing department hires contract programmers. A contract programmer is hired to program for a fixed time period. Whether the time is six months, a year, or longer is negotiable.

Generally, contract programmers are paid a large salary because the company does not have to pay for the contract programmer's benefits and retirement. There are software companies that hire programmers full-time, giving them benefits and insurance, and then those companies do nothing but hire out their programmers to other companies who need contract programming. Do not rule out an opportunity for contract programming if you are looking for a job. The pay is good, the experience is better, and often a company eventually hires the contract programmers it uses if they turn out to be productive workers.

Computer Jobs

Several times a year, leading magazines and newspapers list the job outlook for the coming year, five years, and ten years. For the last decade, computer jobs have been high on the lists for the best job environments, pay, long-term stability, and so forth. That trend will continue for many years. Despite advancements, computer technology is still in its infancy. There are a lot more programs to write than those that have been written in the past.

Companies sometimes allow data processing managers and personnel to work in more relaxed conditions than other departments. Whereas a company's accounting department reports in at 8:00 a.m., clocks out for exactly 60 minutes for lunch, and leaves at 5:00 p.m. on the dot, its DP staff may not arrive and leave at a uniform time.

The reason working conditions can be more relaxed is that programmers, analysts, and computer technicians often need to pursue a problem or programming task until its conclusion, even if that means staying awake in the computer room for 52 hours straight. Programmers love to burn the midnight oil. As Chapter 3 pointed out, programming is not a science yet, and it might never be one. A large part of programming reflects a person's style and involves a personal commitment to a project. There is a creative side to programming that programmers often find addictive. A programmer who drags in at 11:00 a.m. might be doing so because he or she stayed up until 4:30 a.m. trying to debug some code for the company.

DP managers understand that the creative spirit that programming brings often comes in spurts. When a programmer gets involved on a programming project, that programmer spends more voluntary overtime than any other type of worker would consider. The trade-off seems to be worth the relaxed attitude in many programming organizations.

Reward: Another primary advantage of the programming field over many others is its equal opportunity. Because the business computer industry didn't really begin until the mid-1960s—when the idea of equal pay for equal work was coming into acceptance—equal opportunity was already a part of the computer industry. There are many female and minority employees in data processing departments, from the lowest-paid job to the highest, and the norm has always been for their job and pay to be equal to that of others among them.

Job Titles

You should understand the kinds of jobs that are out there for programmers. Then when you look in the help-wanted ads of the newspapers, you'll have an idea of the qualifications and experience needed for the different jobs being advertised.

Warning: The titles described in this section are fairly common in the computer industry, but they are not necessarily universal. Whereas the title for a job in one company might be *Programmer Analyst*, another company might give the same duties a title of *Senior Programmer*. The specific titles mentioned here, although open to change and interpretation, are common enough to describe most of the responsibilities and titles in most computer departments.

Most computer jobs require some kind of college degree (except for the first one, Data Entry Clerk, described in the next section). There is debate as to whether a two-year associate degree or a four-year bachelor's degree is best. The four-year degree is always better in one respect: you are more founded in the theory behind how computers work and will be able to learn new computer skills faster because of it. However, a four-year degree keeps you out of the work force two years longer than a two-year degree, and two years is a long time in the rapidly changing field of computers.

A two-year programming degree simply does not give you enough time to learn much about foundational computing theory. In two years, a college will teach you as many hands-on skills as possible. You'll pick up one or two programming languages (as opposed to four or more in a four-year curriculum). Furthermore, you'll find that you can enter the programming marketplace at the same job rank and get paid just as much as someone with a four-year degree. The drawback to a two-year degree is that you will not progress through the ranks as fast as someone with a four-year degree.

Perhaps the best of both worlds is possible. You can get a two-year degree, go to work for a company in an entry-level programming job, and get the last two years part-time to finish a four-year degree (most four-year colleges give credit for classes taken for a two-year degree with only a few exceptions here and there). Often a company will pay for, or at least supplement, its employees' continuing education.

> **Reward:** If you have time and money to spare (and who doesn't? Seriously, there are always scholarships, grants, and loans), consider getting a second degree, either an additional two-year degree or a master's in a field other than programming. A second degree will augment your programming skills. In addition to understanding programming, you will be able to apply those programming skills more readily to an area such as accounting or engineering.

Data Entry

There are some computer jobs that do not require any programming skills. On the low end of the computer ranks fall the *Data Entry Clerks* (often called *Data Entry Operators*). Data Entry Clerks typically need only a high school diploma or its equivalent and some keyboarding skills. Data Entry Clerks, except for the ones who have been with a company for a long time and have often received pay raises, make the lowest salaries of any of the computer jobs in the company.

The life of a Data Entry Clerk is simple; he or she sits in front of a computer screen typing data into the computer. Typically, as Figure 13.3 shows, all the Data Entry Clerks type on terminals (keyboard and screen combinations) attached to a central computer, usually a mainframe. Eight hours a day, five days a week, the data entry department enters data.

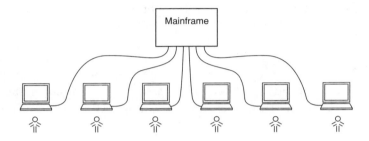

Figure 13.3. Data Entry Clerks normally enter data into the same computer.

A company's data-entry requirements are massive. Payroll figures, sales figures, government figures, competing statistics, market trends, industry trends, projections, and so forth all must be factored into the company's working atmosphere. The computer programs that process that large amount of data need it entered somehow. The larger the organization, the larger the data needs; some companies have hundreds of full-time Data Entry Clerks. Someone has to enter the data, and it is the job of the Data Entry Clerk to do so.

At first glance, you may want to stay away from such a job. The data-entry position, however, can be a powerful first step into a computing career for some people. People with little or no computer training who need experience can begin as a Data Entry Operator. While with the company, they can show a positive attitude, meet others within the company, and receive the typical company insurance and benefits. If the clerk pursues the proper training, the clerk can move into higher programming positions.

> **Reward:** As mentioned earlier, a company will often pay for some or all of an employee's part-time education. Therefore, Data Entry Clerks, with no programming background at all, can take night classes to begin training in programming skills. Once they finish a degree, or are trained adequately enough, the company can move them into one of the entry-level programming jobs. Such a person might never have been able to get a programming job if he or she had not started out in data entry.

There is nothing at all wrong with keeping a data-entry job for many years. Some people enjoy it and make a long-term career out of it. Although the money may not start out being great, over the years the annual raises can turn the job into a comfortable profession.

Programming

A person with knowledge of programming, either a self-taught programmer who has a degree in another area, or a person who received programming training in a two-year or four-year institution, will bypass the data-entry job and move straight into a job related to actually programming. The first job title given to a new programmer hired fresh out of college (or one with little professional programming experience) is usually *Assistant Programmer* (also known as *Junior Programmer* or *Programmer I*). Assistant Programmer is generally considered the entry-level job for anyone without experience as a programmer in another company.

A person typically does not remain as an Assistant Programmer for more than six or eight months. The job is really a trial period so the company can determine the employee's work attitude, skills, and general benefit to the company. An Assistant Programmer does no new programming. Instead, the Assistant Programmer works on programs others have written, often doing routine program maintenance.

Clue: During the trial period, an Assistant Programmer learns how the company operates, gets acquainted with the other computer personnel, and generally "learns the ropes" of the company's working environment.

Once a person stays in the Assistant Programmer role for a while, he or she is usually promoted to *Programmer*, along with a small raise and a pat on the back. The Programmer title means that the company expects good things in the coming years and has trust in the person. It is rare for a person to hold an Assistant Programmer title for several years and still be with the same company.

The Programmer earns a respectable salary for someone with little experience. As mentioned earlier, the computer field pays well, and its titles tend to command higher pay when ranked with similar experience titles in other departments. Therefore, if a person graduates with a programming degree at the same time as someone with a different type of degree, and they both go to work for the same company, the programmer usually has a higher salary after the first year. Of course, this depends on many factors and does not always hold, but on the average it does.

The Programmer does little more than the Assistant Programmer. The title of Programmer is a little misleading. The Programmer's primary job is to work on programs written by others, maintaining them and modifying them when the need arises. The Programmer rarely gets to write a program from scratch for the first year or two.

After a year or two of success, the Programmer's supervisor will begin to have the Programmer write programs from scratch. Of course, the specifications of the program (the flowchart, output definition, and possibly pseudocode) will already be done and the programmer only has to implement those specifications into a new program. After a while, the Programmer's attitude and on-the-job learning can justify moving into a more advanced job, with the title *Senior Programmer* (sometimes called a *Programmer Analyst*).

The Senior Programmer is primarily responsible for writing new programs after being given specifications to follow. The Senior Programmer does not have to worry much about maintaining older code because the new Assistant Programmers and Programmers take care of that. (There is nothing wrong or unfair about maintaining programs, but when you train for writing programs, you cannot wait to get your hands on new programming projects.)

The Senior Programmer title usually commands a pay raise (over the normal annual cost-of-living raise) and maybe an office of his or her own instead of sharing an office with another Assistant Programmer or Programmer. A person is a Senior Programmer for a few years, writing code and getting to know the workings of the company, its users' needs, and the base of programs already in existence.

After a few years of success (the time is based on an individual's abilities, but two to three years is typical), the company will probably give that programmer the next higher programming title (along with a raise): *Programmer Analyst.*

A Programmer Analyst begins to work more closely on the front-end of programming: the program design. Chapter 4, "Designing the Program," explained a lot about the analysis and design steps that must take place before you can write a program. Although Programmer Analysts do not do a lot of design work, they work closely with those who do. By working with designers (whose jobs are described in the next section), supervisors can learn just how apt that Programmer Analyst will be at program design. The Programmer Analyst does more programming than analyzing, but he or she does receive on-the-job training for the next step up the organizational ladder.

Clue: Before a Programmer Analyst moves to the next level, the company may opt to promote the Programmer Analyst to a Senior Programmer Analyst. This title is common in organizations that have large DP staffs and that may not yet have an open position higher up the DP organization chart, but that want to reward a Programmer Analyst for a job well done. The promotion brings a raise with it.

The Analysis and Design Staff

Once you make it to the next level of job, *Systems Analyst*, you know you've made the big time. You'll probably never have to write another program again; instead, you'll analyze and design programs that others will write.

Clue: Isn't it strange that you train for a long time to be a computer programmer and work hard at programming for several years, just so you don't have to program anymore? Actually, the programming experience is a must for the high-level Systems Analyst. Without the understanding that programming brings, one cannot design systems for others to program.

The Systems Analyst is the liaison between the users and the other departments who need data processing work performed. As Figure 13.4 shows, the Systems Analyst talks to both the users and the programming staff. The users do not understand computer requirements; they only know what they want (or what they think they want). The users must work with the Systems Analyst to design the needed computer system. The Systems Analyst has worked in the company for many years. The Systems Analyst understands the needs of the programmers and the needs of the users in the company. The programmers might appear too technically oriented to the users; sometimes the users themselves do not even know what they want. The Systems Analyst must be able to produce the output definition and logic design through numerous conversations with the users.

Figure 13.4. The Systems Analyst is the go-between for the users and the programmers.

353

The job of the Systems Analyst is one of the most respected jobs in the computer industry. The Systems Analyst is paid a lot and often has high-level benefits only available to supervisory-level positions within the firm. Often, a person becomes a Systems Analyst and retires from that position instead of moving to another job. Some companies reward years of excellent performance by promoting a Systems Analyst to *Senior Systems Analyst*. The Senior Systems Analyst often does nothing different from the other Systems Analysts, however, and the new title is more of a "thank you" from the company than anything else.

Clue: In smaller programming departments, one person might wear lots of hats, but that person's job title does not accurately reflect the range of jobs performed. For example, some companies have only two or three people in the entire computer department. All of them might program and also perform systems analysis and design duties. Smaller companies give you the opportunity to perform a wider range of programming tasks, improve your skills, and give you the opportunity to gain an understanding of the responsibilities of lots of job titles. Larger companies, however, usually offer better benefits, pay, and job security, but it will take you longer to broaden your skills.

Management Possibilities

By the time a person has been a Systems Analyst for a few years, he or she understands the company and the data processing department very well. The Systems Analyst knows most of the users and all the computer people in the company because the Systems Analyst has interacted so closely with users and programmers for so long. A person at the Systems Analyst level might decide that he or she is ready to move into a management-level position.

The higher salaries offered in the computer field can be a mixed blessing. Once you've been in data processing for a few years, your salary becomes much higher than that of others who have been with other departments for the same amount of time. A person who makes it to Systems Analyst and then decides that computers are no longer a challenge often finds it difficult to move to another position within that company. Companies rarely let people move to a position that requires a pay cut; such employees soon miss the money they were used to, and they start looking elsewhere for a job. The Systems Analysts find themselves locked into a job from which they cannot escape if they stay too long. Their only recourse when this happens is to move to a completely different company.

Warning: This section is not trying to steer you away from hopes of becoming a Systems Analyst. After all, being paid too much is a good problem to have! Most people are perfectly content to reach the level of Systems Analyst and stay there until retirement. It often means continued high pay raises, travel, and great benefits.

You should know, however, that being a Systems Analyst too long can lock you into that position. Make sure you want to stay there when the time comes to make a move or stay in the Systems Analyst's job.

The company is able to keep more people on the DP staff by paying higher salaries and locking them into a certain job range. A data processing department must have some kind of long-term personnel to maintain programming consistency and the programming standards that have been put into place.

Often, a Systems Analyst decides that he or she is ready to move into management. One of the first management-level job titles in data processing is that of *Supervisor*. Supervisors manage a small group of programmers and analysts, directing projects from a management point of view (making sure their people have adequate resources to do their jobs, are properly evaluated for raises, and so forth). Data processing departments normally prefer their Supervisors to have data processing experience. That is why so many Supervisors are promoted from within the ranks of Systems Analysts.

From a supervisory position, you might next move into a job called *Data Processing Manager* and be responsible for several Supervisors and their projects. The head manager of a data processing department is typically called the *Director*. The Director is usually even in rank with the Vice Presidents in the rest of the firm.

Reward: One of the advantages to moving into a supervisory or management position is that you can often move to non-DP departments within the company as a Supervisor or Manager. Before reaching a management position, your job rank and salary would make you overqualified for positions within other departments.

Note: There are other computer jobs, but they relate more to the hardware side of corporate computing than to the software and programming side. Some of these jobs are *tape librarians*, *disk librarians*, *computer operators*, and *computer technicians*.

The Standards Manual

Almost every programming department develops its own way of doing things. Over time, a company realizes that it should document the accepted company programming standards, and the result is usually a thick tome: the *standards manual*. The standards manual is updated regularly by the department as new languages and techniques are mastered. Typically, the standards manual dictates that structured programming techniques and proper documentation (remember QBasic's REM statements?) are required, and that standard naming conventions for files and variables are followed. Every programmer is assigned a standards manual and is expected to follow the coding guidelines within it.

Pitfall: The standards manual is handed down from higher management. Its use by the programming staff is mandated, yet the standards manual often sits unopened on the shelf for most of a programmer's career.

In a way, a standards manual is self-defeating. Nobody can read it from cover to cover without risking nodding off. Few people have the need to apply any of the standards when they read them, and when they're in the middle of a program, they don't feel they have time to look up every standard way of doing something. Nevertheless, the standards manual is important; it provides strong suggestions that, although not followed to the letter all of the time, improve the future maintenance of the systems.

It is the role of the Systems Analyst to review code written by the programming staff and make sure that the important standards are being followed. Perhaps the Systems Analyst does not know a majority of the information in the standards manual, but by the time they have progressed to the ranks of Systems Analyst, people have a good idea of what is important within the company and what the major standards are that need to be followed.

Structured Walkthroughs

The programming standards within the company are most often in focus during a *structured walkthrough*. A structured walkthrough has nothing to do with structured programming. A structured walkthrough is a review of a newly written program by some of the programming staff.

You might recall from Chapter 4 that a program follows these steps when the programmer is done writing it:

1. The programmer tests the program at his or her desk, trying to get as many bugs out as possible.

2. The programmer passes on the program to the user for testing (often, a parallel test is performed).

3. The user puts the program into use.

Now that you are familiar with the roles of the programming staff, you might be interested to know about an extra step that often takes place between steps 1 and 2. Once the programmer is satisfied that the program is as accurate as possible, he or she prints listings of the program for several people and prepares for the structured walkthrough.

In the structured walkthrough, several other Programmers and Systems Analysts get together with a copy of the original listing, with the Programmer in the room, and they pick apart the program in detail trying to find errors, weak spots, broken standards, and poor documentation. Along the way they make suggestions on how to improve the code.

Clue: A structured walkthrough often produces what is known in the industry as *egoless programmers*. Programmers are often known for their egos; a good structured walkthrough often shows that a program is not as well written as the original programmer might have thought at first.

The structured walkthrough is not an attempt to point fingers. Its only purpose is to produce the best code possible. The other programmers are not going to be critical of the programmer personally; after all, they are going to be at the center of a future structured walkthrough themselves.

Once a programmer implements many of the suggestions from the structured walkthrough, that programmer finds that he or she agrees that the program is better written than it was originally. After many such walkthroughs, the programmer develops better programming skills and the company gets better programs.

Putting a Program into Production

Figure 13.5 shows all the steps needed to get a program into use by the user. When the user is finally convinced that the program works as well as originally asked for, and the user is convinced that the parallel testing went smoothly, the program is then *moved into production.*

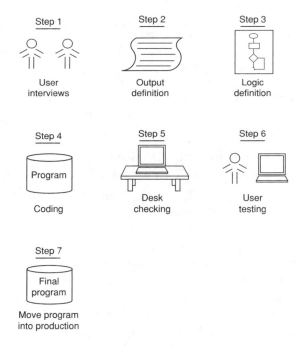

Figure 13.5. *The steps for designing, writing, and installing programs.*

Warning: The steps in Figure 13.5 are not necessarily followed in the strict sequence shown. Although the overall sequence is adhered to, there are many loops in the process.

For instance, when the structured walkthrough is finished, the programmer goes back to the program, implements the structured walkthrough's suggestions, and begins desk checking those corrections. When the users find bugs during the parallel testing (and they *always* find them), the programmer must go back to the original source code and fix the bugs. As you look at Figure 13.5, keep in mind that review, corrections, and retesting are part of the overall programming process.

When a program moves into production, it is considered complete. The user begins to use the program in a working, non-test environment. The program's results are considered reliable within reason. (Over time, a program's reliability improves as it is used and continues to work well.)

Being in production hardly implies that the program needs no changing and updating over the years. Nevertheless, a production program is one that is considered fixed and usable until a user makes a request to update the program or scrap it for a completely new one. If changes are made to a program that is in production, the Systems Analyst goes back to user interviews and determines what the user wants. The entire systems analysis and design stage is then repeated for the revised program. Depending on the extent of the changes, a program's revision might take more or less development time that its ancestor program took to write. As you have read throughout this entire book, the maintenance of programs is critical in our ever-changing world. The better you write your code, the more documentation you supply, and the more you follow your company's programming standards, the better chance you will have at locking in your career in the computer field.

Pitfall: *Job security* is an overused term. Often, you hear programmers jokingly talk about the cryptic code they write so that "only they will be able to understand it." Modern programmers are only too aware of the fact that the better employers seek programmers who write clear, clean code, are more concerned with proper programming, and follow as many of the company's programming standards as possible.

Some people can write programs very quickly, but the spaghetti code they produce is unreadable for future maintenance. You do not want to fall into the trap of thinking that speed is more important than clear programs.

Many companies have a formal procedure for moving programs into production. When a program is ready to be moved into production, the programmers finalize the program's documentation and prepare a source code file with a filename added to the production program list's records. That program is then stored on tapes and disks in what are known as production areas.

There are some mainframe systems that do not even allow programmers to change a program once the system is instructed to treat that source program as a production program. Programmers are able to make copies of the program's source code, but the program is read-only and cannot be changed. If an update has to be made, the programmer copies the source code and makes changes to the copy. Once the updates are made and the new version is ready for production, the production records are changed to reflect the new source code. From that point, the production system treats the new version of the code as the production version, but the original remains in place as a backup.

This tight control over production source code enables a company to ensure that it always has an unmodified copy of every program used by every user in the company. Without such control, a programmer could write a program, compile and test it, and install it on the user's system. Once installed, the programmer might inadvertently change the program. Because it is virtually impossible to reproduce source code from compiled code, the data processing department would have no way to generate the original source code if the users wanted a change made to the program they are using.

The Data Processing Department's Equipment

Throughout a large organization, many people work on many different computers. People are working on microcomputers, minicomputers, mainframes, and (possibly) supercomputers. Microcomputers on every desktop—networked to each other and also attached to the larger computer systems—require lots of coordination, but the flexibility makes the setup worthwhile.

In the old days, when *central computing* was the only thing possible and all of the company's personnel used one big mainframe, everybody's work stopped when the computer broke down. With *distributed computing*, people work on microcomputers connected to one or more central mainframes. The mainframe acts as the repository for large databases and for computing-intensive jobs. Individual users can use the microcomputers to process whatever data they need to process. Another advantage of distributed computing is that when the mainframe breaks down or is brought down for routine maintenance, people can continue working with their word processors, database programs, and spreadsheets on their PCs.

Figure 13.6 shows the direction of data flow in an organization's distributed computing system. Often, data processing management dictates that corporate data can be *downloaded* (data being sent to a smaller computer from a larger one), but not *uploaded* (data being sent to a larger computer from a smaller one). With the downloading capability, employees that have their PCs attached to the mainframe can retrieve any data from the central repository of data. They then can process the data, look at it, and print it. (Of course, in-place security measures ensure that sensitive data such as payroll figures do not fall into unauthorized hands.) Once the data is copied to the user's microcomputer, however, the user is rarely allowed (again, through security control on the mainframe) to send data back to the mainframe's files unless authorization has been given.

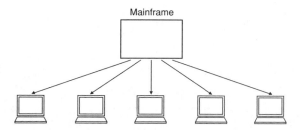

Mainframe

Figure 13.6. Data can be downloaded from a mainframe to a microcomputer.

The reason for the tight upload control is simple. The company's primary data records are stored on its largest computer, because that computer holds the most data. If users are allowed to read and write that data freely, the data's integrity would be lost forever. One user would download a file a split second before another user replaced the file with a change. There would be too many versions of the (supposedly) same data floating around on everyone's microcomputer, and decisions would be made based on that data. There is nothing to keep a user from downloading data and changing it once it gets to the microcomputer, but the original is still secure on the mainframe for the rest of the company's use.

Along these same lines, it is interesting to note that today's microcomputer software and hardware vendors are sporting their wares (*soft-* and *hard-* that is!) and boasting that theirs is one of the first to *multitask* (run two programs at once) and allow for multiple users. What they fail to realize is that the PC world is just beginning to catch up to what the mainframe and minicomputer world has been doing for many years. Multiuser, multitasking computers have been the norm for many years—only in the microcomputer world are they the leading edge.

Consulting

Many programmers find an enriching life as a computer consultant. Too many businesses and individuals buy a computer thinking all their problems will be solved, and they do not realize the amount of training that is often needed to use the computer effectively. There has been a growing niche for computer consultants over the last several years, and you might find success as a consultant yourself.

As a consultant, you can be a hero or a heroine to your clients. So many times, computer consultants rush to help someone with a problem getting a report completed, only to find that the client is inserting a disk upside-down or forgetting to press the online button on the printer. The computer is still a mystery to a vast number of people.

As a consultant, you can take on as much or as little work as you want. Many programmers moonlight as consultants, sometimes finding that their consulting business grows enough to do it full time. They might give up the benefits that a company can provide, but they like having full say-so over what they do.

Getting started as a consultant takes little more than word-of-mouth coverage. Offer to help your accountant, attorney, or anyone you know who uses a computer. Tell them that you'd like to start doing some consulting and that you'd be glad to give them an hour or two free of charge just to see how they like the work (and how you like the work). Often, these initial free calls turn into a long-term proposition that is good for both you and your clients.

Chapter Highlights

You now have an understanding of computer departments and their people. There are many jobs in the computer industry, both for entry-level and advanced programmers. A computer job is a fun, well-respected, and needed occupation; you'll be glad you're a part of the computer industry.

✖ A data processing department is known by many names. Some examples are *Information Services*, *Information Systems*, and *MIS*.

✖ The data processing department writes programs for the rest of the company.

✖ The entry-level job into the computer field is the Data Entry Clerk. A Data Entry Clerk enters data into a computer. Large companies require massive amounts of data entry.

✖ Although a data-entry job is not very high in the organization, it does get someone's foot in the door who otherwise would have no chance at a computer career.

✖ Most entry-level programmers begin at the Assistant Programmer level. The Assistant Programmer's primary responsibility is to help with program maintenance and to get to know how the data processing department works.

✖ The Assistant Programmer is soon promoted to the job of Programmer, a title that denotes a higher level and a passing of the trial stage of an Assistant Programmer. Despite the title, the Programmer does not write many new programs, but instead maintains and updates programs already in use.

✖ As a Programmer proves his or her skills and shows enthusiasm, a promotion to Programmer Analyst is in the offing. Programmer Analysts write new programs from the specifications given to them. In their later years, Programmer Analysts begin to work more closely with the Systems Analysts and learn the skills needed for their next promotion.

✖ A Systems Analyst is considered one of the highest levels of professional computing in a data processing department. The Systems Analyst is the go-between for the user who wants a program written and the Programmer Analysts who will eventually write the programs. Once a person reaches the Systems Analyst level, that person often considers some kind of supervisory position. Nevertheless, many Systems Analysts retain that job until retirement. A Systems Analyst gets paid a lot, has a nice office (large companies are especially preoccupied with office space and rank within the company's organization), and usually enjoys the job very much. When in the middle of rush projects, a Systems Analyst doesn't always view the job with happiness, but overall, the Systems Analyst position is a deserved reward for years of hard work.

✖ Most computer departments have large manuals called *standards manuals* that provide guidance for programmers in the company. Rarely is the standards manual followed in great part, but it does offer a source of clarity and some recourse when a programmer finds that spaghetti code seems to be the only way.

✖ A structured walkthrough is a meeting with other Programmers and Systems Analysts who look over a programmer's code and make suggestions for improving it.

✖ A company usually moves a program into production when the program is finished and tested. The source code of production programs is kept secure so it can be regenerated if the user has problems.

✖ A company's data processing equipment is often networked together. With networking come data responsibilities. One common control is to allow the downloading of data from the mainframe to a microcomputer, but not allow uploading from the microcomputer to the mainframe. The integrity of the data would easily be damaged if everyone could change the central repository of data on the mainframe.

The Future of Programming

In the jungle, Perilous Perry instructed a group of beginning programmers. What can our hero's young charges accomplish? What lies over the horizon of their programming future?

1. Will there be a need for programmers in the future?

2. What is a program generator?

3. What does CASE stand for?

4. How does CASE differ from a program generator?

5. What is an object?

6. How does object-oriented programming differ from non-object-oriented programming?

7. Which OOP language is best?

8. What is a macro language?

9. Why do end-user programs such as spreadsheets and database programs include their own programming languages?

10. Why is continued education important for programmers?

The future of programming is bright. Programming computers will continue to fill scores of hours for those who program. The demand for quality computer software should continue to grow. There will continue to be backlogs in programming departments. Your programming skills will be in high demand and your pocketbook will contain the fruits of your labors. The best advantage of a programming career is that it is even more fun than it is financially rewarding.

This book has walked you through the steps of program design and creation. You now know some of the highlights of the QBasic programming languages. You understand the procedures that companies put into place to develop programs and put them into production. As you look for a programming job, you will be able to decipher the various programming job titles such as Systems Analyst and Assistant Programmer.

I would be amiss if I did not address the future of programming and give you an idea of what some of the nontraditional areas of programming provide. This chapter describes some of the new programming language features. You will also see how non-programmers write simple programs from inside an application such as Lotus 1-2-3. There is even a programming language in MS-DOS called the *batch file language*.

This chapter concludes the *Absolute Beginner's Guide to Programming*, but begins your future as a programmer. Once you read about some of the sideline, nontraditional programming tools, you will be ready to chart your own programming course and head to the area of programming you most prefer.

Program Generators

There are programs that actually write programs for you, called *program generators*. Today's program generators are simple and do not produce extremely powerful programs. Nevertheless, they portend an important niche in the future of programming. They improve a programmer's productivity by helping with screen and report design.

In a way, the Visual Basic programming language is a program generator. Although you must do some programming to create complex Visual Basic programs, you can create simple programs by moving elements on the screen and choosing options with the mouse. The Visual Basic compiler takes your visual requests and converts them to a program that the computer will run.

The Windows program you see in Figure 14.1 was created using Visual Basic. It requests an invoice number and then produces the detail lines from the invoice. Some programming was required for the application in Figure 14.1. Today's program generators are little more than screen, report, and simple data processing code generators. You must often wrap more specific code that you write within and around a program generator's code to make the program do all that you want it to do.

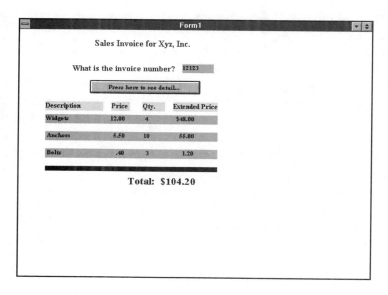

Figure 14.1. *A program created with Visual Basic's help.*

Pitfall: Don't let the prospect of program generators get you down if you want a future in programming. Because program generators create such generic programs, they will probably never replace programmers—certainly not anytime soon. Program generators are tools that *help programmers*. The programmer can use program generators to take care of all the screen and report elements, as well as some simple data processing. The programmer then has more time to devote to the specifics of the user's request and can concentrate on making the computer perform tasks so detailed that a program generator could never accomplish the same results.

Program Development with CASE

CASE is an acronym for *Computer-Aided Software Engineering*. CASE is like a program generator, only instead of helping programmers write programs, CASE tools help create programs starting at the initial design level. A Systems Analyst can use CASE from the inception of a program request to the program's movement into production. CASE is a massive program on the computer that the Systems Analyst can use for the initial output design, data definitions, logic definition (some CASE programs even draw flowcharts from a flowchart description entered by the Systems Analyst), and program generation. CASE often produces code based on the Analyst's logic definition, but heavy programmer intervention is needed to implement any but the most general of programs and to ensure the project's overall success.

CASE became widely used in the 1980s. Its proponents promised that CASE would revolutionize the programming environment and decrease the time and resources needed to produce a finished program. (Most of the newer programming advances promote quicker development time and easier maintenance as their primary goals.) The promise of CASE, however, never materialized. Although CASE has achieved some success, it has yet to produce the advances in software development that were originally hoped.

The failure of CASE, however, may not be the fault of the product's own short-comings. Rather, the ways Systems Analysts designed systems in the past may have been the wrong approach. As you see in the next section, a new programming technique called *object-oriented programming* (*OOP*) is rapidly becoming accepted as a language philosophy that will shorten the programming time needed for any given project. Along with object-oriented programming is object-oriented analysis and design. CASE tools should make a comeback in the 1990s as more of them are integrated with object-oriented methodologies.

Clue: The CASE products of the 1980s were not bad tools. The problems that resulted from them were due to the fact that CASE helped Systems Analysts and Programmers do faster what the Systems Analysts and Programmers already did incorrectly. Pre-OOP programming methods suffer from difficult maintenance and documentation problems that OOP does not introduce. CASE could not eliminate the inherent problems that non-OOP programming contains. (OOP has its own set of problems as well, however, but it is viewed as an improvement over other traditional methods.)

CASE is probably in your future as you learn more about programming and go to work for a programming department. CASE is most helpful for large programming projects that involve many people. Often, a small programming project will not need the administration, direction, and support that a CASE tool can give to a project.

Because of the complexity and requirements of CASE programs, they are most-often available only for large computers such as mainframes. There are some PC-based CASE products, but they are limited in scope and do not include some of the more common components. Here is a list of items found in a typical CASE product:

✖ Documentation tools for the user interviews, including an integrated word processor and database

✖ Systems analysis and design tools such as flowchart and pseudocode generators

✖ Project management administration, including PERT diagrams and resource allocation charts

✖ A data dictionary that keeps track of all the data items in the system and gives programmers the ability to use consistent naming conventions in their programs

✖ A program generator for simpler and routine code

Clue: Think of CASE as a program that helps you and others design and write programs. CASE is good for handling the minute details throughout the system's development so you and the other Programmers and Systems Analysts can work on implementing all of the user's request.

OOPs, It's Object-Oriented Programming

The world of programming is changing dramatically. People who have programmed for years are returning to schools and to the bookstores to hone up on the newest direction in the field: object-oriented programming. It seems as if OOP will make as much or more of an impact on programming as structured programming did in the 1960s.

OOP streamlines that which regular programming languages make difficult. Object-oriented programming helps you program better and faster. The more object-oriented programs you write, the more code you will be able to reuse later to make future development go even more smoothly.

Warning: Not everything advertised as being *object-oriented programming* is really object-oriented programming. Sometimes a program is

considered to be object-oriented just because it has graphics, but all objects are not graphics and all graphics are certainly not objects. (There are some very good graphics programs that are object-oriented, but many are not.)

Objects

Objects are program variables and nothing more. All of the variables in the QBasic chapters are objects. Even though those programs have variables, they are not considered to be object-oriented. The objects of OOP do much more work than those of non-OOP programs. The object variables of OOP become *active*.

A non-OOP variable has properties. The variable might hold strings or numbers, and it also has a name and holds a data value. A true object variable has *behaviors* in addition to the properties of a regular variable. Object variables not only contain data, but they also contain code that manipulates that data. Object variables know how to do work as well as hold data. Objects can initialize themselves, print themselves, and calculate with their own data values. An object has a miniature program embedded within it.

Reward: A program that contains object variables exists primarily to send messages to the objects, telling the objects what to do. The programs you saw earlier had to directly manipulate all of the variables because the variables could do nothing but hold data.

Your data more accurately reflects the real world that it represents because the data has both behaviors and characteristics. If you were writing an object-oriented program to control a stoplight, you could create a stoplight object that behaves in the program just like a real stoplight behaves; the stoplight object could change its value from green to yellow to red when the program instructs it to do so. If you had to write a non-object-oriented program for the stoplight, your program would have to worry about the details of changing the contents of the variable from color to color. Your primary program would be doing all the detailed work, but it is that detailed work that introduces bugs in code and takes the programmer's attention away from the primary purpose of the program.

Pitfall: Internally, objects are nothing more than computerized representations. You have to write all the code for what you want the object to be able to do. In other words, you have to write the code to change the stoplight object variable or there is no way it knows how to do that. Once you give the object its behaviors by writing code for it, you never have to worry about those details again. You can concentrate on the overall objectives of the program using that object.

Objects take away a layer of abstraction from your programs. The objects become more like the data in the real world they are trying to represent. If you were writing an invoicing program, you would have invoices that contain lines for the invoice detail that can be filled in and printed. The more like the real world your programs are to you, the faster you will be able to take the real world requirements of the project and write a program that manipulates those objects.

Objects take the tedium out of programming. OOP contains object variables and uses them to their fullest extent. An object-oriented program contains active data, not just passive data. The objects you write have another advantage that other non-OOP variables do not have. You can easily use objects from one program inside another program. Also, if objects are similar to each other (for example, a *vice-president* is just a special kind of *employee*), you can *inherit* the active properties of one and create another, making changes to the new objects to make them suit their new roles. By inheriting objects, you can reuse them without having to rewrite all the code from scratch.

Objects in an OOP program are like components inside a car or television. You do not have to know how a motor works to drive a car and you do not have to know how a television tube produces color to watch color TV. When you use objects that you or someone else has written, you do not have to look at the code inside the object. (Through an OOP process known as *data-hiding*, you cannot even always see the code inside the object.) There are software companies that sell nothing but objects. You buy these pre-compiled objects (which means you cannot look at the source code) and use them in your own programs without knowing anything about their internal workings. Writing a program then becomes little more than putting together pieces until you have the program you want.

OOP and Non-OOP Programming

The opposite of object-oriented programming is *procedural programming*. You used procedural programming in the chapters on QBasic programming. There is nothing wrong with procedural programming, but it is not as maintainable as OOP.

Object-oriented programming is not a panacea, although the current array of programming publications might lead you to believe that OOP is the only way to program. A badly written object-oriented program is worse than a well-written procedural program. If you follow the spirit of reusable objects, and if you write programs that follow some accepted OOP-industry guidelines, you will find fewer program errors and finish the programs you write in less time.

Learning OOP

There is much debate about the best way to learn object-oriented programming. Some feel that you should already know how to write procedural programs well before you tackle OOP. Others feel that there is too much to "un-learn" when moving from a procedural language to an object-oriented language. Most agree, however, with the first argument and feel that learning OOP is easier if you already know how to program computers.

Pitfall: Moving from a procedural programming language to an object-oriented language takes some time, whether or not you know how to program computers. Do not underestimate the learning curve needed to tackle OOP. Appendix A suggests some books that can help you learn an object-oriented language.

The world is not a world of objects—not just yet, anyway. Many companies' data processing departments plan to move to the OOP environment. A company's conversion is not affected so much by technical decisions as it is by upper-level management's decisions. A retooling must take place before a data processing department converts its programming teams to objects. Not only do new OOP compilers need to be purchased, but the programmers need to be trained. Because of the costs involved, management is slow to react to any new computer technology.

A programming department should never attempt to rewrite all of its existing systems just to become object-oriented. There is no good reason to do that if the systems in place are adequate. New programming projects will be good OOP training for programmers; the benefits of rewriting existing systems do not justify the costs involved in doing so.

OOP Languages

The most common object-oriented language is C++. C++ is not the best object-oriented language by any means, but its widespread use makes it the hands-down winner in OOP languages today. C++ is a hybrid object-oriented language; C++ is the C programming language with some additions that include the ability to support object-oriented programming.

C++ is successful because C is so successful. It is only natural that C programmers will move on to C++ programming instead of a completely different object-oriented programming language. C++ is now available on all classes of computers, from PCs to supercomputers.

Other OOP languages include *SmallTalk*, *Effiel*, and *Pascal with Objects*. Of these, SmallTalk is probably used in industry more than the others, although Borland's Pascal with Objects is popular among home computer programmers. It is impossible to say which object-oriented programming language is best to use. If you learn C, C++ is a logical OOP choice because the bridge between C and C++ is easier to cross than one between two unrelated OOP languages.

> **Warning:** When you first begin to learn object-oriented programming, you will be inundated with silver-dollar sized words such as *encapsulation*, *polymorphism*, and *multiple inheritance*. It seems that the programming community never uses an easy word when a difficult one will do just as nicely! Don't let the new terms frighten you. As you learn about the language, you will see that their meanings fit their titles.

Non-Traditional Programming Languages

When a computer professional hears the words *programming language*, he or she often thinks of COBOL, FORTRAN, C, C++, Pascal, and BASIC. The traditional high-level languages are the foundation of programming computers. A person needs training to be able to write programs in a programming language.

There is, though, some programming that you and anyone else can do that does not require any knowledge about programming languages at all. Many of today's most popular computer applications come with their own built-in programming language that is of a much higher level of abstraction than the languages you have seen described in this book.

The following sections describe some of the ways people program computer applications. By taking the time to learn the built-in language of the application, even users with few computer skills can customize their applications to make them perform a little more like they want.

Macro Languages

The term *macro* is used for many things in computers. A macro is a programming routine in either assembler or a high-level programming language that a programmer writes and then includes later in other programs. (A macro is a form of a subroutine, although it does not allow as much flexibility as a subroutine does.)

The word *macro* is also applied to many end-user's application commands that come with many of today's popular spreadsheets and word processing applications. For example, Lotus 1-2-3, one of the most popular electronic spreadsheets on the market and the biggest-selling spreadsheet program in computer history, has its own built-in macro language. As with most applications' macro language, the one with Lotus 1-2-3 is two-tiered; it is both a keystroke repeater and a miniature programming language.

The first form of the Lotus 1-2-3 macro language is the easiest to use. If a user with Lotus 1-2-3 types the same keystrokes over and over to perform a certain task such as printing a report, those repeated keystrokes would be good candidates for a macro program. For example, if you have used Lotus 1-2-3, you may remember that the following keystrokes produce a printed listing of an area from the spreadsheet:

```
/ppra1..g17{Enter}agq
```

These one-character keystroke combinations select the following commands from the Lotus 1-2-3 menu:

```
Print
Printer
Range
a1..g17
Align
Go
Quit
```

Although printing the range of cells from a1 to g17 is not difficult, the keystrokes can be tedious if you have to do it often. Because you use the same keystrokes for the same task over and over, the keystrokes are good candidates for the macro keystroke recorder. Instead of issuing these keystrokes every time, you can type them into a spreadsheet cell, out of the way of the main spreadsheet area, as Figure 14.2 shows.

Using the Lotus 1-2-3 menu, you then can assign a single keystroke, usually an Alt keystroke combination, to the spreadsheet's macro cell. If the user assigns the printing macro shown earlier to the Alt-P keystroke, Lotus 1-2-3 automatically performs the printing of the spreadsheet whenever the user presses Alt-P.

```
A:A20:                                                        READY

A      A              B         C         D         E         F         G
1
2                     Rental Property Analysis
3                     --------------------------------
4                     For Month of March              Monthly
5                                                      Profit
6                     Gross     Gross     Gross     Increase/
7  Location           Expenses  Income    Profits   Decrease
8  --------------------------------------------------------------
9  1013 E. Illinois   $234.32   $450.00   $215.68     11.0%
10 4146 West 57th       90.00    400.00    310.00      4.0%
11 857 Old Oak Road    314.54    415.00    100.46      8.0%
12 209 NW Highway        0.00    275.00    275.00     13.3%
13 6104 E. 48th St.    500.00    475.00    -25.00     -2.0%
14                     ---------------------------------
15                   $1,138.86 $2,015.00   $876.14     34.30%
16                     =================================
17
18
19
20                                       /ppral..g17~agq
RENTAL.WK3
```

Figure 14.2. *Entering the keystroke macro.*

Note: This section is not trying to teach you how to program Lotus 1-2-3. You may not even be a user of Lotus 1-2-3, or of any other spreadsheet product. Nevertheless, a programmer should be aware of all of the things end-users can do. Almost certainly, the users will call on the programmer to get them out of the mess they created themselves in an unsuccessful attempt at macro programming!

Most programs like Lotus 1-2-3 that have a macro keystroke recorder also provide more powerful macro commands. These commands mirror a high-level programming language's commands. Lotus 1-2-3 has a built-in macro language that loops, makes decisions, and calculates values, just like regular programming languages do. The languages that come with end-user applications such as Lotus 1-2-3 are never as flexible as a programming language because they have to be safe for users to use. However, they do provide some fairly advanced (for users) programming techniques that someone can take advantage of if they want to automate very complex functions.

> **Reward:** Although users might have a difficult time programming with anything other than a keystroke macro recorder, your programming skills can come in handy for the user. Because you are becoming adept in programming languages, application macro languages such as the one with Lotus 1-2-3 will pose little challenge to you. You'll be able to add menus and powerful selection code to your company's user applications, making the users' lives simpler and making you a hero in their eyes.

Many word processors such as Microsoft Word also support macro language features. Routine tasks such as mail merging, printing, and file saving are even easier with macro programming. Microsoft Word for Windows uses a form of QBasic as its built-in macro language, a macro language that now you should be able to master in no time.

The concepts of macro programming are simple. You only have to familiarize yourself with the specifics of the language. Here is a listing from a Word for Windows word processing macro:

```
If InStr(WindowName$(), ": ") = 0 Then FilePrintPreview 0
If Files$("examples.doc") <> "" Then
    FileOpen.Name = "examples.doc"
Else
    Dim dlg As FileOpen
    GetCurValues dlg
    dlg.Name = "EXAMPLES.DOC"
again:
    On Error Goto bye
    Dialog dlg
    On Error Goto again
    FileOpen dlg
End If
bye:
```

Although it is similar to QBasic, the macro does have some of its own style and notation. Nevertheless, after a few minutes with a manual, any QBasic programmer will feel at home writing powerful macros to help users do what they need.

Database Languages

Most of today's popular database programs have their own language for automating common database tasks. Some database languages have progressed to being almost as powerful as a programming language, although not quite as flexible. There are many reporting, updating, and processing procedures needed with a large database that a built-in language helps automate.

> **Note:** As with Lotus 1-2-3, many database programs have both a keystroke-recording macro language as well as a programming language.

Most database programs attempt to supply as much capability as possible through its menus. Figure 14.3 shows a dBASE IV menu that helps the user through a file structure modification. As with Lotus 1-2-3 and other application programs, the built-in menus do not provide as much power as a customized version can offer.

Here is a partial listing of a dBASE IV program using its built-in programming language:

```
Ans = ""
DO WHILE .NOT. LOWER(Ans)$"sre"
   @10,0
   WAIT "Enter selection (s-sort, r-report, e-exit)" TO Ans
   IF .NOT. lower(Ans)$"sre"
      @12, 1 SAY "You must answer s, r, or e"
   ENDIF
ENDDO
```

As you can see, the language is not that different from QBasic. This routine is trying to limit the user's input to three letters—*s*, *r*, or *e*—and repeats the prompt if the user enters anything else.

Programming a database application helps those who do not know the database to use it. A database, even with its helpful built-in menus, takes a while to learn how to use, and even longer to learn how to program. If there are users in your company who need to use a database to keep track of data, but they are computer illiterate to the point of not understanding the database concepts or menus, you can design an application that guides them through the use of the database for their specific application.

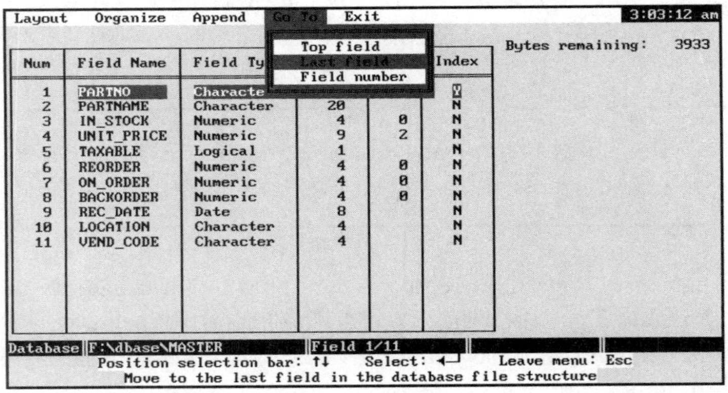

Figure 14.3. The dBASE IV menu helping the user through a database modification.

DOS Programming

Most operating systems have their own programming language, although it is not as sophisticated or flexible as a regular programming language. Mainframe programmers have used *JCL* (for *Job Control Language*) since the 1960s to automate operating systems tasks. Minicomputer users and programmers have also used operating system programming languages. The most common is the *UNIX shell script*.

PC users with MS-DOS have their own version of an operating system language as well. You can automate certain operating system tasks with the MS-DOS *batch language*. Instead of repeating the same operating system commands over and over, you can type them into a file called a *batch file*. A batch file is nothing more than a file with MS-DOS commands listed in it. When you want MS-DOS to perform each of the commands, you only have to type the name of the batch file and not the individual commands.

Suppose that every morning you wanted to clear the screen, display a wide directory listing of your files, and then look to see how much disk space is remaining on your computer. You could store the following commands in a file named MORNING.BAT (all batch files must end in the .BAT extension):

```
CLS
DIR /W
PAUSE
CHKDSK
```

As in QBasic, the MS-DOS CLS command clears the screen. DIR /W displays a wide directory listing (the files are listed across the screen instead of down the screen). PAUSE causes MS-DOS to pause and display the following message:

```
Press any key to continue...
```

Finally, the CHKDSK command displays the free space on your disk drive.

Over the years, you will develop lots of batch files that help you do your work more efficiently. If you routinely back up the same files, compile the same programs, or do any repetitive task from the MS-DOS prompt, a batch file will save you a lot of time.

Your Training Needs

There is a tremendous need for trainers in the programming field. As you learn more about programming, you should consider sharing your knowledge with others through training, consulting, or teaching. You will find that your own programming skills improve when you teach them to someone else.

The need for training is never as apparent as it is in virtually every programming department in the world. Programmers are often called to offer a training class for others who do not posses some needed skills. In-house training enables a company to keep a cap on their training costs and control the material being covered.

Your own computer training does not stop. The computer industry changes rapidly. The skills you have today can be obsolete in ten years, so part of your job is to continue your own training. It is incumbent upon you to stay up with current trends if you want to secure your computer position in the future.

Warning: Not every new breakthrough in computer hardware and software becomes an industry standard. You do not have to be on the "bleeding edge" of technology (a programmer's pun describing very new and unproven technology), learning everything there is to learn. You do not even have to be on the leading edge of computer programming innovations. For instance, object-oriented programming is now considered by the industry as the best way to program, yet the majority of computer programmers haven't learned how to program with objects. It appears, someday soon, they will have to master OOP. There is rarely a need to stay on top of the latest trends, however, because today's breakthrough might be tomorrow's flop.

You will find your own niche in the computer field. Specialization is almost a must these days. It is so very difficult to master everything. Some people choose to specialize in networking, object-oriented programming, or graphical user interfaces. As you learn more about programming, you will find the area that best fits your own interests and you will master that area.

Every month, take a trip to your local library or bookstore to scan the shelves for the latest computer magazines. Try to read one good computer book every month or two (Appendix A lists some excellent titles that you are ready for after finishing this book). Every six months, research a new topic of computer programming to improve your skill levels. Most computer people find that self-study is not a job they balk at; the field of programming is exciting. It never gets old. The new innovations everywhere you look are always exciting and hold promise of powerful computing power in the future.

Chapter Highlights

There are many tools on the market, such as program generators and CASE programs, that make a programmer's life easier. Perhaps none have made as great an impact as object-oriented programming. OOP should help make programmers more productive in the coming years.

* The business of programming will continue to grow throughout the coming decades.

* Program generators actually write programs for you.

* Because program generators have to be so generic, they do not produce extremely detailed code. Program generators are useful for tedious, time-consuming areas of programming, such as screen and report design.

* CASE stands for Computer-Aided Software Engineering.

* CASE helps software developers move quicker through the entire program design and writing process.

* Object-oriented programming uses variables that have behaviors. Those variables are called objects.

* The most popular OOP language today is C++. Its popularity stems from the widespread use of C.

* OOP helps speed the programming process by letting you reuse existing code and leave the tedious details to the objects so they take care of themselves.

✖ Built-in programming languages help end-user application programs such as spreadsheets, word processors, and database programs become more automated.

✖ A macro keystroke recorder reads the user's keystrokes and creates a miniature program that mimics those keystrokes when the user requests the macro to run. This enables a user to issue several keystroke commands via a single keypress.

✖ Application programs also include their own macro programming language. The application languages must be high-level enough for end-users (meaning non-programmers) to be able to master, so they are not always as powerful as regular programming languages.

✖ Continuing education is almost as vital in the field of computers as it is in the medical profession. The rapidly changing computer technology requires that programmers stay on top of current trends by reading books and magazines, and taking courses when possible.

Appendix

Where Do You Go from Here?

Now that you have a more solid foundation than almost any other beginning programmer has ever had, you are ready to direct your education toward more specific goals. You should now begin tackling a programming language in depth. Mastering a programming language takes a while, and different people learn at different rates. Nevertheless, the biggest problem budding programmers face is that they jump in too fast. After reading *Absolute Beginner's Guide to Programming*, you will not have that problem; you will be surprised at how well this book's concepts prepare you for your programming future, whether that future is just for fun or for a career.

The following sections contain popular book titles that you are now ready to master. They were specifically chosen to get you up to speed in a specific area of computer programming. You will notice that there are also a couple of hardware books and operating system books. This is because any programmer worth his or her salt has a primary understanding of the operating system and the hardware with which it interacts. Don't worry, you don't have to learn to solder a wire to understand your computer's hardware or how it integrates with the operating system in harmony.

Pascal

Turbo Pascal Programming 101

Readers take an active approach to learning Turbo Pascal in this step-by-step tutorial/workbook. Special features such as *Find the Bug, Try This, Think About, Finish the Program,* and *Still Confused* give the reader a thorough understanding of the programming language. Covers Turbo Pascal 7. (Beginning)

Turbo Pascal 6
Object-Oriented Programming

Learn how to integrate Borland's Turbo Vision classes with the Turbo Pascal compiler by using this book/disk set. (Intermediate to Advanced)

QBasic

QBasic Programming 101

Readers take an active approach to learning QBasic in this step-by-step tutorial/ workbook. Special features such as *Find the Bug, Try This, Think About, Finish the Program*, and *Still Confused* give the reader a thorough understanding of the language. This book discusses the PLAY and graphics features discussed in Chapter 11 of *Absolute Beginner's Guide to Programming*. Available in April, 1993. (Beginning)

Teach Yourself QBasic in 21 Days

Users can achieve QBasic success now! Each lesson can be completed in 2–3 hours or less. Shaded syntax boxes, Q & A sections, and "Do's and Don'ts" sections reinforce the important topics within QBasic. Available in April, 1993. (Beginning to Intermediate)

Generic C

> **Note:** The next few books are considered to be generic C books. The term *generic* means that the source code can be ported to any C compiler, depending on the book.

Teach Yourself C in 21 Days

With this best-selling book, users can achieve C success now! Each lesson can be completed in 2–3 hours or less. Shaded syntax boxes, Q & A sections, and "Do's and Don'ts" sections reinforce the important topics within C. (Beginning to Intermediate)

C Programming Proverbs and Quick Reference

This quick, expert guide to writing better programs will help programmers speed up their program development with at-a-glance commands, functions, and statements. Code snippets give readers a head start on developing elegant C code. (Beginning to Intermediate)

Programming in ANSI C

A no-nonsense introductory approach to the C language. Written for programmers, systems analysts, and students, this book teaches the basics of programming in ANSI C. Highlights specific ANSI standards. (Beginning to Advanced)

Advanced C

Here's the next step for programmers who want to improve their C programming skills. This book gives efficiency tips and techniques for debugging C programs and improving their speed, memory usage, and readability. (Intermediate to Advanced)

Generic C++

> **Note:** The next few books are considered to be generic C++ books. The term *generic* means that the source code can be ported to any C++ compiler, depending on the book.

C++ Programming 101

Readers take an active approach to learning C++ in this step-by-step tutorial/workbook. Special features such as *Find the Bug, Try This, Think About, Finish the Program,* and *Still Confused* give the reader a thorough understanding of the language. (Beginning)

Tom Swan's C++ Primer

The expert tutorial and reference for C++ programmers! The book/disk set combines an easy-to-read style with thorough review material and covers all major C++ compilers. (Beginning to Intermediate)

Advanced C++

This comprehensive guide is the next step for programmers who have achieved proficiency with the basics of C++ and want to learn about advanced topics. (Intermediate to Advanced)

Microsoft C++

Do-It-Yourself Microsoft C++ 7

A hands-on tutorial, this book is written for readers with little C programming experience. This book explains the features of the Microsoft compiler as well as all the fundamental programming structures. (Beginning to Intermediate)

Microsoft C/C++ 7 Developer's Guide

This is a must-have for all C programmers using C/C++ 7. The extensive tutorials explain how to create DOS and Windows applications using C++, OOP, and the Microsoft Foundation Class Libraries. The disk features example programs that help readers learn Microsoft C/C++ 7. (Intermediate to Advanced)

Turbo C++

Do-It-Yourself Turbo C++

Beginning and intermediate C/C++ programmers can become proficient with this complete introduction to the Turbo C++ compiler. (Beginning to Intermediate)

Turbo C++ Programming 101

Readers take an active approach to learning C++ in this step-by-step tutorial/ workbook. Special features such as *Find the Bug, Try This, Think About, Finish the Program,* and *Still Confused* give the reader a thorough understanding of the language. (Beginning)

Turbo C++ for Windows Programming for Beginners

This is the complete guide to Windows programming with the Turbo C++ compiler! This valuable book/disk set shows C and C++ programmers how to use Windows for more powerful computing. This book includes in-depth information on advanced Windows programming techniques and provides specific information on the Borland programming extensions. Available in February, 1993. (Beginning to Intermediate)

Mastering Borland C++

Designed for every programmer, this example-packed tutorial ensures instant productivity. The book covers Borland C++, Turbo Vision, and ObjectWindows, and features a massive reference section of sample programs. (Beginning to Advanced)

Secrets of the Borland C++ Masters

This is the ultimate book of tips, techniques, and shortcuts for intermediate and advanced programmers. The book helps programmers produce faster programs, use less memory, optimize the Turbo Debugger and Turbo Profiler, and more. (Intermediate to Advanced)

Borland C++ 3.1 Object-Oriented Programming, Third Edition

This best-selling book is ideal for computer science students, professional programmers, and serious hobbyists. It presents powerful examples of object-oriented applications plus complete how-to instructions for Windows programming with Borland C++. It also features extensive coverage of Turbo Vision and the ObjectWindows Library. (Intermediate to Advanced)

Programming Windows Games with Borland C++

Learn how to use object-oriented programming to write computer games. This book shows how to use C++ classes for image manipulation and sound generation. It includes a disk containing shareware Windows games as well as source and executable versions of SPUZZLE and BLOCKADE. Available in April, 1993. (Intermediate to Advanced)

Visual Basic

Teach Yourself Visual Basic in 21 Days

Users can achieve Visual Basic success now! Each lesson can be completed in 2–3 hours or less. Shaded syntax boxes, Q & A sections, and "Do's and Don'ts" sections reinforce the important topics within Visual Basic. Available in Summer, 1993. (Beginning to Intermediate)

Do-It-Yourself Visual Basic for Windows, Second Edition

Beginning programmers will find this book to be a simple introduction to the Visual Basic environment and the BASIC language within Windows. This book provides extensive information on debugging and error handling. (Beginning to Intermediate)

Do-It-Yourself Visual Basic for MS-DOS

Beginning programmers will find this book to be a simple introduction to the Visual Basic environment and the BASIC language within DOS. This book provides extensive information on debugging and error handling. (Beginning to Intermediate)

Secrets of the Visual Basic Masters

The one book that makes programmers Visual Basic masters! The book includes two disks that feature all source code used in the text, as well as third-party tools for more efficient complex applications. (Intermediate to Advanced)

Extending Visual Basic

Anyone who has purchased or is thinking about purchasing an extension product needs this book. This book features over 30 of the most popular extension products. The two disks included contain modified versions of these third-party extension products. (Intermediate to Advanced)

Visual Basic for DOS Developer's Guide

This book/disk set helps programmers get the full power and maximum productivity from Visual Basic for DOS. It contains tips and techniques to help developers maximize the power of Visual Basic. Available in April, 1993. (Intermediate to Advanced)

Visual Basic for Windows Developer's Guide

This book/disk set helps programmers get the full power and maximum productivity from Visual Basic for Windows. It contains a disk with source code and executable example applications as well as third-party tools and utilities. It also provides a reference for functions, objects, properties, and Custom Libraries. (Intermediate to Advanced)

Moving... (Series)

The *Moving...* series appeals to current programmers of one particular language who want to learn another programming language. Each book compares the languages and their syntax to make a smooth transition from one language to another.

Moving from C to C++

An invaluable guide for C programmers wanting to learn how to move from C to C++. This book shows how one application written in C is converted to C++ with more efficient code. It includes tips and techniques for making the transition from C to C++. It also shows the "why" of object-oriented programming before teaching the specifics. (Beginning to Intermediate)

Moving into Object-Oriented Programming with Turbo C++

This book focuses on learning Turbo C++ and object-oriented programming with no prior knowledge of C. This book takes the reader step-by-step in a friendly, easy-to-follow style through lessons about classes, objects, and all the aspects of object-oriented programming. The book also covers Borland's BGI graphics.

Numerous line-drawings show relationships between objects' data and their member functions. Too many OOP books rely solely on code to teach C++, but OOP is not just code—it is a process that programmers must understand conceptually before being able to grasp the OOP code. Available in June, 1993. (Beginning to Intermediate)

Moving from Turbo Pascal to Turbo C++

Here's the perfect how-to book for Turbo Pascal programmers wanting to learn Turbo C++. This book introduces readers to Turbo C++ with complete coverage of object-oriented programming. It shows how a Turbo Pascal program is converted to Turbo C++ with more efficient code. (Beginning to Intermediate)

Moving from Basic to C

This book begins with a comparison of interpreters and compilers. Then the book features a general "look" comparison of the languages. The book then shows how one application written in BASIC is converted into C. This book is a complete step-by-step guide for moving a BASIC programmer into C. Available Summer, 1993. (Beginning to Intermediate)

DOS

1-800-HELP with DOS

Readers get their own DOS technical support system in this problem/solution guide. The "Directory Assistance" jump table lets readers identify problems by error message or symptom. The "Secrets and Surprises" notes point out undocumented features of DOS. Available in March, 1993. (Beginning to Intermediate)

Absolute Beginner's Guide to Memory Management

This book is targeted toward people who want to know the very basics of memory management and where they can apply that knowledge. Available in March, 1993. (Beginning)

Alan Simpson's DOS Secrets Unleashed

This book is the power user's guide to DOS! This comprehensive how-to guide is filled with practical tips, advice, tricks, and secrets for getting the most out of DOS. The three disks included contain Visual Basic for DOS programs, shareware utilities, and DOS enhancements. Available in March, 1993. (Intermediate to Advanced)

Windows

1-800-HELP with Windows

Readers get their own Windows technical support system in this problem/solution guide. The "Directory Assistance" jump table lets readers identify problems by error message or symptom. The "Secrets and Surprises" notes point out undocumented features of Windows. Available in April, 1993. (Beginning to Intermediate)

Tricks of the Windows Masters, Deluxe Edition

This edition of the best-selling book takes readers beyond the basics to the most advanced features of Windows. It provides numerous tips and tricks to help the reader maximize Windows performance. The book covers Windows 3.1 and Windows for Workgroups. The 3 disks included feature shareware packages specially designed for Windows 3.1. Available in March, 1993. (Intermediate to Advanced)

Windows Revealed

The most complete tutorial and reference for powerful PC results! This book contains virtually all the information Windows users need to know. It discusses desktop accessories and many best-selling Windows programs. (Beginning to Advanced)

Windows Resource and Memory Management

A behind-the-scenes look at how to develop an effective memory management strategy for Windows! This book/disk set is aimed at Windows users who want to eliminate the frustration of slow-running programs and running out of memory in Windows. (Intermediate to Advanced)

Absolute Beginner's Guide to DOS and Windows

This book is perfect for the person who wants to use DOS and Windows but needs a good starting point! It gives a thorough discussion of the two main operating systems in use today. Available in Spring, 1993. (Beginning)

Windows Programming

Teach Yourself Windows Programming in 21 Days

Users can achieve Windows success now! Each lesson can be completed in 4–5 hours or less. Shaded syntax boxes, Q & A sections, and "Do's and Don'ts" sections reinforce the important topics with Windows programming. Available Spring, 1993. (Beginning to Intermediate)

Uncharted Windows Programming

This book contains a fun collection of "how-to" essays on advanced Windows programming topics. Information is presented in a Problem, Solution, Secret format. The book includes a disk containing all the source code from the book, plus additional Windows shareware. Windows 3.1 and Win32 compatible. Available in April, 1993. (Advanced)

Windows Programmer's Guides

This series provides the most comprehensive information of specific topics of Windows programming. While most other Windows programming books just touch on topics such as OLE and DDE, DLLs and Memory Management, and Resources, Windows Programmer's Guides devote full attention to these areas. Experienced Windows programmers will find all they need to add power to their programming in these books. (Advanced)

Titles available:

> **Windows Programmer's Guide to Microsoft Foundation Class Library**
>
> **Windows Programmer's Guide to DLLs and Memory Management**

Windows Programmer's Guide to OLE and DDE

Windows Programmer's Guide to ObjectWindows Library

Windows Programmer's Guide to Resources

Windows Programmer's Guide to Borland C++ Tools

Windows Programmer's Guide to Serial Communications

Windows NT

Migrating to Windows NT

This book gives complete information on downsizing or migrating to Windows NT. It clarifies what moving to Windows NT means to end users, managers, and businesses. It contrasts Windows NT with other operating systems and enables readers to assess the impact Windows NT will have on their organization. Available in February, 1993. (Beginning to Advanced)

UNIX

The Waite Group's UNIX System V Primer, Second Edition

This book is a hands-on introduction to using UNIX! The text provides an updated, detailed overview of the UNIX operating system. The step-by-step introduction, numerous examples, exercises, and chapter reviews make this book ideal for beginners. (Beginning to Intermediate)

403

C Programming for UNIX

This book is intended for those with some prior knowledge of the C programming language, but who are unfamiliar with the UNIX development environment. The tutorial sections provide a fairly comprehensive introduction to the ANSI C language for beginners. The book is divided into three sections, covering C, UNIX, and reference material in great depth. (Beginning to Intermediate)

Networking

Absolute Beginner's Guide to Networking

This book is designed for anyone who needs to know about networking personal computers. Whether you are a beginning PC user or a "power" user, if you are interested in acquiring a network or are going to be using one, *Absolute Beginner's Guide to Networking* clearly and concisely explains the background, technologies, and possibilities that networking offers. It has numerous illustrations, an extensive LAN terminology glossary, many network product feature comparisons, and decision-making checklists. Available in May, 1993. (Beginning)

Technology

FractalVision: Put Fractals to Work for You

This book/disk combination shows users how to use fractals and teaches the mathematics behind fractal theory. The hands-on approach encourages readers to experiment using the fractal images on the disk. It is ideal for computer users, graphics enthusiasts, and programmers. (Beginning to Intermediate)

Multimedia Madness!

Comprehensive coverage of multimedia for the high-tech enthusiast! This book/CD-ROM/disk set provides a complete introduction for end-users as well as programmers. It provides step-by-step instructions for authoring multimedia projects. The CD-ROM and 3.5" disk includes multimedia creations, tools, and utilities. (Beginning to Intermediate)

Creating Virtual Reality

This book is perfect for computer users who want to experiment with virtual reality and high-tech graphics. It covers the history, state of the art, and future directions of virtual reality. The authors lead readers through all the steps in building a virtual world. The disk contains real-world simulations. (Intermediate to Advanced)

Other Titles of Interest

Memory Management for All of Us, Deluxe Edition

Maximize your PC performance with memory management! This national best-seller covers issues from the early PCs to the latest 486 speed demons. Boxed tips, notes, and cautions simplify the reader's search for answers to common problems. The disk contains utilities to help increase hard disk memory. Available in April, 1993. (Beginning to Advanced)

Programming Sound with DOS and Windows

The objective of this book is to teach the reader how to write DOS and Windows applications that incorporate playing real voices and music through the PC speaker while simultaneously moving text and graphic objects on the screen. Covers SoundBlaster. Available Spring, 1993.

Appendix

ASCII Table

Dec X_{10}	Hex X_{16}	Binary X_2	ASCII Character
000	00	0000 0000	null
001	01	0000 0001	☺
002	02	0000 0010	☻
003	03	0000 0011	♥
004	04	0000 0100	♦
005	05	0000 0101	♣
006	06	0000 0110	♠
007	07	0000 0111	●
008	08	0000 1000	■

Dec X_{10}	Hex X_{16}	Binary X_2	ASCII Character
009	09	0000 1001	○
010	0A	0000 1010	■
011	0B	0000 1011	♂
012	0C	0000 1100	♀
013	0D	0000 1101	♪
014	0E	0000 1110	♪♪
015	0F	0000 1111	☼
016	10	0001 0000	►
017	11	0001 0001	◄
018	12	0001 0010	↕
019	13	0001 0011	‼
020	14	0001 0100	¶
021	15	0001 0101	§
022	16	0001 0110	–
023	17	0001 0111	↨
024	18	0001 1000	↑
025	19	0001 1001	↓
026	1A	0001 1010	→
027	1B	0001 1011	←
028	1C	0001 1100	FS
029	1D	0001 1101	GS
030	1E	0001 1110	RS
031	1F	0001 1111	US
032	20	0010 0000	SP
033	21	0010 0001	!
034	22	0010 0010	"
035	23	0010 0011	#
036	24	0010 0100	$
037	25	0010 0101	%
038	26	0010 0110	&
039	27	0010 0111	'

Dec X_{10}	Hex X_{16}	Binary X_2	ASCII Character
040	28	0010 1000	(
041	29	0010 1001	)
042	2A	0010 1010	*
043	2B	0010 1011	+
044	2C	0010 1100	,
045	2D	0010 1101	-
046	2E	0010 1110	.
047	2F	0010 1111	/
048	30	0011 0000	0
049	31	0011 0001	1
050	32	0011 0010	2
051	33	0011 0011	3
052	34	0011 0100	4
053	35	0011 0101	5
054	36	0011 0110	6
055	37	0011 0111	7
056	38	0011 1000	8
057	39	0011 1001	9
058	3A	0011 1010	:
059	3B	0011 1011	;
060	3C	0011 1100	<
061	3D	0011 1101	=
062	3E	0011 1110	>
063	3F	0011 1111	?
064	40	0100 0000	@
065	41	0100 0001	A
066	42	0100 0010	B
067	43	0100 0011	C
068	44	0100 0100	D

continues

Dec X_{10}	Hex X_{16}	Binary X_2	ASCII Character
069	45	0100 0101	E
070	46	0100 0110	F
071	47	0100 0111	G
072	48	0100 1000	H
073	49	0100 1001	I
074	4A	0100 1010	J
075	4B	0100 1011	K
076	4C	0100 1100	L
077	4D	0100 1101	M
078	4E	0100 1110	N
079	4F	0100 1111	O
080	50	0101 0000	P
081	51	0101 0001	Q
082	52	0101 0010	R
083	53	0101 0011	S
084	54	0101 0100	T
085	55	0101 0101	U
086	56	0101 0110	V
087	57	0101 0111	W
088	58	0101 1000	X
089	59	0101 1001	Y
090	5A	0101 1010	Z
091	5B	0101 1011	[
092	5C	0101 1100	\
093	5D	0101 1101	]
094	5E	0101 1110	^
095	5F	0101 1111	–
096	60	0110 0000	`
097	61	0110 0001	a
098	62	0110 0010	b

Dec X_{10}	Hex X_{16}	Binary X_2	ASCII Character
099	63	0110 0011	c
100	64	0110 0100	d
101	65	0110 0101	e
102	66	0110 0110	f
103	67	0110 0111	g
104	68	0110 1000	h
105	69	0110 1001	i
106	6A	0110 1010	j
107	6B	0110 1011	k
108	6C	0110 1100	l
109	6D	0110 1101	m
110	6E	0110 1110	n
111	6F	0110 1111	o
112	70	0111 0000	p
113	71	0111 0001	q
114	72	0111 0010	r
115	73	0111 0011	s
116	74	0111 0100	t
117	75	0111 0101	u
118	76	0111 0110	v
119	77	0111 0111	w
120	78	0111 1000	x
121	79	0111 1001	y
122	7A	0111 1010	z
123	7B	0111 1011	{
124	7C	0111 1100	¦
125	7D	0111 1101	}
126	7E	0111 1110	~
127	7F	0111 1111	DEL

continues

411

Dec X_{10}	Hex X_{16}	Binary X_2	ASCII Character
128	80	1000 0000	Ç
129	81	1000 0001	ü
130	82	1000 0010	é
131	83	1000 0011	â
132	84	1000 0100	ä
133	85	1000 0101	à
134	86	1000 0110	å
135	87	1000 0111	ç
136	88	1000 1000	ê
137	89	1000 1001	ë
138	8A	1000 1010	è
139	8B	1000 1011	ï
140	8C	1000 1100	î
141	8D	1000 1101	ì
142	8E	1000 1110	Ä
143	8F	1000 1111	Å
144	90	1001 0000	É
145	91	1001 0001	æ
146	92	1001 0010	Æ
147	93	1001 0011	ô
148	94	1001 0100	ö
149	95	1001 0101	ò
150	96	1001 0110	û
151	97	1001 0111	ù
152	98	1001 1000	ÿ
153	99	1001 1001	Ö
154	9A	1001 1010	Ü
155	9B	1001 1011	¢
156	9C	1001 1100	£
157	9D	1001 1101	¥

Dec X_{10}	Hex X_{16}	Binary X_2	ASCII Character
158	9E	1001 1110	Pt
159	9F	1001 1111	ƒ
160	A0	1010 0000	á
161	A1	1010 0001	í
162	A2	1010 0010	ó
163	A3	1010 0011	ú
164	A4	1010 0100	ñ
165	A5	1010 0101	Ñ
166	A6	1010 0110	a̲
167	A7	1010 0111	o̲
168	A8	1010 1000	¿
169	A9	1010 1001	⌐
170	AA	1010 1010	¬
171	AB	1010 1011	½
172	AC	1010 1100	¼
173	AD	1010 1101	¡
174	AE	1010 1110	«
175	AF	1010 1111	»
176	B0	1011 0000	░
177	B1	1011 0001	▒
178	B2	1011 0010	▓
179	B3	1011 0011	│
180	B4	1011 0100	┤
181	B5	1011 0101	╡
182	B6	1011 0110	╢
183	B7	1011 0111	╖
184	B8	1011 1000	╕
185	B9	1011 1001	╣
186	BA	1011 1010	║

continues

Dec X_{10}	Hex X_{16}	Binary X_2	ASCII Character
187	BB	1011 1011	╗
188	BC	1011 1100	╝
189	BD	1011 1101	╜
190	BE	1011 1110	╛
191	BF	1011 1111	┐
192	C0	1100 0000	└
193	C1	1100 0001	┴
194	C2	1100 0010	┬
195	C3	1100 0011	├
196	C4	1100 0100	─
197	C5	1100 0101	+
198	C6	1100 0110	╞
199	C7	1100 0111	╟
200	C8	1100 1000	╚
201	C9	1100 1001	╔
202	CA	1100 1010	╩
203	CB	1100 1011	╦
204	CC	1100 1100	╠
205	CD	1100 1101	=
206	CE	1100 1110	╬
207	CF	1100 1111	╧
208	D0	1101 0000	╨
209	D1	1101 0001	╤
210	D2	1101 0010	╥
211	D3	1101 0011	╙
212	D4	1101 0100	╘
213	D5	1101 0101	╒
214	D6	1101 0110	╓
215	D7	1101 0111	╫
216	D8	1101 1000	╪

Dec X_{10}	Hex X_{16}	Binary X_2	ASCII Character
217	D9	1101 1001	⌟
218	DA	1101 1010	⌐
219	DB	1101 1011	█
220	DC	1101 1100	▄
221	DD	1101 1101	▌
222	DE	1101 1110	▐
223	DF	1101 1111	▀
224	E0	1110 0000	α
225	E1	1110 0001	β
226	E2	1110 0010	Γ
227	E3	1110 0011	π
228	E4	1110 0100	Σ
229	E5	1110 0101	σ
230	E6	1110 0110	μ
231	E7	1110 0111	τ
232	E8	1110 1000	Φ
233	E9	1110 1001	θ
234	EA	1110 1010	Ω
235	EB	1110 1011	δ
236	EC	1110 1100	∞
237	ED	1110 1101	ø
238	EE	1110 1110	∈
239	EF	1110 1111	∩
240	F0	1111 0000	≡
241	F1	1111 0001	±
242	F2	1111 0010	≥
243	F3	1111 0011	≤
244	F4	1111 0100	⌠
245	F5	1111 0101	⌡

continues

415

Dec X_{10}	Hex X_{16}	Binary X_2	ASCII Character
246	F6	1111 0110	÷
247	F7	1111 0111	≈
248	F8	1111 1000	°
249	F9	1111 1001	•
250	FA	1111 1010	·
251	FB	1111 1011	√
252	FC	1111 1100	η
253	FD	1111 1101	^{2}
254	FE	1111 1110	■
255	FF	1111 1111	

Note: The last 128 ASCII codes listed in this table, numbers 128 through 255, are specific to IBM PCs and IBM compatibles.

Glossary

accumulator   A variable in a program which keeps track of a running total.

address   The numeric location of a certain byte in memory.

APL   A programming language that requires a special keyboard because of its large character set. APL is excellent for scientific and engineering programming.

append   To add data to the end of a file.

array   A list of data items in memory that all have the same name and whose elements are differentiated by a subscript.

artificial intelligence   The science of programming computers so they can learn on their own and interpret a spoken language.

ASCII table   The American Standard Code for Information Interchange table that assigns each of the possible computer characters to a unique bit pattern.

assembler   A program that translates mnemonics into their binary equivalents.

BASIC   A programming language that is easy for beginning programmers to learn.

batch programming language   The language that lets you automate MS-DOS.

beta testing   The term applied to giving the user a copy of a preliminary program to test.

binary   The two states, on and off, that electricity can become.

binary digit   Also known as a *bit*. A 1 or a 0 that represents the on or off state of electricity.

binary search   The process of searching a sorted list of items for a value, starting at the midpoint and eliminating one half of the remaining list every time you look for a match.

bit   See *binary digit*.

branching   Jumping from one part of a program to another.

bubble sort   A specific way to sort data in a list that is easy to implement, but not as efficient as some of the other more advanced data-sorting methods.

bug   A program error that causes undesirable behavior from the computer.

byte   A single character inside the computer, which is comprised of eight bits.

C   A programming language that is extremely efficient.

C++   An improved version of the C programming language that incorporates object-oriented programming techniques.

carriage-return key   The key on your computer, often labeled Enter, that signals the end of a command or line of text.

CASE   Stands for *Computer-Aided Software Engineering*. CASE is a computer software system that helps you develop other software from the design stage through the implementation stage.

central processing unit   See *CPU*.

chargeback   An effective way to pay for a company's data processing department expenses by charging each department that uses the data processing department for the amount of the expense it incurs.

COBOL   A programming language designed for use in business.

code   The name given to program statements.

compiler   A program that converts a program's source code, written by you, into machine language.

computer information system   The collection of hardware, software, people, data, and procedures that must all be in place for a successful implementation of a computer project.

construct   A control statement in a programming language.

CPU   Stands for *central processing unit* and is the primary processor inside your computer's system unit that performs all computations and controls the rest of the computer.

CRAY   The name applied to supercomputers built by the Cray Research Company, the makers of most of the supercomputers today.

CRT   Stands for *cathode ray tube*, and is another name for the monitor.

cursor   The blinking line or box on your computer screen that tells you where the next character will appear on the screen.

data   Raw facts and figures. Data is the plural of *datum*, but is often used in the singular.

data entry   The process of entering data into a computer.

data processing   The act of taking raw data and turning it into meaningful information via a computer program.

data processing department   The department in a company that operates the computers and writes programs for the rest of the company.

database management   Using the computer to enter, edit, report, and track a large collection of related data.

debugging   The process of removing errors from a computer program.

decision   One of the three structured programming techniques where the program logic tests a relational value and executes one of two possible program paths.

default disk drive   The disk drive that is active before you begin a program.

desk check   The testing done by the programmer before giving the program to the user to test.

desktop computers   Another name often applied to microcomputers.

difference engine   The first computer, designed by Charles Babbage, which was never actually completed.

disassembler   Program that attempts to convert a compiled program back into a semblance of its source code. Disassemblers are inaccurate, but they do offer some help in reverse engineering for a compiled program.

disk drive   The magnetically recorded memory-storage device that holds non-volatile, long-term data for your computer.

DOS   Stands for *disk operating system.* See *operating system.*

downloading   The act of retrieving data from one computer to another.

downtime   The term applied to the time a computer is broken or is shut down for routine maintenance.

DP   An acronym for *data processing.*

editor   The text-entering program that looks like a word processor and is used by programmers to enter and correct program listings. There are two kinds of editors—line editors and full-screen editors.

Edlin   The MS-DOS line editor.

electronic spreadsheets   See *spreadsheets.*

end-user   The non-computer person who uses a computer and the programs on it to do work (also called *user*).

event-driven   The process used in Windows programs of responding to different events such as mouse movements and keystrokes.

extension   The optional three-letter part of a filename, separated from the first part with a period.

fields   A screen field is a place on the screen where the user answers a question or fills in a blank. In a disk file, a field is a column of data.

file handle   A number assigned to a file for use in a computer program.

first generation computers   The earliest, tube-based computers.

flowchart   A graphical representation of program logic.

flowchart template   A plastic outline of common flowchart symbols that helps you draw better looking flowcharts.

FORTRAN   A programming language good for scientific and engineering programming.

free-form   In reference to a programming language, one that does not require commands to begin in a specific column and one that allows placement of extra lines and spaces in the code to make it more readable.

full-screen editor   A program editor that gives you full control over the movement of the cursor for entering and changing text on the screen.

function   A built-in routine inside a programming language.

function keys   The keys labeled *F1* through *F10* (some keyboards go as high as *F12*) that perform a program-specific set of commands. Often used as shortcut keys for long strings of other commands.

GIGO   Stands for *garbage-in, garbage-out*, and is the term used when bad data entered into the computer results in bad information coming out.

GUI   Stands for *Graphical User Interface* and is used generically for Windows-like operating environments.

hardcopy   The name applied to printed output.

hardware   The physical components of a computer system such as the printer, screen, and keyboard.

hertz   The number of cycles per second that a note vibrates.

hexadecimal   The base-16 representation of numbers.

high-level language   A programming language closer to spoken instructions than either assembler or machine language.

I/O   Stands for *input/output* and is used for peripheral devices connected to your computer that perform both input and output, such as the disk drive and modem.

infinite loop   A program loop that has no way to end. The computer continues performing the loop until the programmer or user intervenes in some way.

information   Processed data; the output from computer programs.

input device   A peripheral device, such as the keyboard, that gets data from the outside world and sends it to the CPU for processing.

input validation   The process of writing a program so it checks a user's input for valid data.

integer   A whole number.

integrated circuit   The wafer-thin silicon chip inside your computer's system unit that holds the CPU and performs the computing.

interpreter   The translator that takes your program's source code and converts it into machine language one statement at a time. An interpreter is slower than a compiler, but is sometimes easier for beginners to use.

JCL   Stands for *Job Control Language* and is the name applied to the grouping of mainframe operating system commands.

K   Stands for *kilobyte* and is 1,024 characters of memory (often approximated as 1,000 characters of memory).

keyboard   The typewriter-like keys attached to your computer for the input of data.

kilobyte   See *K.*

line editor   A program editor that lets you edit only one line at a time and that allows no cursor control.

logic errors   Syntactically correct computer program instructions that make no sense when carried out.

loop   A repetitive sequence of program, flowchart, or pseudocode instructions.

looping   One of the three structured programming techniques where the program logic repeats until a certain condition is met.

low-level programming   Assembler or machine language programs.

machine   A name loosely applied that refers to a computer.

machine language A program translated into its binary form. Machine language is the only language computers can actually understand. All programming languages must be translated into machine language before the computer can carry out the instructions.

macro language An end-user application's built-in programming command language.

mainframe The second largest and fastest class of computers used by large businesses for data processing. Mainframes require large data processing staffs to maintain, operate, and program them.

megabyte Approximately one million characters of memory (1,048,576 bytes).

menu A list of program options from which you can select.

microcomputer The smallest and least expensive class of computers that are desktop-sized and house a microprocessor for the CPU.

microprocessor The name given to the integrated circuit chip inside PCs that comprises the computer's CPU.

minicomputer The second smallest class of computers that have multiple-user capabilities and that are used by smaller businesses for data processing.

mnemonic An abbreviation for a binary command name that is easier to remember than its binary counterpart.

modem A device that connects your computer to a phone line so the computer can communicate with other computers.

monitor The video screen connected to your computer that displays information for the user.

monochrome A monitor that can only display one color on a black or white background.

MS-DOS Stands for *Microsoft Disk Operating System* and is the operating system used by most IBM-compatible computers.

multimedia The combination of sound and graphics in a computer system.

multitasking When a computer can perform more than one task at the same time.

non-volatile   Applied to memory that is not erased when the computer's power is turned off.

numeric keypad   The section on most computer keyboards that has the numbers *0* through *9* arranged in a calculator-like arrangement for easy input of numbers.

object-oriented programming   A new programming style that uses active data and that speeds the program-writing process.

off-site   Used to indicate that backups of important computer software are kept away from the location of the computer.

online services   Computerized bulletin boards to which you can connect your computer and collect information, pay bills, and shop electronically.

OOP   Acronym for *object-oriented programming*.

operating system   The program that acts as the go-between for your hardware and software.

operator   In a programming language, an operator is a symbol that indicates an action must be performed (operated) on data, such as a plus or minus sign. Mainframes have human operators that monitor their resources and run the computer.

operator precedence table   Also called a *hierarchy chart*, describes the order that a programming language evaluates math operators in an expression.

output definition   The first step when designing a computer program; involves determining exactly what the user wants the program to produce.

output device   A peripheral device, such as the monitor, that sends data from the CPU to the outside world.

overhead   A way a company pays for its data processing department's activities by taking a portion out of each of the other departments' budgets.

overtype mode   In a program editor, overtype mode is active when the characters you type replace those on the screen.

parallel arrays   Arrays with the same number of elements where each element in one array corresponds to an element in the other one.

parallel test   When the user tests a program using regular manual procedures to ensure that the program produces the correct results.

Pascal   A programming language that supports structured programming very well.

PC   Stands for *personal computer* and is the name generically given to micro-computers, especially those that are IBM-compatible.

people year   A time measurement used in the computer industry for estimating the amount of time needed to complete a computer project.

peripheral devices   The I/O devices connected to your computer that collect or display data in some fashion.

pixel   Stands for *picture element* and represents one graphic dot on the computer's screen.

PL/I   A massive programming language that IBM had hoped would replace all the others in the late 1960s. It did not.

print zone   A column on your screen or printer that BASIC uses to separate data. A new print zone occurs every 14 columns.

printer   The peripheral device attached to your computer that sends results to paper.

procedural language   The opposite of an object-oriented language; one that performs its instructions in a step-by-step fashion with the program instructions operating separately from the data.

profiler   A program that measures another program's execution and that gives hints about possible efficiency improvements you can make.

program   A list of detailed instructions the computer requires to perform a task.

program generator   A program that writes simple programs for you, thus saving you work.

programmer   A person who writes computer programs.

prompts   The messages that describe the next input needed by the program.

prototype   A model of a computer program that simulates what the final computer program will look like.

425

pseudocode   Structured and rigid English-like writing that describes program logic.

punch cards   Cards that are punched with holes by a card-punch machine and that were used for input and output in earlier computers.

RAM   Stands for *random-access memory*, which is volatile memory that holds data and programs that your computer processes.

random-access control   Reading and writing to a data file in any order, not necessarily in sequence.

random-access memory   See *RAM*.

read-only memory   See *ROM*.

records   The lines of related data in a datafile.

relational test   The process of testing a program relation to determine the next program path to take.

resolution   The crispness of graphics elements on the screen.

ROM   Stands for *read-only memory*, which is memory that holds a test and startup program for your computer's power-up sequence. You cannot change the contents of ROM.

RPG   A programming language that is good for generating reports, but is more cryptic than most of the other programming languages.

screen generators   Programs that help you design user screens by arranging the screen text and entry fields; implemented so the user does not need to know how to program.

second generation computers   Computers based on solid-state transistor electronics which were faster, cheaper, and more reliable than the first generation computers.

sequence   One of the three structured programming techniques where the program logic flows from one statement to the next in sequence.

sequential file processing   Reading, writing, and appending to a datafile in sequence from the first record to the last.

sequential search   The process of searching a list of values, from the beginning of the list, until you find a match.

shared program   The concept of storing both the program and data in memory at the same time.

site license   A special kind of software license that allows you and others in your company to use the software you purchase without having to buy a separate copy for each user.

software   Computer programs and data.

software license   You purchase and agree to a software license when you buy a disk with a program on it. The software license ensures that you will use the software for your own use and will not distribute it to others without approval.

sort   The process of putting a list of values in order, such as alphabetizing names and putting numbers into ascending or descending sequence.

source code   The program listing that you write before it is translated into machine language.

spaghetti code   A method of writing programs that are unorganized and difficult to follow.

spreadsheet   A program that allows fast and easy analysis of numbers in an accountant's rectangular worksheet format. A spreadsheet is like a word processor for numbers.

standards manual   A book that describes the company's recommended way to write programs.

statements   The lines of instructions in a program.

string   A group of characters strung together and referred to as a group.

structured programming   A methodology of writing programs so they are easier to read and maintain. Structured programs contain three constructs: sequence, decision, and looping.

structured walkthrough   When a committee of programmers and analysts study a program looking for improvements that can be made to the code.

subroutine A stand-alone section of a program that you execute from another part of the program.

supercomputers The largest, fastest, and most expensive computer, the speed of which is improved by supercooling its internal components with liquid gases.

syntax The ordering, grammar, and spelling of a spoken or programming language.

system A collection of interrelated parts that work together to accomplish a task.

systems analysis and design The method of analyzing a user's needs and designing a computer system to fulfill those needs.

Systems Analyst The liaison in a company that acts as a go-between for the users and the programmers.

third generation computers The computers based on integrated circuit chips that are still in use today and that offer advanced processing power in a small space at a low cost.

TLA Stands for *three-letter acronym*, used humorously by computer professionals as a label for all the acronyms in the business such as CPU, IBM, RAM, and ROM.

top-down design The process of starting at the overall objective and breaking it down until all the details fall out.

2's complement The negative representation of a number at the binary level.

UNIX A multiple-user operating system used on minicomputers and some microcomputers.

uploading The act of sending data from one computer to another.

user See *end-user*.

user-friendly An often overused term that software and hardware vendors use to describe their products while implying the products are easy to use.

variable A storage location in memory used by a program to hold data.

vi Stands for *visual editor* and is a full-screen editor available on most UNIX minicomputer systems.

Visual Basic   A special version of BASIC that enables you to create Windows applications by moving graphical elements on the screen and doing very little programming.

volatile   A term applied to memory that is erased when your computer is turned off.

Windows   A graphical user interface to make operating a computer easier. Windows is written and distributed by Microsoft, Incorporated.

word processor   A program that turns your computer into a powerful electronic typewriter with advanced text-editing capabilities.

word wrap   A feature of most word processors that automatically wraps a partial word at the end of a line down to the next line as you type it.

Index

Symbols

: (semicolon)
    displaying question marks, 223
    displaying values, 210-211
2's complement, 141, 428
7-bit ASCII tables, 137
8-bit ASCII tables, 137

A

A Programming Language, *see* APL
  language
abacus, 30, 34
access
    disk files, 264-266
    random-file, 275-276
accumulators, 307-310, 417
ADA language, 160-161
adapter cards, 280
addresses, 204, 417
algorithms, 306
    accumulator variables, 307-310
    counter variables, 307-310
    data swapping, 310-312
    sorts, 312-317
Alt key, 48
ANSI (American National
  Standards Institute), 37, 152
APL language, 160, 417
append mode, 266
appending to data files, 273-274

Apple computer, 36
arithmetic
    binary, 139-144
    QBasic language, 214-218
arrays, 254-258, 417
    elements, 256
    erasing, 260-262
    parallel, 260, 316, 424
    reserving space, 258-260
    searching, 317-327
        binary, 324-327
        improved sequential,
            320-324
        sequential, 319-320
artificial intelligence, 68, 417
ascending order sorts, 312
ASCII tables, 137, 407-417
    7-bit, 137
    8-bit, 137
assemblers, 146, 417
assigning values, 206-208
Assistant Programmers, 350

B

backups, 25, 275
base-2 numbering system, 143
base-10 numbering system, 143
base-16 numbering system, 148
BASIC language, 36, 417
    original version, 178-180
    QBasic version, 180-184
        assigning values, 206-208
        clearing screens, 214
        comparing data, 232-234

displaying values, 208-213
entering and running
    programs, 199-202
exponentiation operator, 216
inputting keyboard data,
    222-231
integer division, 216
math, 214-218
math operators, 215
MOD operator, 216
printing values, 213
relational tests, 234-236
remarks, 202
storing data, 204-206
Visual Basic version, 184,
    187-189
    for DOS version, 190
    graphical orientation, 187
    relationship with Windows,
        185
    runtime interpreter, 186
batch programming language, 418
BEEP statement, 281
beta testing, 131, 418
binary, 418
    arithmetic, 139-144
    digits, see bits
    numbers, 142
    searches, 324-327, 418
bits, 136, 418
bottom-up design, 86
boxes, drawing, 295-296
branching, 418
bubble sorts, 313-317, 418

bugs, 74, 418
  logic errors, 75
  syntax errors, 75
bytes, 47, 137, 418

C

C language, 37, 418
  commands, 173
  creation of, 169-170
  growth of, 170-172
  operators, 173-174
  publications, 391-392
C++ language, 37, 176-177,
  393-394, 418
CALL statement, 329
calling subroutines, 329
carriage return key, 48, 418
CASE (Computer-Aided Software
  Engineering), 372-374, 418
cash register program, 227-228
cathode ray tubes (CRT), 49, 419
central computing, 362
central processing unit (CPU), 45,
  418
character string data, 150
chargebacks, 344-345, 418
chips, 33
CIRCLE statement, 297
circuits, integrated, 33, 422
clauses, *see* options
clearing screens, 214
CLOSE statement, 266
closing disk files, 266-267
CLS statement, 214

COBOL language, 36, 152-156,
  418
  data division, 153
  environment division, 153
  identification division, 153
  procedure division, 153
code, 419
  pseudocode, 105-108
  source, 70, 427
  spaghetti, 125, 427
combining PRINT and INPUT
  statements, 226-231
comma-separated data, 267
command strings, 285
commands
  macro, 381
  see also, statements
commas, displaying values, 211
Commom Business Oriented
  Language, *see* COBOL language
comparing data, 232-234
compilers, 71-74, 419
computer consultants, 363-364
Computer-Aided Software Engineering (CASE), 372-374, 418
computers
  abilities, 4
  Apple, 36
  business uses, 14-16
  compared to people, 18
  desktop, 43, 420
  EDSAV, 36
  EDVAC, 36
  ENIAC, 35

fifth generation, 38
first generation, 30-31
fourth generation, 38
historical milestones, 34-38
household uses, 11-14
IBM PC, 37
information systems, 19, 419
    data, 23-24
    data processing procedures,
      24-25
    hardware, 19-22
    people, 23
    software, 22-23
  mainframes, 41-42
  Mark I, 35
  microcomputers, 34, 43-44
  minicomputers, 42-43
  misconceptions, 6-11
  personal, 43, 425
  second generation, 32, 426
  supercomputers, 40-41
  third generation, 33-34, 428
  TRS-80, 36
  tube-based, 30
computing
  central, 362
  distributed, 362
constructs, 125, 419
contract programmers, 345
controlling FOR loops, 242-245
coordinates, 288
counters, 307-310
CPU (central processing unit), 45,
  418

Cray Research Company, 40
CRAY supercomputers, 419
creating output files, 267-270
CRT (cathode ray tube), 49, 419
CRT Display Layout Forms, 91
Ctrl key, 48
cursors, 48, 300-301, 419

D

data, 4, 23-24, 419
  character string, 150
  comma-separated, 267
  comparing, 232-234
  downloading, 362
  entry, 419
  processing, 419
  storing, 136-139, 204-206
  swapping, 310-312
  uploading, 362
Data Entry Clerks, 348-350
data files, appending to, 273-274
data processing departments,
  340-343, 419
  chargeback, 344-345
  contract programmers, 345
  equipment, 362-363
  jobs
    Assistant Programmers, 350
    Data Entry Clerks, 348-350
    educational requirements,
      347-348
    management, 354-356
    outlook, 346-347

Programmer, 351
Programmer Analyst, 352
Senior Programmer, 351
Senior Programmer Analyst, 352
Senior Systems Analyst, 354
Systems Analyst, 353
moving programs into production, 359-361
overhead, 343-344
resources, 342
standards manuals, 356-357
structured walkthroughs, 357-358
database
languages, 383-384
management, 16, 419
DEBUG program, 147
debuggers, 119
debugging, 75, 419
decision flowcharting symbol, 98
default disk drives, 265, 419
definition, output, 91-93
demonstration and prototyping programs, 94
descending order sorts, 312
design, 82-85
bottom-up, 86
defining output, 85-86
tools, 91-93
top-down approach, 86-91
working with users, 93-94
developing logic, 94-95
flowcharts, 95-105
pseudocode, 105-108

top-down, 86-91
writing the program, 107-108
desk checks, 130, 420
desktop computers, 43, 420
devices
input, 46, 422
output, 46, 424
peripheral, 46, 425
difference engines, 35, 420
DIM statement, 258
disassemblers, 58, 420
disk operating system (DOS), 50
disks
drives, 47, 265, 420
files, 254, 262-263
closing, 266-267
fields, 263
opening, 264-266
reading, 271-273
records, 263
floppy, 47
hard, 47
displaying values, 208-210
with commas, 211-213
with semicolons, 210-211
distributed computing, 362
divide and conquer approach, 324
division, integer, 216
DO-UNTIL loop, 247-249
DO-WHILE loop, 246
DOS (disk operating system), 50, 399-400, 420
dot matrix printers, 49
downloading, 362, 420
downtime, 41, 420

drawing
   boxes, 295-296
   lines, 293-295
drives, default disk, 265

E

EBCDIC table, 138
editors, 112-113, 420
   free-form, 421
   full-screen, 116
      debuggers, 119
      editing window, 117
      integration, 118
      menus, 118
      navigating, 118
      profilers, 120
   line, 113-116, 422
      Edlin, 113-115, 420
      vi, 113
Edlin editor, 113, 420
   asterisk prompt, 114
   commands, 115
EDSAV computer, 36
EDVAC computer, 36
egoless programmers, 358
electronic spreadsheets, *see*
   spreadsheets
elements, array, 256
ELSE option, 234
ELSEIF statement, 235
END statement, 209
end-users, 5, 420
engines, difference, 35
ENIAC computers, 35
Enter key, 48

entering programs, 199-202
EOF() function, 271
ERASE statement, 260
erasing arrays, 260-262
errors
   logic, 75, 422
   syntax, 75
Esc key, 48
event driven programs, 185, 420
EXIT FOR statement, 244
expansion slots, 46
exponentiation operator, 216
extensions, 262, 420

F

fields, 92, 263, 420
fifth generation computers, 38
file handles, 420
filenames, 262
files
   backups, 275
   data, appending to, 273-274
   disk, 254, 262-263
      closing, 266-267
      fields, 263
      opening, 264-266
      reading, 271-273
      records, 263
   handles, 265
   multiple, opening, 274-275
   non-volatile, 262
   output, creating, 267-270
   records, writing, 267-270
first generation computers, 30-31
floppy disks, 47

flow connector flowcharting
symbol, 99
flow direction flowcharting
symbol, 99
flowcharting symbols
decision, 98
flow connector, 99
flow direction, 99
I/O, 98
off-page, 98
process, 98
terminal, 98
flowcharts, 95-99, 421
examples, 103-105
rules, 99-103
templates, 95
FOR-NEXT loop, 238-245
Formula Translator, *see*
FORTRAN language
FORTRAN language, 36, 149,
421
fourth generation computers, 38
free form languages, 168, 421
frequency, 282
full-screen editors, 116, 421
debuggers, 119
editing window, 117
integration, 118
menus, 118
navigating in, 118
profilers, 120
function keys, 48, 421
functions, 421
EOF(), 271
funny money, 344

G

games, number-guessing, 247-248
garbage in, garbage out (GIGO),
23, 421
generators, program, 370-372
GIGO (garbage in, garbage out),
23, 421
GOSUB statement, 329-332
GOTO statement, 125
grade-printing program, 241
graphical user interface (GUI), 51,
166, 421
graphics, 286-287
graphics adapter cards, 280
graphs, text-based, 298-300
grouping routines, 332
GUI (graphical user interface), 51,
166, 421

H

handles, file, 265
hard copies, 49
hard disks, 47
hard-wired programming, 144
hardcopy, 421
hardware, 19-22, 44-45, 421
disk drives, 47
hard disks, 47
monitors, 49
printers, 49
system units, 45-47
hertz, 281, 421
high-level languages, 149, 421

I

I/O (input/output), 421
  devices, 46
  flowcharting symbol, 98
IBM PC computers, 37
IC (integrated circuit), 33
IF statement, 232-234
improved sequential searches,
  320-324
incremeting variables, 307
infinite loops, 128, 422
information, 4
information systems, 19, 419
  data processing procedures,
    24-25
  hardware, 19-22
  people, 23
  software, 22-23
input, 5
  devices, 46, 422
  mode, 199, 265
  validation, 236, 422
INPUT # statement, 271
INPUT statement, 222-224
  combined with PRINT
    statement, 226-231
  inputting strings and multiple
    variables, 225-226
input/output, see I/O
Insert key, 199
integer division, 216
integers, 422
integrated circuits (IC), 33, 422
interfaces, GUI, 51, 166
interpreters, 71, 422
  runtime, 186

J-K

Job Control Language (JCL), 422

K (kilobyte), 422
keyboards, 48, 422
  sending input, 222-224
keypads, numeric, 48
keys
  Alt, 48
  carriage-return, 418
  Ctrl, 48
  Enter, 48
  Esc, 48
  function, 48
  Insert, 199
  PageDown, 199
  PageUp, 199
keystroke recorders, macro, 380
keywords, LET, 206
kilobyte (K), 47, 422

L

language translators, 71
  compilers, 73-74
  interpreters, 71-73
languages, 67-70, 131
  ADA, 160-161
  APL, 160, 417
  BASIC, 36, 417
    original version, 178-180
    QBasic version, 182-184,
      199-206, 391
    QuickBASIC version,
      180-182
    Visual Basic version,
      184-190, 396-398, 429

batch programming, 418
C, 37, 418
    commands, 173
    creation, 169-170
    growth of, 170-172
    operators, 173-174
    publications, 391-392
C++, 37, 176-177, 418
    publications, 393-394
COBOL, 36, 152-156, 418
FORTRAN, 36, 149, 421
free form, 168, 421
high-level, 149, 421
low-level, 147
machine, 71, 423
macro, 423
non-traditional, 379
    database, 383-384
    macro languages, 379-383
    MS-DOS batch, 384-385
Pascal, 166-169, 425
    publications, 390
PL/I, 157-158, 425
procedural, 159, 425
RPG, 158-160
RPM, 426
self-documenting, 151
Turbo C++, publications,
    394-396
laser printers, 49
LET keyword, 206
licensed software, 58
licenses
    site, 22
    software, 22

line editors, 113-116, 422
    Edlin, 113
        asterisk prompt, 114
        commands, 115
    vi, 113
LINE INPUT statement, 270
line printers, 213
LINE statement, 293
lines, drawing, 293-295
listings
    6.1. A sample FORTRAN
        program, 150-151
    6.2. A sample COBOL
        program, 153-155
    6.3. A sample PL/I program,
        158
    6.4. A sample RPG program,
        159
    7.1. A sample Pascal program,
        168
    7.2. A sample C program, 175
    7.3. A sample C++ program,
        177
    7.4. A sample original BASIC
        program, 178-179
    7.5. A sample QuickBASIC
        program, 181-182
    8.1. The QBasic program with
        shortcut remarks, 203-204
    9.1. Demonstrating INPUT, 224
    9.2. A cash register program for
        a small store, 227-228
    9.3. Demonstrates various PRINT
        USING options, 230

9.4. Improving the look of dollar values, 230-231

9.5. Using an IF statement, 232

9.6. An IF within the ELSE must become ELSEIF, 236

9.7. Using SELECT CASE to select from several tests, 237

9.8. Using FOR and NEXT to control a counting loop, 238-239

9.9. Printing without a FOR-NEXT loop, 240

9.10. Printing a message several times, 240

9.11. A teacher's grade-printing program, 241

9.12. Counting down from 10 to 1, 243

9.13. Printing the first few even and odd numbers, 243-244

9.14. Demonstrating the EXIT FOR statement, 245

9.15. Controlling the grade printing with a DO-WHILE loop, 246

9.16. A number-guessing game, 247-248

10.1. A partial program that requests student names and grades without using arrrays, 255-256

10.2. Improving the grade program with arrays, 257

10.3. The grade program that stores data and prints it later, 259

10.4. A program that erases an array, 261

10.5. Using WRITE # to write a record to a file, 268

10.6. Writing the file based on more user input, 269

10.7. Reading a data file from the disk, 272

10.8. Appending to the end of a file created earlier, 274

10.9. Creating a backup file, 275

11.1. Getting a beep from the speaker, 281

11.2. Producing every note possible on a PC, 283

11.3. Producing a rising and falling siren, 283-284

11.4. Generating strange sounds with SOUND, 284

11.5. Turning on some graphics pixels, 289

11.6. Turning on and off some graphics pixels, 290-291

11.7. Turning on lots of pixels with nested FOR loops, 292

11.8. Drawing lines with LINE, 294-295

11.9. Drawing boxes on the screen, 296

11.10. Drawing several running circles, 297

11.11. Producing a text graph without graphics, 299

11.12. Using LOCATE to print a word at different locations on the screen, 301

12.1. A number-guessing game with a counter variable, 308

12.2. A grade-reporting and averaging program, 309-310

12.3. Sorting a list of values with the bubble sort, 314

12.4. Sorting names is as easy as sorting numbers in QBasic, 316-317

12.5. Using a sequential search in an inventory application, 319-320

12.6. Improving the sequential search, 322

12.7. Using a binary search, 325-326

12.8. A program outline that does not use subroutines, 329-330

12.9. A program outline that does not use subroutines, 331

12.10. A program that uses subroutines for everything, 333-334

LOCATE statement, 300
logic errors, 75, 422
look-up routines, 317-318
looping, 128-130, 422
loops, 237-238, 422
   DO-UNTIL, 247-249
   DO-WHILE, 246
   FOR-NEXT, 238-245

   infinite, 128, 422
   nesting, 292
low-level programming, 147, 422
LPRINT statement, 213

M

M (megabyte), 47, 423
machine languages, 71, 423
machines, 34, 422
macro languages, 379-383, 423
macros, 15
   commands, 381
   keystroke recorders, 380
mainframes, 41-42, 423
Mark I computers, 35
megabyte (M), 47, 423
memory, 64, 136
   measurements, 47
   non-volatile, 424
   RAM, 46
   ROM, 47
   volatile, 429
menus, 423
microcomputers, 34, 43-44, 423
microprocessors, 34, 45, 423
minicomputers, 42-43, 423
mnemonics, 145
MOD operator, 216
modems, 46, 423
modes
   append, 266
   input, 265
   insert, 199
   output, 266
   overtype, 199, 424

monitors, 49, 423

monochrome monitors, 49, 423

moving programs into production, 359-361

MS-DOS operating system, 44, 385, 423

multimedia, 12, 423

multitasking, 363, 423

N

naming variables, 204-206

nesting loops, 292

networking, publications, 404

non-volatile files, 262

non-volatile memory, 424

null value, 225

number-guessing game, 247-248

numbering systems
    base 2, 143
    base 10, 143
    base 16, 148

numeric keypads, 48, 424

O

object-oriented programming, *see* OOP

off-site, 424

online services, 13, 424

OOP (object-oriented programming), 37, 66, 373-375, 424
    learning, 377-378
    objects, 375-377
    support languages, 378-379

OPEN statement, 264, 273

opening
    disk files, 264-266
    multiple files, 274-275

operating systems, 49-51, 424
    DOS, 50
    MS-DOS, 44, 385, 423
    UNIX, 42, 170, 428
        publications, 403-404

operators, 424
    exponentiation, 216
    MOD, 216
    precedence, 215, 424
    relational, 235

OPTION BASE statement, 259

options
    ELSE, 234
    STEP, 288, 294
    THEN, 233
    USING, 228

output, 5, 63
    definition, 91-93, 424
    devices, 46, 424
    files, creating, 267-270
    mode, 266

overhead, 343-344, 424

overtype mode, 199, 424

P

PageDown key, 199

PageUp key, 199

parallel
    arrays, 260, 316, 424
    tests, 131, 425

parentheses, and operator precedence, 215

Pascal language, 166-169, 425
    publications, 390
Pascalines, 35
passwords, 25
PCs (personal computers), 43, 425
people year, 425
peripheral devices, 46, 425
picture elements, *see* pixels
pixels, 286, 425
    turning on and off, 288-293
PL/I language, 157-158, 425
placing text, 300-301
PLAY statement, 285
precedence, operator, 215
PRESET statement, 288
PRINT statement, 208, 300
    combined with INPUT
        statement, 226-231
print zones, 211, 425
printer spacing charts, 91
printers, 49, 425
    dot matrix, 49
    laser, 49
    line, 213
printing
    to screens, 211
    values, 213
procedural
    languages, 159, 425
    programming, 377
process flowcharting symbol, 98
processing, sequential file, 275
profilers, 120, 425
program generators, 370-372, 425
Programmer Analyst, 352

programmers, 425
    Assistant Programmers, 350
    contract, 345
    egoless, 358
    Programmer, 351
    Programmer Analyst, 352
    Senior Programmer, 351
    Senior Programmer Analyst,
      352
programming
    hard-wired, 144
    high-level, 149
    low-level, 147, 422
    OOP, 66
    procedural, 377
    shared-program, 144
    structured, 66, 121-126, 427
        decision, 127-128
        looping, 128-130
        sequence, 126, 426
Programming Language I, *see* PL/I
programs, 5, 59, 425
    array erasing, 261
    cash register, 227-228
    DEBUG, 147
    debugging, 75
    demonstration and prototyping,
     94
    design, 83-85
        defining output, 85-94
        developing logic, 94-108
        writing program, 107-108
    entering, 199-202
    event driven, 185
    grade-printing, 241

moving into production, 359-361

number-guessing game, 247-248

running, 199-202

shared, 427

source, 70

storing, 62, 136-139

testing, 130-131

   beta testing, 131

   desk checking, 130

   parallel testing, 131

prompts, 92, 425

prototypes, 94, 425

PSET statement, 288

pseudocode, 105-108, 426

publications

   C language, 391-392

   C++ language, 393-394

   DOS, 399-400

   Moving... series, 398-399

   networking, 404

   Pascal language, 390

   QBasic language, 391

   technology, 404-405

   Turbo C++ language, 394-396

   UNIX operating system, 403-404

   Visual Basic language, 396-398

   Windows, 400-403

   Windows NT, 403

punch cards, 35, 426

Q

QBasic language, 182-184

   comparing data, 232-234

   inputting keyboard data, 222-231

   integer division, 216

   math, 214-218

   MOD operator, 216

   operators

      exponentiation, 216

      math, 215

   programs, entering and running, 199-202

   publications, 391

   relational tests, 234-236

   remarks, 202

   screens, clearing, 214

   storing data, 204-206

   values

      assigning, 206-208

      displaying, 208-213

      printing, 213

QuickBASIC language, 180-182

R

RAM (random-access memory), 426

random-access control, 318, 426

random-access memory (RAM), 426

random-file access, 275-276

read-only memory (ROM), 47, 426

reading disk files, 271-273

receiving keyboard input, 222-224

records, 263, 426
  writing to files, 267-270

relational
  operators, 235
  tests, 234-236, 426

REM statement, 202

remarks, 179, 202
  shortcut, 203

Report Program Generator, *see* RPG language

reserving array space, 258-260

resolution, 286, 426

RETURN statement, 329, 332

ROM (read-only memory), 47, 426

routines
  grouping, 332
  see also subroutines

RPG language, 158-160, 426

RPG specification sheets, 160

running programs, 199-202

runtime interpreters, 186

S

screen generators, 92, 426

SCREEN statement, 287-288

screens
  clearing, 214
  video, 49

SDK (Software Developer's Kit), 186

searching
  arrays, 317-327
    binary, 324-327
    improved sequential, 320-324
    sequential, 318-320, 427
  divide and conquer approach, 324

second generation computers, 32, 426

security, 24-25

SELECT CASE statement, 236-237

self-documenting languages, 151

semicolons (:)
  displaying question marks, 223
  displaying values, 210-211

Senior Programmer, 351

Senior Programmer Analyst, 352

Senior Systems Analyst, 354

sequence, 426

sequential file processing, 275, 426

sequential searches, 318-320, 427
  improved, 320-324

shared programs, 427

shared-program programming, 144

shortcut remarks, 203

site licenses, 22, 427

slots, expansion, 46

software, 20-23, 427
  licensed, 58
  licenses, 22, 427

Software Developer's Kit (SDK), 186
sorts, 312-317, 427
 ascending order, 312
 bubble, 313-317, 418
 descending order, 312
SOUND statement, 281-284
 duration, 282
 hertz, 282
source code, 427
source programs, 70
spaghetti code, 125, 427
spreadsheets, 14-16, 427
standards manuals, 356-357, 427
statements, 427
 BEEP, 281
 CALL, 329
 CIRCLE, 297
 CLOSE, 266
 CLS, 214
 DIM, 258
 ELSEIF, 235
 END, 209
 ERASE, 260
 EXIT FOR, 244
 GOSUB, 329-332
 GOTO, 125
 IF, 232-234
 INPUT, 222-224
  combined with PRINT statement, 226-231
  inputting strings and multiple variables, 225-226
 INPUT #, 271
 LINE, 293

LINE INPUT, 270
LOCATE, 300
looping, see loops
LPRINT, 213
OPEN, 264, 273
OPTION BASE, 259
PLAY, 285
PRESET, 288
PRINT, 208, 300
 combined with INPUT statement, 226-231
PSET, 288
REM, 202
RETURN, 329, 332
SCREEN, 287-288
SELECT CASE, 236-237
SOUND, 281-284
 duration, 282
 hertz, 282
SUB, 329
STEP option, 288, 294
storing
 data, 136-139, 204-206
 programs, 62, 136-139
strings, 427
 command, 285
 inputting, 225-226
structured English, 105
structured programming, 66, 121-126, 427
 decision, 127-128
 looping, 128-130
 sequence, 126, 426
structured walkthroughs, 357-358, 427

SUB statement, 329
subroutines, 328-334, 428
  calling, 329
subscripts, 257
supercomputers, 40-41, 428
symbols, flowcharting
  decision, 98
  flow connector, 99
  flow direction, 99
  I/O, 98
  off-page, 98
  process, 98
  terminal, 98
syntax, 68, 428
  errors, 75
systems, 428
  analysis and design, 82, 428
  information, 19
    data, 23-24
    data processing procedures,
    24-25
    hardware, 19-22
    people, 23
    software, 22-23
  units, 45-47
Systems Analyst, 353, 428

T

tables
  ASCII, 137, 407-417
  EBCDIC, 138
templates, flowchart, 95
temporary variables, 312

terminal flowcharting symbol, 98
testing programs, 130-131
  beta testing, 131
  desk checking, 130
  parallel testing, 131, 425
  relational testing, 234-236, 426
text, placing, 300-301
text-based graphs, 298-300
THEN option, 233
third generation computers, 33-34,
  428
TLAs (three-letter acronyms), 18,
  428
top-down design, 86-91, 428
transistors, 32
translators, language
  compilers, 73-74
  interpreters, 71-73
TRS-80 computer, 36
tube-based computers, 30
Turbo C++ language, publications,
  394-396

U

UNIX operating system, 42, 170,
  428
  publications, 403-404
uploading, 428
  data, 362
user-friendly, 10, 428
users, 420
USING option, 228

V

validation, input, 236
values
    assigning, 206-208
    displaying, 208-210
        with commas, 211-213
        with semicolons, 210-211
    null, 225
    printing, 213
    swapping, 310-312
variables, 428
    accumulator, 307-310
    counter, 307-310
    incrementing, 307
    multiple, inputting, 225-226
    names, 204-206
    temporary, 312
    values, swapping, 310-312
VGA (Video Graphics Array), 280
vi (visual editor), 113, 428
Video Graphics Array (VGA), 280
video screens, 49
Visual Basic language, 184-189, 429
    for DOS version, 190
    graphical orientation, 187
    publications, 396-398
    relationship with Windows, 185
    runtime interpreter, 186
volatile memory, 429

W

walkthroughs, structures, 357-358
"what if" analysis, 14
whitespace, 168
Windows, 10, 429
    publications, 400-403
    relationship with Visual Basic, 185
Windows NT publications, 403
word processing, 13
word processors, 429
word wrap, 48, 112, 429
WRITE # command, 267
writing records to files, 267-270

X-Y-Z

x-coordinates, 288

y-coordinates, 288

zones, print, 211

Order Your Program & Tutorial Disk Today!

Instead of typing the code you find in *Absolute Beginner's Guide to Programming*, you can load the programs from a companion disk and forget about the tedious typing errors that plague so many first-time programmers. As you learn QBasic with this book's text, you will appreciate not having to fight the keyboard as you type, edit, and test each program.

As a bonus, you will also receive a set of *Tutorial Example Programs*, a new concept that beginning programmers will find invaluable as they move into intermediate and advanced QBasic programming. The disk contains over 200 programs that highlight *every* QBasic command and function. As you progress with QBasic, learning more of its advanced commands, you will be able to turn to this TEP companion disk and find a program that spotlights any QBasic command, no matter how common or obscure.

Disks are available in 3 ½-inch format. The cost is $12 per disk. (When ordering from outside the U.S., please add $5 for extra shipping and handling and make sure funds are drawn on a U.S. bank.)

Just fill in the blanks on this page or a copy of this page, and mail it with your check or postal money order (sorry, no credit card orders) to:

Greg Perry
QBasic Companion Disk
P.O. Box 35752
Tulsa, OK 74153-0752

Please print the following information:

Number of Disks: _____ @ $12.00 = _____

Name: _____

Address: _____

City: _____ State: _____

ZIP: _____

(On foreign orders, please use a separate page
to give your mailing address in the
format required by your post
office.)

Checks and money orders should
be made payable to **Greg Perry**.

*(This offer is made by the author,
not by Sams Publishing.)*